DATE DUE

DEMCO 38-296

Politics in the
Third Turkish Republic

Politics in the Third Turkish Republic

EDITED BY

Metin Heper
and Ahmet Evin

Westview Press
BOULDER • SAN FRANCISCO • OXFORD

Copyright © 1994 by Westview Press, Inc.

Published in 1994 in the United States of America by Westview Press, Inc., 5500
Central Avenue, Boulder, Colorado 80301-2877, and in the United Kingdom by
Westview Press, 36 Lonsdale Road, Summertown, Oxford OX2 7EW

A CIP catalog record for this book is available from the Library of Congress.
ISBN 0-8133-8674-8

Printed and bound in the United States of America

The paper used in this publication meets the requirements
of the American National Standard for Permanence of Paper
for Printed Library Materials Z39.48-1984.

10   9   8   7   6   5   4   3   2   1

Contents

PART EIGHT

Conclusion

Preface and Acknowledgments

The Third Republic (from 1982 to the present) ushered in a new chapter in Turkish politics. Turkey's economy has undergone a major transformation, and economic cleavages have become increasingly salient. The central political philosophy governing Turkish republicanism has become increasingly muted: The effect of Atatürkism as an ideology, or as a political manifesto, has somewhat diminished. New issues, such as the environment and feminism, have cropped up as items in the political agenda. The military appears to be increasingly reluctant to interfere in politics. The political parties and the press came to have leading roles in the polity. These developments, among others, have given a new twist to efforts to consolidate democracy in a milieu long dominated by an omnipresent, if not always an omnipotent, state.

An earlier volume, *State, Democracy and the Military: Turkey in the 1980s* (Berlin: Walter de Gruyter, 1988), compiled by the present editors, dealt with the developments leading up to the 1980 military intervention and the restructuring of politics in the early years of the Third Republic. In the present volume, we examine the trials and tribulations involved in consolidating democracy in Turkey since the early 1980s.

The editors are grateful to Professor Udo Steinbach, Director of the Deutches Orient Institut in Hamburg, for his support of the project leading to this volume. The preparation of the manuscript for publication was made possible through generous grants from the Deutches Orient Institut and the Stiftung Volkswagenwerk in Hannover.

Rüşdü Saracoğlu's chapter on the economy is based on his paper, "Economic Stabilization and Structural Adjustment," published previously as a World Bank Economic Development Institute paper. The chapter by Metin Heper on Turgut Özal's presidency is an updated version of his article, "Consolidating Turkish Democracy," which appeared in the *Journal of Democracy* 3 (1992): 105-117. The editors wish to thank the officers of the World Bank and the editors of *Journal of Democracy* for granting us permission to publish the revised versions of these two articles.

Metin Heper and Ahmet Evin
Ankara and Hamburg

Acronyms

ANAP	Turkish acronym for the Motherland Party
AP	Turkish acronym for the Justice Party
CHP	Turkish acronym for the Republican People's Party
DISK	Turkish acronym for the Confederation of Revolutionary Labor Unions
DP	Turkish acronym for the Democratic Party
DSP	Turkish acronym for the Democratic Left Party
DYP	Turkish acronym for the True Path Party
EC	European Community
GNP	gross national product
HP	Turkish acronym for the Populist Party
IBRD	World Bank
ICFLU	International Confederation of Free Labor Unions
ILO	International Labor Organization
IMF	International Monetary Fund
IPI	International Press Institute
MHP	Turkish acronym for the Nationalist Action Party
MIT	Turkish acronym for the National Intelligence Agency
MP	Turkish acronym for the Nation Party
MSP	Turkish acronym for the National Salvation Party
NATO	North Atlantic Treaty Organization
NSC	National Security Council
OECD	Organization for Economic Cooperation and Development
OIC	Organization of the Islamic Conference
PKK	Kurdish acronym for the Worker's Party of Kurdistan
PLO	Palestinian Liberation Organization
PTT	Turkish acronym for the Post, Telephone, and Telegraph Agency
SEE	state economic enterprises
SHP	Turkish acronym for the Social Democratic Populist Party
SPO	State Planning Organization
TGNA	Turkish Grand National Assembly
TKKOİ	Turkish acronym for Mass Housing and Public Participation Agency
TİP	Turkish acronym for the Worker's Party of Turkey
TOBB	Turkish acronym for the Union of Chambers and Stock Exchanges of Turkey
TÜRK-İŞ	Turkish acronym for the Worker's Confederation of Turkey
TÜSIAD	Turkish acronym for the Turkish Association of Industrialists and Businesspersons
UN	United Nations
VAT	value added tax
YÖK	Turkish acronym for the High Board of Education

PART ONE

Turkish Democracy, the 1980 Military Intervention and Beyond

1

Turkish Democracy in Historical and Comparative Perspective ·

Dankwart A. Rustow

The difficulties faced by Turkish democracy are well illustrated by the periodic interventions of the armed forces at roughly ten-year intervals–in 1960-1961, 1971-1973, and most recently in 1980-1983. Yet there seems to be a fundamental contrast between those temporary interventions in Turkey and long-term military interventions in other Third-World or Mediterranean countries, such as Francisco Franco in Spain (1936-1975), Gamal Abdel Nasser in Egypt (1954-1970), and Reza Shah in Iran in the 1950s; various leaders in Korea, the Philippines, Argentina, and Brazil in the 1960s and Chile in the 1970s; or the 1967 colonels' junta in Greece. Whereas these other coups established repressive authoritarian or personalist regimes, on each occasion the Turkish military assumed power for a strictly limited period, relinquishing it as soon as law and order were restored and efforts were made to strengthen democratic institutions.

Officers, Bureaucrats, and Modernization

The political role of the military, of which General Kenan Evren's 1980-1983 regime may well be the last example, has deep roots in Ottoman and Turkish history. For the Ottoman-Turkish military, the century and a half of defeat from 1774 to 1918 at the hands of Austria, Russia, and eventually the Allies of World War I, meant a profound transformation. No longer the vanguard of irresistible conquest, the military's major task now became to acquire the technology and organization of a superior European power. From the late eighteenth century onward, military instructors and specialists were invited from Europe–Italian shipbuilders, French artillerists, German staff officers, even an Italian brass-band conductor to compose the appropriate martial music. By the mid-nineteenth century, the Ottoman military college had been transformed into the leading Western-style edu-

3

cational institution for a new Ottoman elite.

Increasingly, too, young Ottoman officers were sent to Europe for tours of training extending beyond military matters. One young officer, İbrahim Şinasi (1826-1871)–sent to Paris to further his training in French, mathematics, and artillery–returned to Istanbul and developed new poetic idiom in the European romantic style and founded the first non-official Turkish-language newspaper in Istanbul. One of Şinasi's journalistic-poetic disciples, Namık Kemal, actively cooperated in the secret conspiracy of the Young Ottomans, who in 1876 deposed two successive sultans and forced on the third Turkey's first European-style written parliamentary constitution–a constitution soon abrogated by Sultan Abdülhamit II (1876-1908) but reimposed by another military conspiracy under the Committee of Union and Progress in 1908.

The Westernizing reforms–designed by nineteenth-century sultans to defend their traditional realms more effectively and had filtered down from viziers and pashas to lieutenants and cadets–had come to encompass, willy-nilly, railroads, telegraphs, a daily press, romantic verses, European law codes, and written constitutions. Following the final military defeat of the Ottoman Empire in World War I, those same railroads and telegraphs enabled another Turkish military leader, Mustafa Kemal (later Atatürk), to organize a desperate War of Independence in defense of the Turkish-speaking heartland of the defeated empire against a Greek invasion.

This implied a radical transition from Ottoman imperial to Turkish national consciousness. As Atatürk declared in a programmatic speech in 1919, "Today the nations of the whole world recognize only one sovereignty: national sovereignty."[1]

Following the nationalist victory in the Turkish War of Independence (1919-1922), Atatürk ruled the Turkish Republic (from 1923 to 1938) as a benevolent one-party dictator. He briefly allowed an opposition party in 1924-1925 and encouraged the formation of another in 1930. However, he soon called off these experiments when they gave rise to strong expressions of traditionalist Islamic and even separatist sentiments. The sustained effort to make the transition to democracy came later, when a new generation of leaders had been educated along Atatürk's Western, secular, nationalist principles. Specifically, in 1945 Atatürk's successor, İsmet İnönü, allowed a free press and the formation of opposition parties and by 1948 committed the single-party bureaucracy to scrupulous fairness between the government and opposition.

Once again–as in the days when the sultans' military reforms hastened the transformation of their traditional, dynastic empire into a modern, republican nation-state–developments soon ran ahead of the cautious in-

---

[1] The speech was given upon Mustafa Kemal's arrival in Ankara, his later headquarters and capital, in December 1919; cf. Dankwart A. Rustow, "Atatürk as Founder of a State," in *Philosophers and Kings: Studies in Leadership*, Dankwart A. Rustow, ed. (New York: G. Braziller, 1970), p. 214.

tentions of the original sponsors. Atatürk had consolidated Turkey as a nation by creating a parliamentary machinery within a one-party state. İnönü, in allowing opposition, intended to bring Turkey closer to the Western powers; above all, he was hoping to relieve the pressures on a wartime economy while securing his party's further stay in power. But, to İnönü's surprise, the voters eagerly seized the opportunity to change governments as soon as it was offered.[2] That very process of competitive elections since 1950 has provided the major mechanism by which Atatürk's cultural and educational reforms have been spread from a small, urban elite to the Turkish people as a whole.

It has been widely assumed that social accomplishments of advanced industrial countries–such as urban residence, universal literacy, and a high standard of living–are among the essential preconditions for the advent of democracy. Instead, Turkish experience confirms the likelihood of a converse causal nexus: Political parties competing for the ballots of an illiterate peasantry will soon be forced to offer their constituents more schools, as well as better roads and other economic amenities. In Turkey's first free election in May 1950, the voter turnout was an astonishing 89 percent, with illiterate voters helped by pictorial symbols on the party ballot; average participation in national elections since that time has been well over 70 percent.

The resulting social transformation has been truly remarkable. In 1935, only one out of three Turkish children went to elementary school; by 1950, this number was two out of three. Today schooling is virtually universal. Similarly, the proportion of literacy–which was 20 percent in 1935 and 32 percent in 1950–had jumped to 67 percent in 1980, with four out of five men and half of the women literate. Attendance at high schools (or *lycées*) has increased tenfold between 1950 and 1990. The ratio of urban population (inhabitants of cities and towns of over 10,000 to the total population) was virtually unchanged during the one-party period–16 percent in 1927, 19 percent in 1950–but since then has increased 50 percent. In the remaining rural half of the population, by 1968, every other village (49.6 percent) had sent some of its residents to work abroad–mostly to Germany. Throughout Turkey, newspaper circulation has quadrupled during the forty years since 1950; although television was not introduced until 1970, in the early 1980s as many television sets were found in both rural and urban regions as the number of printed copies of daily newspapers in circulation.[3]

Taken together, the Ottoman legacy, Kemal Atatürk's national revolution, and İnönü's move toward democracy in the late 1940s seemed to

---

[2] For details on Turkey's transition to democracy and İnönü's role, see Dankwart A. Rustow, *Turkey: America's Forgotten Ally* (New York: Council on Foreign Relations, 1987), Ch. 4, esp. pp. 62ff.

[3] For data through the late 1970s, see the convenient statistical summaries in Walter F. Weiker, *The Modernization of Turkey: From Atatürk to the Present Day* (New York: Holmes and Meier, 1981).

give Turkey a uniquely favorable climate for the achievement of a stable and thriving democracy on the eve of the 1980s. And the importance of each of these factors becomes clearer when Turkey's situation is compared, point by point, with that of other developing Third-World countries as to governmental tradition, national identity, and the social basis of political competition.

Most Third-World countries have had much difficulty in developing a governmental bureaucracy; and only a few, such as India, embarked upon political independence with a functioning, indigenously staffed civil service bequeathed by their colonial rulers. Turkey inherited its governmental tradition, including sizable cadres of a civilian and military bureaucracy, from the Ottoman Empire; indeed, when that empire collapsed in 1918, over half of the civilian bureaucrats and 90 percent of the trained military staff officers continued their service in the Turkish Republic, with only a small minority serving in other successor states such as Syria, Iraq, or Libya.

Throughout most of the Third World, the present borders of would-be nation-states were drawn by European colonial rulers and do not coincide with any spontaneous sense of national identity. Only in Southeast Asia do those boundaries include solid, homogeneous ethnic communities. For the Arabs, the problem is one of a single language spoken in a score of countries from Oman to Morocco; hence, the aspiration of Pan-Arab nationalism actively competes with a basket of loyalties within existing state borders. In India and in most of tropical Africa, the postcolonial borders bring together many different ethnic and linguistic groups. Typically, there is no linguistic majority, so the language of the outgoing colonial rulers (English or French) must continue to serve as a lingua franca. Not surprisingly, political parties tend to divide along ethnic-linguistic lines, and democratic institutions often mask the reality of rule by one of the ethnic minorities over the rest. Too often, the heavy inflow of arms to the Middle East and Africa has reinforced this pattern of domination by tribal or sectarian minorities, such as the Alawites of Syria or the Sunni Arabs of Iraq.

Turkey, by contrast, was never a colony. Its army is one of the few in the Third World that is recruited by universal conscription, and its officer corps has long been one of Turkey's chief avenues of social mobility. Under Atatürk's leadership, this national citizens' army established the boundaries of the Turkish Republic by averting the threat of colonial partition. Specifically, the regions Atatürk set out to defend in the War of Independence corresponded to the Turkish-speaking heartlands of the former Ottoman Empire; thus, within those national borders, over 90 percent of the population speaks Turkish and over 98 percent of the people are Muslims.[4]

---

[4]The remainder are Muslim Kurds and Arabs in the southeast section of the country (efforts have been made to gradually assimilate them through an organic process of social mobility); and a small Greek, Armenian and Jewish minority mostly in Istanbul.

In short, except for the lingering Kurdish intransigence in the south-east and the relatively less significant Sunni-Alevi cleavage, Turkey represents the exceptional phenomenon of an almost complete coincidence of national and state identities. As a result, democratic competition has occurred basically among parties backed by different social strata and disagreeing over issues of economic policy–town versus country, business versus agriculture, military versus civilians, rich versus poor; yet those divisions have been attenuated by the processes of economic development and social mobility, which democracy itself has done much to accelerate.

Revolution at the Ballot Box

When President İnönü inaugurated the Turkish experiment with competitive party politics in the mid-1940s, the division that immediately came to the fore can be described as one of "outs" versus "ins." The Republican People's Party (CHP) in Atatürk's day had been founded by former military officers and government officials who had taken the lead in organizing Turkish national resistance during the War of Independence. Many of the top leaders of the CHP had started–like Atatürk and İnönü themselves–with military careers, although Atatürk, in a dramatic showdown with some of his former military-political associates in 1924, had forced everyone to choose between further service in the army or in politics.[5] Other early leaders of the CHP had been recruited from the civilian branches of government or from among educators in the public school and state university systems.

The exceptional leader during the one-party period was Celal Bayar, whose background was neither military nor administrative but was in private banking. After serving briefly as minister of reconstruction in 1922-1924, he became the founder in 1924 of the İş Bank, Turkey's first and most successful private bank. He reentered the government as minister of economy in 1932 and prime minister in 1937-1939 and reemerged in 1946 as chairman of the Democratic Party (DP), the first to challenge the CHP's political monopoly.

The 1950 election was thus Turkey's first step toward overcoming its most deeply entrenched social-political divisions–that between the urban bureaucracy and the population at large. In moving the capital from Istanbul to Ankara, Atatürk thoroughly reorganized the traditional bureaucracy inherited from Ottoman times, staffed it with graduates of the new Westernized educational system, and supplemented it with the new bureaucracy of the CHP. Meanwhile, Atatürk's revolution intensified the contacts between the capital and the hinterland by expanding governmental functions into such spheres as popular education and industrial

---

[5]See Dankwart A. Rustow, "The Army and the Founding of the Turkish Republic," *World Politics* 11 (1959): 547.

development.

In its quarter century of unchallenged rule, the CHP had formed a network of local alliances–with the chiefs of nomadic clans or hereditary landowners in some of the more backward regions of the southeast, with affluent merchants or local notables in the towns of central Anatolia, and with village elders in rural areas throughout Turkey. The emerging DP also built its own rather heterogeneous network of local supporters: leaders of rival clans or owners of smaller estates in the east, rich cash-crop farmers (such as Adnan Menderes) in western Anatolia, businesspeople, university teachers, and trade union leaders in Istanbul–in short, of socially, educationally, or economically prominent personages who had been left on the outside of the official government-CHP network.

A glance at the changing occupational background of Turkish legislators since the 1950s shows the effectiveness of the democratic challenge to the old bureaucratic monopoly. Thirty years of electoral politics have served to break the closed circuit of government officialdom, the pattern whereby former military officers and civil servants in the legislature would enact the laws and budgets to be administered by their bureaucratic colleagues on continuing assignment. In the single-party period, roughly half of the legislators had come from civil service or military backgrounds. In the first competitively elected Parliament of 1950, the proportion of former government officials (including military officers and educators from state schools) was still as high as 35 percent in the CHP but was only 19 percent among the incoming DP majority. (Significantly, it was this new nongovernmental majority of assemblymen that elected Celal Bayar as Turkey's first president whose background was completely civilian.) Yet after a quarter of a century of party competition, the percentage of former government officials among parliamentarians elected in 1977 was only 18 percent in Bülent Ecevit's CHP and was as low as 12 percent in the Justice Party (AP).

In the perspective of a half-century, the Atatürk revolution clearly served to unify the country and to bring government closer to the people; yet in the short run, Atatürk's innovations inevitably increased the distance between the Western-educated administrators and the still-traditional population at large. A generation later, the ballot box revolution of the 1950s and 1960s stimulated social mobility, raised the level of popular expectations, and in that sense brought the people closer to the government. Nonetheless, the advent of democracy coincided with a vast expansion of the bureaucracy, which now had to channel the massive inflow of foreign aid into the economy, supervise the building up of the economic infrastructure, and administer the growing patchwork of piecemeal economic regulations.

Deadlock of Ideology and Victory of Pragmatism

In the election campaigns that have been fought in Turkey since 1950, mostly at four-year intervals, the usual ephemeral attention–so familiar from other democratic settings–has been given to the personalities of leaders and their rivalries, to charges of corruption and misrule, and to promises of redress of all manner of specific grievances. In the political contest itself, the personal element has always been prominent. İnönü and Bayar, who faced each other as leaders of the CHP and the DP, respectively, in 1950, had been political rivals since the days of Atatürk. When the Justice Party was founded in 1961, its very name implied a bitter protest against the hanging of ex-Premier Menderes by the military regime of General Cemal Gürsel the previous year. From the late 1960s onward, the quadrennial elections became an increasingly acrimonious contest between Ecevit of the CHP–poet, journalist, and eloquent spokesperson for the grievances of the lower classes–and Süleyman Demirel of the AP, the engineer and father figure with the traditional folksy touch.

Beneath this surface level of personalities and mutual allegations, the extent to which Turkish politics has steered clear of ideology is remarkable. In this important respect, Turkish politics has departed sharply from the continental European model, with its Christian Democratic, Socialist, and Communist parties–not to mention from the Israeli precedent of parties based on intensely shaded varieties of socialism, Zionism, and religious orthodoxy. Rather, the pattern that has emerged in Turkey resembles that of the United States, with its national alliances of regional and local groupings dedicated to more progressive or conservative social policies: It was perhaps no mere coincidence that Turkey's first national elections were fought between groups calling themselves the Republican People's and Democratic parties.

There was a widespread anticipation among both Turkish and foreign observers that any such contest between parties in the late 1940s and early 1950s would turn into a battle for the continuation or reversal of Atatürk's secular reforms, which had been the most intensely controversial issue of the preceding period. It soon became clear, however, that both parties shared the commitment of the Turkish elite to Atatürk's Western and secular values but were also eager to appeal to the more traditional rural electorate. As a result, İnönü's outgoing CHP found itself taking pride in adding a faculty of Islamic theology to the secular University of Ankara and Menderes's incoming DP taking pride in restoring the right of *müezzins* to chant the daily prayer call from the minarets in the original Arabic rather than in the "pure Turkish" version prescribed since 1932. In short, a competition began in adopting specific, minor measures that softened the sharper edges of Atatürk's secularism, neutralized the issue of religion versus secularism as between the major parties, and effectively isolated minority groups, such as the Nation Party (MP), that concentrated their appeal on

Islamic issues alone.

The Islamic-conservative groups, to be sure, have at times had to face various constitutional and legal provisions that prohibit the restoration of an Islamic caliphate or the advocacy of such restoration–provisions that, broadly interpreted, were used to prohibit the MP in 1953 and the National Salvation Party (MSP) in 1980. Yet the MP was reopened almost immediately under a slightly modified program and leadership, as was the Republican Nation Party (1954). It is equally significant that these various Islamicist parties typically mustered no more than 3 to 9 percent of the national vote. The one exception was Necmettin Erbakan's MSP, founded in 1972 by an engineer (who had received his graduate training in Germany and was fond of claiming that Islam was the most modern religion that was compatible with advanced technology) and made respectable through its governmental alliance in 1973 with Ecevit's CHP and later with Demirel's AP. Nonetheless, even under these most favorable circumstances, and in the polarized political climate of the 1970s, it is significant that the percentage of the vote the MSP received declined from an initial high of 11.8 percent in 1973 to 8.5 percent in 1977.

It is important to guard against the tendency of some observers in classifying such groups as Erbakan's MSP with the followers of of the Ayatollah Khomeini in Iran under the loose and comprehensive label of *Islamic fundamentalism*. Iran is a Shi'i Muslim country and Turkey is Sunni Muslim; since the Sunni-Shi'i split goes back to the earliest days of Islam, it is far more pervasive than any such division, say, between Catholics, Orthodox, and Protestants among Christians. Turkish religious-conservative groups such as the MSP are profoundly Sunni in orientation and are greatly repelled by any Shi'i regime of Ayatollahs.

Interestingly, Turkey contains a small group of Alevi Muslims–a religious tendency related to, but by no means identical with, Shi'ism–roughly estimated as between 5 to 20 percent of the population. They have been staunch supporters of the CHP and Atatürk's principle of secularism, in which they see a guarantee against any discrimination the Sunni majority might inflict on them.[6]

A half-century ago, the defenders of the Ottoman theocratic establishment deeply resented secularism as an attack on religion itself whereas Atatürk insisted that his policy of separation of religion and politics and of secular education did not imply any such enmity toward religion. By now, however, Atatürk's concept of religion as a private matter has become well enough established to have removed religion from the political agenda. In contrast to the United States, there are no religious chaplains in the army and no religious invocations at government ceremonies. As in most Western countries, indifference and religious observance alike are socially acceptable, with indifference prevailing among the urban upper

---

[6]Cf. Dankwart A. Rustow "Turkey's Travails," *Foreign Affairs* 58 (1979): pp. 98ff.

strata and religious observance among the villagers.[7] Yet even among the lower classes, social mobility and migration–both within Turkey and to jobs in Europe–have tended to loosen patterns of orthodoxy and traditional behavior.

Two other ideological tendencies have played an even lesser role in electoral politics than has Islamic conservatism. One of these is the fascism of Alparslan Türkeş, whose nationwide vote rose from 3 percent in 1969 and 1973 to 6 percent in 1977. The program of the Türkeş's Nationalist Action Party (MHP) espouses a corporate state and the policy of pan-Turkism–that is, the ideal of political unification of Turkey with the Turkic-speaking populations of western China and what used to be Soviet Central Asia.[8]

The other extremist tendency is revolutionary Marxism, as was represented in the Worker's Party of Turkey (TİP). The TİP had briefly obtained enough of a following to gain 3 percent of the popular vote and fifteen parliamentary seats in 1965. In 1969, it was reduced to only two seats, and by 1973, the shift of the CHP toward democratic socialism largely undercut the electoral appeal of the far left.

Meanwhile, the parliamentary importance of both the MSP and the fascist MHP was enhanced through the deadlock among the major parties throughout the 1970s. Thus, the MSP was able to enter into a coalition with Ecevit's CHP in the period January-September 1974. The MSP and the MHP were both represented in the Demirel governments of 1975-1977 and 1977-1978 and lent parliamentary support to Demirel's minority government of 1979-1980. In one of these coalition governments, the MHP gained control of the Ministry of Customs–at the very time it was known to be engaged in massive smuggling of drugs and arms.

Still, the major significance of both fascism and communism in Turkish politics was felt outside of the electoral and parliamentary processes. Marxism found a stronghold in the Confederation of Revolutionary Trade Unions, which split off from the mainstream Turkish Workers' Confederation in 1967 and intermittently tried to organize political strikes and violent May Day demonstrations in the 1970s. Marxist ideology in its Stalinist, Maoist, and even Albanian versions proved popular in the 1970s among certain urban strata, particularly among some teachers and many students on university campuses. And the economic crisis of the late 1970s, along with the growing paralysis of the governmental system, encouraged the growth of left-wing and right-wing terrorism–the former supplied with

---

[7] For example, private social surveys in the early 1970s found that 64 percent of all Turkish couples combined religious and secular wedding ceremonies, with one-half of the couples in the major cities, but only one out of ten in the villages, having purely secular weddings (My calculations are from Weiker, *The Modernization of Turkey*, p. 74.) Similarly, 70 percent of the population of the smallest villages, but only 24 percent of those in the largest cities, performed the Muslim prayer at least once a day (ibid., p. 57).

[8] On Pan-Turkism, see Jacob M. Landau, *Pan-Turkism in Turkey: A Study of Irredentism* (London: C. Hurst, 1981).

arms smuggled from Bulgaria or across the Black Sea and the latter with arms smuggled from abroad or leaked to the MHP by friendly elements in the armed forces.

The suppression of this double wave of terrorism, and the collection of the vast amounts of small arms that had accumulated in private hands, was one of the major achievements of the Evren regime of 1980-1983. The victory of Turgut Özal's Motherland Party in the 1983 election helped Turkey overcome the parliamentary paralysis that was the other major source of the violent extremism of the 1970s.

In the 1920s, Kemal Atatürk established the political identity of the new Turkey as a Westernizing nation-state. In the late 1940s, İsmet İnönü set Turkey on a course toward political democracy. By the 1980s, the Turkish citizenry at large had made clear its commitment to the full practice of these Western and democratic ideals.

2

Transition to Democracy in Turkey: Toward a New Pattern

Metin Heper

As the preceding chapter shows, from the inception of the republic in 1923 to the 1990s, Turkey experienced a cautious but steady progress in democratization. This evolution was punctuated, however, by three military interventions, but these were brief; they aimed at restructuring Turkish politics so as to bring about a viable system of democracy. In order to place Turkey's travails concerning democracy in perspective, we must dwell on two dimensions of democracy, as well as describe recent thinking about a successful transition to democracy.

Two Dimensions of Democracy

The *problematique* democracy faces is the necessity of striking a balance between political participation and prudent political leadership. By definition, increased participation democratizes political regimes, but the consolidation of democracy necessitates the less dramatic but equally significant process of the emergence of a prudent, not merely a responsive, government.[1]

It is for this reason that C. H. Dodd in Chapter 14 of this volume refers to democracy as a type of state. It is a type of state that looks after the long-term interests of the community rather than one that represents authoritarian rule, isolated from civil society yet imposing itself upon civil society. Translated into structural-functionalist terms, when political participation is concomitant to social differentiation, democratic consolidation can be said to depend on prudent leadership, a characteristic that provides

---

[1] Giovanni Sartori, *The Theory of Democracy Revisited: Part Two: The Classical Issues* (Chatham, N.J.: Chatham House, 1987); Robert A. Dahl, *Dilemmas of Pluralist Democracy: Autonomy vs. Control* (New Haven: Yale University Press, 1982).

a high degree of political integration.[2]

Historically, what amounted to a spontaneous form of political integration had been prescribed by some English pluralists as well as Guild Socialists. Their view, based on the assumption that sovereignty was widely dispersed among social groups and not merely within "spheres of government," anticipated the later articulation of the notion of social pluralism.[3] Accordingly, social groups were to act as agencies of "social coordination" through horizontal relations of adjustment and exchange.[4]

A suitable context in which this view could take root was Alexis de Tocqueville's America, where numerous politically efficacious intermediary structures stood between the individual and central authority. Emphasis was placed on civil societal elements at the virtual expense of central authority. It was further assumed that governmental and nongovernmental actors had their own basically nonaltruistic views and that the public policies formulated, and the particular patterns in which those policies were implemented, reflected the outcomes of essentially self-interested contests within and outside the government.[5]

This particular notion of government was adopted by nearly all of the Founding Fathers of the United States. According to James Madison, for instance, an elected executive was a "delegate" who would either seek to promote the interests of his constituents or use his position to advance his own personal interests. The first option was more desirable, and Madison recommended frequent elections as a check on the elected executive. James C. Calhoun improved the original model by introducing the idea of a concurrent majority. What was desirable was the presence of a plurality of groups, each politically efficacious to impinge upon the government.

Consequently, in America sovereignty was *pluralized,* and its fragments were transferred to the various power groups. In contrast, sovereignty in Europe was *divided* between the state and civil society. It was in the European context, in fact, that concepts such as "general will," "universal will," "common will,", and "common interest" were coined. In Europe, representation was not viewed as mere delegation; the relationship between the people and the elected representative was essentially one of trust. Elected representatives were expected to use their own judgment, because they were expected to represent not only interests but also opinions. It was

---

[2]This notion of the state is elaborated inter alia, in Bertrand Badie and Pierre Birnbaum, *The Sociology of the State,* trans. by Arthur Goldhammer (Chicago: University of Chicago Press, 1979); Peter B. Evans, Dietrich Rueschemeyer, and Theda Skocpol, eds., *Bringing the State Back In* (Cambridge: Cambridge University Press, 1985); and Metin Heper, "Introduction," in *The State and Public Bureaucracies: A Comparative Perspective,* Metin Heper, ed. (New York: Greenwood Press, 1987).

[3]Andrew Wincent, *Theories of the State* (Oxford: Basil Blackwell, 1987), p. 37.

[4]Kenneth H.F. Dyson, *The State Tradition in Western Europe: A Study of an Idea and Institution* (Oxford: Martin Robertson, 1980), p. 193.

[5]Patrick Dunleavy and Brendon O'Leary, *Theories of the State: The Politics of Liberal Democracy* (London: Macmillan, 1987), pp. 43-44, 47-51.

assumed that there were differing levels of opinion as well as of interests.[6]

Thus, "mixed" constitutions developed in Europe, because pluralism there was not viewed essentially as social pluralism but perceived primarily as institutional pluralism. Some governmental institutions were saddled with the responsibility of looking after the long-term interests of the community. Institutional pluralism came to have two versions. The state as an idea and an institution was entrenched more strongly in continental Europe than in Britain. On the continent an idealistic attitude toward representation developed. This approach was derived from a belief in the organic unity of society, which was considered a community of persons who shared certain values and aspirations. Consequently, there was emphasis on leadership and on the exchange of opinions about what should be done by those people who were familiar with the needs of the community.[7]

In continental Europe, responsibility for looking after the long-term interests of the community was generally assigned to the politically nonrepresentative agents: kings, strong presidents, courts, and the bureaucratic elites. In Britain, only the politically representative agents were supposed to play that role. The Whigs pointed out that Parliament represented the entire nation; its decisions were to be more than a mere aggregate of sectional interests. The Tories essentially saddled the cabinet with the responsibility in question.[8]

Even those pluralists who explicitly and effectively brought the state back in continued to place emphasis on social groups. The polity they had in mind incorporated maximum diversity of civil societal life along with some form of central authority. Still, they did pay attention to the requirement of achieving a balance between political participation and prudent government.

Theories of Transition to Democracy

When the pluralists turned their attention to the Third-World countries, on the whole they emphasized political participation rather than prudent government. This was not surprising: Faced with charismatic or patrimonial autocrats, they placed priority on democratization. They stressed the prerequisites for democracy; their aim was to make politically efficacious citizens out of submissive subjects.[9]

---

[6] A. H. Birch, *Representation* (London: Macmillan, 1971), pp. 78-86; Martin Carnoy, *The State and Political Theory* (Princeton: Princeton University Press, 1984), pp. 33ff.

[7] Birch, *Representation*, p. 94.

[8] Ibid., pp. 38-46.

[9] The representative advocates of this view include S. M. Lipset, "Some Social Requisites of Democracy," *American Political Science Review* 53 (1965): 69-105; Gabriel Almond and Sidney Verba, *The Civic Culture* (Princeton: Princeton University Press, 1963).

The so-called genetic approach to transitions to democracy, in turn, fo-
cussed on the elite conflict and the necessity of building up a healthily
functioning democracy. This approach suggested that, with the single
precondition of national unity, a viable democracy would be established
through a process of polarization, crisis, and compromise. It was further assumed that, in the last analysis, a smoothly functioning democracy
would be the handwork of politicians skilled in bargaining techniques.[10]

The proponents of the genetic approach had too much faith in the capacity of politicians in Third-World countries to learn from past mistakes. They
had not considered even institutional pluralism as a means for providing
a balance. Their ideal was Anglo-American adversarial politics, and they
expected political actors to internalize the procedural norms of democracy only. Their optimism bordered on utopia, given the fact that many
Third-World countries evinced strong characteristics of patrimonialism—
that is, they lacked centers with normative systems distinct from the particularisms of the social groups.[11] To many such countries, even the concept of social class was alien. Social class could have brought the idea
of interests—if not general, at least common (as opposed to individual)
interests—the expression of those interests in the form of ideologies, and
the development of coherent policies.[12] But these countries lacked both
autonomous central institutions, which could have contributed to prudent government, and social groups of near-equal powers, which could
have played an active role in social reconciliation and, when necessary,
moderated the conflict at the center. Instead, the dominant pattern of the
structuring of polities in these countries was that of patron-client relations,
which carried intact the peripheral particularisms to the center.[13]

It was the lingering inability of the political actors in these systems to
internalize even the procedural rules of democracy that led the authors of
the Transition Project[14] to propose the drawing up of pacts, "an explicit, but

---

[10]Dankwart A. Rustow, "Transitions to Democracy: Toward a Dynamic Model," *Comparative Politics* 2 (1970): 337-363.

[11]S. N. Eisenstadt, *Traditional Patrimonialism and Modern Neo-Patrimonialism* (Beverly Hills:
Sage, 1978).

[12]I owe this point to Salvador Giner, "Political Economy, Legitimation and the State
in Southern Europe," in *Transitions from Authoritarian Rule: Southern Europe*, Guillermo
O'Donnell, Philippe C. Schmitter, and Laurence Whitehead, eds. (Baltimore: Johns Hopkins University Press, 1986), p. 13.

[13]The situation was no different even in such relatively modernized countries as those in
Latin America. See inter alia Ronald C. Newton, "On 'Functional Groups,' 'Fragmentation,'
and 'Pluralism' in Spanish American Political Society," *Hispanic American Historical Review*
5 (1978): 1-29; Fernando Uricoechea, *The Patrimonial Foundations of the Brazilian Bureaucratic
State* (Berkeley: University of California Press, 1980), pp. 35-36.

[14]Guillermo O'Donnell, Philippe C. Schmitter, and Laurence Whitehead, *Transitions from
Authoritarian Rule: Comparative Perspectives* (Baltimore: Johns Hopkins University Press, 1986);
O'Donnell, Schmitter, and Whitehead, eds., *Transitions from Authoritarian Rule: Southern Eu-
rope*; Guillermo O'Donnell, Philippe C. Schmitter, and Laurence Whitehead, eds., *Transitions
from Authoritarian Rule: Latin America* (Baltimore: Johns Hopkins University Press, 1986);
Guillermo O'Donnell and Philippe C. Schmitter, *Transitions from Authoritarian Rule: Tentative*

not always publicly explicated or justified, agreement among a select set of actors, which seeks to define (or, better, to redefine) rules governing the exercise of power on the basis of mutual guarantees for the 'vital interests' of those entering into it."[15] The parties to these pacts were to be the military, political, and economic elites, not merely the governmental elites. The pacts were to be negative agreements among these elites not to "harm each other's vital interests," rather than "traditional liberal pact[s], based on a strict delimitation of the spheres of the state and civil society."[16] In the last analysis, they were to be merely civil societal arrangements among the parties involved; therefore, they could not by themselves bring about a prudent government, which needed to be based on universalistic norms. It was no coincidence that a pact of this nature contributed successfully to the consolidation of democracy in a country such as Spain, which had a prior class structure, and could not be successfully adopted, for instance, by many Latin American countries that had been characterized by clientelistic politics.[17]

Samuel P. Huntington argued that consolidation of democracy in the Third-World countries depended upon the emergence of centers, with their distinctive norms, so that a prudent government could develop. Huntington considered political institutionalization–that is, the emergence of autonomous political actors adept at bargaining and compromise–to be critical. A viable democracy, according to Huntington, needed political institutions that could "temper, moderate and redirect the relative power of social forces."[18]

Huntington, however, did not deal with the issues relating to the kind and degree of institutionalization required for consolidating democracy. Mark Kesselman and Gabriel Ben-Dor have shown that in different contexts, different degrees of political institutionalization may be observed.[19] Political institutions may not only be too weak, but they may also be too strong; such political institutionalization patterns would also create problems vis-à-vis the consolidation of democracies.[20]

Conclusions About Uncertain Democracies (Baltimore: Johns Hopkins University Press, 1986).

[15]O'Donnell and Schmitter, *Transitions from Authoritarian Rule: Tentative Conclusions About Uncertain Democracies,* p. 37.

[16]Ibid., p. 38.

[17]For an elaboration, see Metin Heper, "Transitions to Democracy Reconsidered: A Historical Perspective," in *Comparative Political Dynamics: Global Research Perspectives,* Dankwart A. Rustow and Kenneth P. Erickson, eds. (New York: HarperCollins, 1991).

[18]Samuel P. Huntington, *Political Order in Changing Societies* (New Haven: Yale University Press, 1968). Also see Otto Kirchheimer, "Confining Conditions and Revolutionary Breakthroughs," *American Political Science Review* 59 (1964): 964-974.

[19]Mark Kesselman, "Over Institutionalization and Political Constraint: The Case of France," *Comparative Politics* 2 (1970): 21-44; Gabriel Ben-Dor, "Institutionalization and Political Development: A Conceptual and Theoretical Analysis," *Comparative Studies in Society and History* 7 (1975): 309-325.

[20]Heper, "Transitions to Democracy Reconsidered."

Too strong a degree of political institutionalization may emerge in polities, where it is brought about by politically unaccountable actors, such as the bureaucratic or the military elites. Thus institutionalization may come not in the form that regularly achieves a modus vivendi among the competing interests (social pluralism) or between the representatives of the latter and those who are saddled with the responsibility of looking after the long-term interests of community (institutional pluralism) but in the form of a state that virtually smothers civil society. This latter situation characterized the Turkish case.

The Turkish Experience

Indeed, the Turkish experience with the transition to democracy differed from those of both the presently viable Western democracies and most Third-World countries that are still struggling to consolidate their democracies. Political institutionalization in most Third-World countries has been too weak; in established Western democracies, it has been neither too strong nor too weak; and in Turkey, it has been too strong.[21] The Ottoman-Turkish state did not develop alongside politically influential social groups but aimed to consolidate all power in the center by rendering all civil societal elements into virtually impotent entities. Even at the pinnacle of their power, the French and Prussian absolutist kings still had to contend with the demands and pressures of the *parlements* and *Stande*. The Ottoman sultans, however, did not face an aristocracy that could impinge upon the affairs of the center. [22]

The center in the Ottoman-Turkish polity came to have its distinct normative system, which was formulated independently from civil societal elements. During the Ottoman centuries, the will, or command, of the sultan as a secular ruler gained prominence. This rule was based on the measuring rods of necessity and reason, not on the personal whims of the sultans. [23] Summed up by the norm of rationality, a particular outlook developed that provided ideals and values for the ruling strata. The bureaucratic elites assimilated these norms through the processes of their recruitment and training, as well as in functions they were assigned–that is, through organizational socialization.[24] Called *adab*, this was "a secular

[21] For some comparisons along these lines, see Metin Heper, "Extremely 'Strong State' and Democracy: The Turkish Case in Comparative and Historical Perspective," in *Democracy and Modernity*, S. N. Eisenstadt, ed. (Leiden: Brill, 1992).

[22] Şerif Mardin, "Power, Civil Society and Culture in the Ottoman Empire," *Comparative Studies in Society and History* 11 (1969): 258-281; Metin Heper, "Center and Periphery in the Ottoman Empire with Special Reference to the Nineteenth Century," *International Political Science Review* 1 (1980): 81-105.

[23] Şerif Mardin, *The Genesis of Young Ottoman Thought: A Study in the Modernization of Turkish Political Ideas* (Princeton: Princeton University Press, 1962), p. 104.

[24] Halil İnalcık, *The Ottoman Empire in the Classical Age: 1330-1666*, trans. Norman Itzkowitz and Colin Imber (London: Weidenfeld and Nicholson, 1973), pp. 65-69.

and state-oriented tradition."[25]

The center continued to be dominant during the Republican period. What later became known as Atatürkism constituted the Republican version of the *adab* tradition. Atatürk wished to substitute reason for "religious dogma." The Atatürkian thought was an outlook; it did not intend to impose a closed system of thought on polity and society in the long run. But when Atatürk died, the bureaucratic elites converted Atatürkian-thought-as-an-outlook into an Atatürkism-as-an-ideology in the Shilsian sense–that is, a closed system of thought. During the 1945-1980 period, the intellectual-bureaucratic and military elites considered as legitimate only that type of political action that conformed to the latter version of Atatürkism. The 1960-1961 and 1971-1973 military interventions were conducted basically because the political elites had drifted from Atatürkism and had, therefore, lost their legitimacy in the eyes of the intellectual-bureaucratic and, particularly, military elites.[26]

Consequently, in the pre-1980 period, the transition to democracy in Turkey had to be carried out within a framework of institutional monism rather than social or institutional pluralism, and in the virtual absence of effective political participation by social groups. [27] After 1954, when the modern urban groups lost their chance of developing into a politically influential force, the fate of the transition to democracy hinged on the outcome of the conflict between the statist elites and the populist political elites.[28] Whereas the former considered democracy as an end in itself–as a technique to find the best solution for the problems the country faced–and argued that Atatürkism should become the sole source for public policies, the latter tried to substitute national will for Atatürkism.

This conflict could not be easily resolved. Consequently, the pendulum kept swinging between a purely statist solution (military interventions) and a purely political formula (a debilitating democracy), and the civil societal elements virtually watched as spectators. As a result, in Turkey, the transitions to democracy were no more than a passage from one type of institutional monism to another: from one in which the center was dominated by the self-appointed guardians of the state to another in which intensely antistatist, populist political elites controlled the center.[29]

---

[25]Carter V. Findley, "The Advent of Ideology in the Islamic Middle East," Part I, *Studia Islamica*, from Fascicle LV, p. 158.

[26]Metin Heper, *The State Tradition in Turkey* (Walkington, England: Eothen Press, 1985), Chs. 3 and 4.

[27]Robert Bianchi, *Interest Groups and Political Development in Turkey* (Princeton: Princeton University Press, 1984); Metin Heper, ed., *Strong State and Economic Interest Groups: The post-1980 Turkish Experience* (Berlin: Walter de Gruyter, 1991).

[28]Faruk Birtek, Ch. 18 in this volume.

[29]Metin Heper, "The Executive in the Third Turkish Republic, 1982-1989," *Governance* 3 (1990): 299-319; Metin Heper "The State, Political Party and Society in Post-1983 Turkey," *Government and Opposition* 25 (1990): 321-333; Metin Heper and Jacob Landau, eds., *Political Parties and Democracy in Turkey* (London: I. B. Tauris, 1991).

This turned out to be the case despite the fact that both the 1961 and 1982 Constitutions attempted to establish institutional pluralism in Turkey, although with significant variations. The 1961 Constitution stacked the judges, bureaucrats, academia, and officers against the parliamentary elites. It created a constitutional court, bolstered the powers of the Council of State, granted autonomy to the universities, and set up the National Security Council. The Constitution was rather programmatic; on many matters, including economic and social goals, it spelled out prescriptive guidelines for the political governments to follow. As already noted, Atatürkism was taken as an ideology in the Shilsian sense and was adopted as the official ideology the political elites were not to transgress.[30]

The 1982 Constitution decreased the number of categories of the state elites. It curtailed the powers of the higher courts and the autonomy of the universities, strengthened the National Security Council, and established a presidency with wide powers. Another significant development was that Atatürkism was no longer perceived as an ideology in the Shilsian sense, which provided further scope for politics.[31]

Thus, whereas the 1960 military intervention led to a situation in which the political arena was strictly circumscribed and the state elites were jealous of their prerogatives, the 1980 military intervention led to a reverse situation. This basic difference between the pre-1980 and post-1980 military interventions provided an opportunity for Turkish politics to extricate itself from the vicious circle of a too-prudent government and a debilitating democracy. There was greater hope for the consolidation of democracy in Turkey, because the difficult-to-resolve conflict between the statist and populist political elites had gradually come to an end. The chapters that follow take up Turkey's experience in transition to a viable democracy in this new post-1980 era. In the concluding chapter we offer a general evaluation of the success of that transition to date.

---

[30] Heper, *The State Tradition in Turkey*, Ch. 4.

[31] For an elaboration, see Metin Heper, "State and Society in Turkish Political Experience," in *State, Democracy and the Military: Turkey in the 1980s*, Metin Heper and Ahmet Evin, eds. (Berlin: Walter de Gruyter, 1988).

PART TWO

Toward a Liberal-Democratic State

3

Demilitarization and Civilianization of the Regime

Ahmet Evin

On 12 December 1983, five weeks after the elections, when the National Security Council (consisting of five generals who had conducted the 1980 military intervention) turned the business of government over to a civilian cabinet, almost no one in Turkey was surprised–even though during the elections the National Security Council had publicly opposed the Motherland Party (ANAP) which won the majority of the seats in the newly formed Parliament, and its leader Turgut Özal, who now emerged as prime minister. The passage from the 1980-1983 military regime to competitive party politics followed unexpected twists and turns.

By early 1983, the military had clearly signaled its intention to establish a representative system that would consist of two parties, one situated slightly to the left and the other slightly to the right of the center, each to be staffed with cadres the military considered to be patriotic moderates. As a result, permission given to Özal by the military to establish a third party came somewhat as a surprise. Özal's sudden popularity, and his success in leading the ANAP to victory at the polls despite the apparent displeasure of President Kenan Evren, was even more of a surprise.

The return of a civilian government in 1983 did not constitute a significant step toward the "civilianization" of politics; it was the beginning of a process that would gain momentum later in the decade. The 1983 elections merely resulted in the reestablishment of a civilian government under the auspices of the military at a time when civil society and civilianization were concepts familiar to only a few people outside the intelligentsia. But throughout the decade, these concepts gained popular currency and came to influence public opinion. Both the nature of the 1980-1983 military regime and the complete change in the cast of political actors it imposed were crucial factors that led to a reorientation of political outlook in Turkey. In this chapter I trace the concrete steps that were taken to establish civilian

23

political control of the government and attempt to evaluate the significance of the changes made in curtailing the military's influence in terms of Turkish political culture.

Toward the 1983 General Elections

The 1980 military intervention and the adoption of a new constitution marked the culmination of a process toward the institutionalization of the military's role in Turkish politics. Over a period of two decades, beginning with the 1960 intervention and punctuated in the middle by the military-controlled "national coalition" regime of 1971-1973, the military gradually assumed an active role as the guarantor of regime stability in Turkey.

During the 1960-1980 period, a succession of presidents with military backgrounds reinforced the privileged position of the military in the polity. The military's direct influence on the executive branch, de facto and de jure, also increased during this period through the National Security Council, which was composed of four cabinet ministers–including the prime minister– and five generals in addition to the president. In 1971, for example, it was the military members of the National Security Council who presented the government with an ultimatum to resign and then appointed a prime minister and cabinet members from outside the Parliament to ensure the implementation of their policies.

Following the 1980-1983 intervention, the military assumed full executive and legislative powers without even attempting to disguise its virtually complete control of the polity. In 1980, unlike the earlier interventions, the military leaders neither claimed to have any backing from, nor attempted to enter into a tacit coalition with, other elite groups. With the closing of all political parties in 1981, the military became the sole actors on the stage, claiming to represent a state that was larger than the sum of its parts.[1]

The military had no plans to close the major political parties at the time of the intervention.[2] It intended to prosecute members of the Parliament who were suspected of illegal activities, and it brought to trial leaders of the ethnic and religious right-wing parties–both of which it had likely planned to shut down. The decision to close all political parties, however, which was taken nearly a year after the coup, seems to have been precipitated by the military's exasperation with the establishment politicians' incessant efforts to influence events behind the scenes. Whatever the reasons behind it, the decision alienated politicians (as well as the bulk of the intelligentsia) and led to the further isolation of the military as an independent executive group, with good or bad results.

---

[1] See Ahmet Evin, "Changing Patterns of Cleavages Before and After 1980," *State, Democracy and the Military: Turkey in the 1980s*, Metin Heper and Ahmet Evin, eds. (Berlin: Walter de Gruyter, 1988), pp. 201-213.

[2] Kenan Evren, *Kenan Evren'in Anıları*, vol. I (Istanbul: Milliyet, 1990), pp. 525-526.

The military's isolation from other elite groups brought into sharp relief the extent of power it had assumed in its self-appointed role as the vanguard of prudent government. In fact, the military was in the process of consolidating more power than it had ever held in the history of the Turkish republic, even as it was preparing for a transition to a parliamentary regime. The paradox was reflected in the 1982 Constitution, the key instrument that began the process of transition. The Constitution made possible the continued influence of the military over the civilian governments to be elected. Provisional Article 1 stated, in effect, that upon the proclamation of the Constitution, the leader of the 1980-1983 military regime would automatically assume the title of president of the republic for a period of seven years. The continued presence of the military at the highest level of decisionmaking was ensured, given the extensive powers of appointment and supervision the Constitution assigned to the president. The 1982 Constitution also provided immunities to members of the National Security Council, "which will have exercised legislative and executive power on behalf of the Turkish nation from 12 September 1980 to the formation of the Grand National Assembly . . . following the first general elections" (Provisional Article 15).

Public attitude toward the military also changed because of its isolation from all other segments of the polity. General Evren was popular among the masses, who voted overwhelmingly in favor of the new constitution and thereby elected him as president for an additional seven years. But popular support for Evren as a distant father figure, who had brought law and order to the country, was not the same as support for populist political leadership, which had close affinity with the masses. Traditional society looked upon the state with a mixture of awe and respect; it was accustomed to having someone revered as head of state. The same society no longer had a traditional attitude toward politics; it was ready for full participation, and preferred to be represented by one of its own in the capital. A strong protest vote in 1983 gave the ANAP an absolute majority in the Parliament and showed, among other things, the electorate's preference for making a distinction between the affairs of the state and the nitty-gritty of politics.

Demilitarization

The results of the 1983 general elections seemed to be a setback for the military, and in retrospect, they can be seen as the first of a series of events that marked the gradual erosion of military authority. They did not, however, entail a comprehensive transfer of power to a civilian regime. Far from returning to the barracks, the military retained considerable influence over governmental policymaking through its majority representation in the National Security Council. It would submit to the Council of Ministers its views on taking decisions and ensuring necessary coordination with regard to the establishment and implementation of the national security policy of the state. "The Council of Ministers" was required, in return, "to give priority consideration to the decisions of the National Security Council concerning the measures it adopted that were necessary for the preservation of the existence and the independence of the state, the integrity and indivisibility of the country, and the peace and security of society" (Constitution: Article 118).

The presidency itself provided a significant means for keeping the military's guiding hand in matters of state. Moreover, with martial law in effect in many provinces at the time of the 1983 elections, the military continued to be highly visible, and it exercised executive powers in its policing function. To some extent, it even exercised judicial powers through the military courts, which presided over the trials of those prosecuted under martial law.

The formation of a civilian government by the ANAP required a modus vivendi between the military leadership, which naturally looked upon the presidency as the locus of the highest authority, and the Özal government, which derived its political power from a comfortable majority in the Parliament. But the ANAP, which included a heterogeneous group of members from widely divergent backgrounds with a broad spectrum of ideologies, ranging from liberal to all shades of right, had neither a critical mass of experienced politicians nor the military's confidence. The fact that some ANAP deputies had been active supporters of the former ethnic nationalist right-wing Nationalist Action Party and of the religious right-wing National Salvation Party was a cause of concern. It is ironic that the military was stuck with less-than-desirable partners in the majority party after having carefully planned the transition and disqualified a number of politicians who, in the final analysis, might have presented less of a problem. Cohabitation, under the circumstances, would hardly be possible; the solution was a tacit division of labor between the presidency and the government.

A successful modus operandi was quickly achieved, with President Kenan Evren taking responsibility over all matters relating to internal and external security, as well as foreign affairs and higher education—matters about which the military commanders were highly sensitive. The prime minister cooperated fully. From the beginning, President Evren took it upon himself to chair the cabinet meetings when the agenda included major national security items, such as the unrest in the southeastern region. At a press conference after one such meeting, when asked about the developments in the region, Prime Minister Özal simply said, "We received the President's directives" regarding the situation.[3] All matters relating to the economy, in turn, came under the purview of the government. President

---

[3]On the relations between the president and the prime minister during the 1980s, see Metin Heper, "The Executive in the Third Turkish Republic, 1982-1989," *Governance* 3 (1990): 299-319.

Evren often avoided answering questions about economic policy and, on at least one occasion, stated tersely that "the economy is the government's problem."[4]

In the initial period of transition, civilianization had not yet become a focus of attention. The issue was confined to the delegation of an autonomous area of responsibility to the elected government, whereas politics remained largely under the supervision of a nonelected authority. Although a complete transition ultimately required the removal of nonelected authority from the political arena, the simultaneous need to build civilian institutions to displace the military in the active guardianship of the state was not brought onto the agenda until 1987. In the intervening years, Prime Minister Özal gradually extended the government's sphere of influence to include the civil bureaucracy and increased his control over economic affairs by appointing a loyal team of technocrats and private-sector managers to top governmental positions.[5] With respect to matters related to internal and external security, as well as foreign affairs and higher education, however, the government appeared to be operating strictly within the framework of the division of labor with the military. It sought and received the president's approval nearly for all of its decisions concerning these matters and their implementation.[6]

The military, in the meantime, began to return to the barracks according to its own timetable for an orderly transition. Beginning in 1984, martial law was gradually lifted, province by province, but the military presence in public life remained strong. Those indicted under martial law continued to be prosecuted in military courts, and the trials, which were reported in the press, increased public awareness of military authority. There remained, in fact, a lingering doubt as to whether the military would completely forego its policing duties, especially in view of the precarious situation in the southeast, where armed resistance by separatists had evolved into a full-fledged guerrilla warfare. General Necdet Üruğ, the chief of general staff, attempted to dispel these doubts and tried to reassure the public that the military would return to its professional duties by the end of 1985. Much to his credit, Üruğ prepared the armed forces for an orderly transition by repeating often, in official communications and briefings, his decision to pull the military back into the barracks.

Such assurances notwithstanding, the process of transition failed to capture public attention. The press dwelt more on the military influence at the center of political authority than on the issue of building credible civilian institutions. Its emphasis on the need for demilitarization (that is, diminishing the role of the military in public decisionmaking) rather than on

---

[4]Ibid.

[5]For these appointments, see Metin Heper, "The State and Debureaucratization: The Case of Turkey," *International Social Science Journal* 42 (1990): 611.

[6]Henri J. Barkey, "Why Military Regimes Fail: The Perils of Transition," *Armed Forces and Society* 16 (1990): 169-192.

civilianization of the regime (that is, devolution of responsibility from the military to civilian institutions for certain governmental functions) gave rise to critical debates on the role of the military in Turkish politics. Public criticism of the actors involved in the 1980 coup, which was somewhat muted at first, grew sharper and louder; these debates ushered in a nation-wide postmortem of the 1980-1983 regime, which has continued unabated to this day.[7]

Demilitarization was high on the agenda of the opposition politicians. Early in 1986, they began raising objections to the continued involvement of the military in decisionmaking and blamed the 1982 Constitution for having institutionalized the military-civilian division of labor at the top level. At the beginning of 1986, the leaders of two of the opposition parties–Hüsamettin Cindoruk of the True Path Party (DYP) and former prime minister Bülent Ecevit of the Democratic Left Party (DSP)–agreed to join forces in calling for a new constitution, one that would be "prepared by the Grand National Assembly, composed of the true representatives of the people" and then submitted to a referendum.[8] Cindoruk further explained that in their view, the new constitution should eliminate the National Security Council, and its preamble ought to exclude passages that might legitimize military interventions. The constitution they envisaged would also make it impossible for any nonelected group, whether from the civil or the military bureaucracy, to share sovereignty with the nation.

Cindoruk and Ecevit took a strongly antimilitarist stand that was as much a matter of political expediency as of personal engagement. Ecevit had refused to cease criticizing the military regime after he was banned from politics; he had even served a brief prison sentence for his outspo-kenness. Now back in politics, he could build on his credentials as an uncompromising opponent of military interventions. Cindoruk was more a caretaker than a leader of the newly formed DYP, holding the helm for another disenfranchised politician, Süleyman Demirel. A former prime minister who had twice been removed from office by military interven-tions, Demirel, too, had his own reasons for raising objections to military involvement in politics. By adopting a tone strongly critical of the armed forces, the opposition politicians hoped to gain popular support at this time when the average citizen had become weary of omnipresent manifestations of military influence.

---

[7]The following books, in addition to a vast number of newspaper and periodical articles, have contributed to the debate on the role of the military: Yalçın Doğan, *Dar Sokakta Siyaset: 1980-1983* (Istanbul: Tekin Yayınevi, 1985); Türker Alkan, *12 Eylül ve Demokrasi* (Istanbul: Kaynak Yayınları, 1986); Celil Gürkan, *12 Mart'a Beş Kala* (Istanbul: Tekin Yayınevi, 1986); Yavuz Donat, *Buyruklu Demokrasi, 1980-1983* (Ankara: Bilgi Yayınevi, 1987); Emre Kongar, *12 Eylül ve Sonrası* (Istanbul: Say, 1987); Nevzat Bölügiray, *Sokaktaki Asker* (Istanbul: Milliyet, 1989); Muammer Yaşar, *Paşalar Politikası* (Istanbul: Tekin Yayınevi, 1990). These debates have gained renewed vigor with the November 1990 publication of Evren's memoirs; see note 2, above.

[8]*Cumhuriyet* (Istanbul daily), 11 January 1986.

Some commentators voiced even stronger objections to any kind of military involvement in political life. İlhan Selçuk, a columnist for the influential Istanbul daily, *Cumhuriyet*, saw militarism as a threat to the established order and even took Cindoruk to task for having as members of his own party retired generals who had held important posts during the 1980-1983 period.[9] With the perceived popularity of antimilitary rhetoric in mind, even the mild-mannered leader of the Social Democratic Populist Party (SHP), Professor Aydın Güven Gürkan, joined the chorus of seasoned opposition politicians by leveling accusations at the ANAP government for "not being a civilian or democratic government."[10]

Accusations against the military were countered by those who emphasized consensual politics as the chief requisite for a properly functioning democracy. "Democracy is contingent on having serious and responsible political parties," stated a retired general in an editorial page, and he argued that past civilian governments had been neither democratic nor prudent. The excesses of the Democratic Party regime (1950-1960), the general continued, had forced the military to intervene in 1960 in order to restore democracy. As for the 1980 coup, it had been the failure to achieve consensus among the political parties, leading to a parliamentary stalemate, that had led to the military intervention in the first place.[11] "Military interventions," posited Mehmet Ali Kışlalı in a weekly editorial, "cannot be prevented by oratorical declamations but by making democracy work as a consensual system."[12]

Those who placed priority on regime stability also took exception to unrestrained attacks on the military. The institution itself had not only been a stabilizing factor during the gradual evolution of competitive politics but it had also been a progressive force throughout modern Turkish history: It was responsible for introducing reforms and upholding the type of republicanism that had enabled the introduction of a multiparty system in the first place. It made no sense, therefore, to try to weaken this institution by attempting to mobilize public opinion against it–especially since without the ballast it provided, the country could once more plunge into turbulence.[13]

The news of religious fundamentalists' infiltration of military schools gave rise to broader public concern with protecting the integrity of the military institution. A December 1986 investigation revealed sectarian affiliation among students of several military *lycées*; and 33 cadets in Istanbul's Kuleli Military *Lycée*, who were found guilty of propagating fundamentalist activities, were immediately dismissed. The chief of general staff,

---

[9]İlhan Selçuk, "Militarizm," *Cumhuriyet*, 15 April 1986.

[10]"Hükümet Sivil Değil," *Cumhuriyet*, 28 April 1986.

[11]Sıtkı Ulay, "Demokrasi Özlemi," *Milliyet* (Istanbul daily), 1 September 1986.

[12]*Haftaya Bakış* (Ankara weekly), 2-8 November 1986.

[13]See inter alia Aydın Yalçın, "Türk Ordusunun Milli Özellikleri," *Forum* (Ankara fortnightly), 15 November 1985.

who had acted swiftly and firmly, gave assurances that the situation was under control; still, liberals and social democrats were greatly alarmed by the news. Although they had little sympathy for the military, they did not wish to see it succumb to "darker forces of fundamentalism," for they implicitly acknowledged the importance of the military as a guarantor of secularism.

None of these groups expected the elected government to take a hard line and act as a bulwark against the spread of religious revival into the state institutions, given the significant representation of Islamicists and their well-established power base within the ANAP. Some of them wondered, perhaps not without some wishful thinking, whether the president and the National Security Council would fully exercise the powers assigned to them by the 1982 Constitution to stem what was perceived as a reactionary tide. Others emphasized the need to find "civilian solutions" for protecting democracy from the forces threatening to undermine the country's secular order.[14] Religious extremism, they warned, could trigger an authoritarian response from the armed forces if adequate measures were not taken to protect the institutions of the state from infiltration by fundamentalists. The issue of fundamentalism is what broke the ranks of those who had been rallying around the banner of demilitarization.

Then, early in 1987, Prime Minister Özal introduced the notion of civil society into the political debate. "In the West," he said in an interview, "where civilianization and civilization are taken to be synonymous, people have fought long battles over centuries to gain the right to govern themselves. In Turkey, on the other hand, civilian institutions were first established during the Atatürk period when there was a transition from community [Ümmetçilik, literally 'religious communitarianism'] to nationhood [milliyetçilik, literally 'nationalism']. However, " continued Özal," the idea that the individual should be subservient to the state remained the prevailing outlook in Turkey until recently." Calling for a revision of this outlook, he advocated the principle that the state should be for the people and not the people for the state as the basis of civil society (sivil toplum).[15]

Özal's discourse on civil society did not relate to social organization or institutions functioning independently of state authority, but in the context of Turkish political sensitivities, it related more immediately to the issue of civilianization than an academically oriented discourse would. There was a neat parallel between the idea of diminishing the state's supervision over society and that of diminishing the military's guardianship of prudent

---

[14]Ali Sirmen, "Sivil Çözümler Üretmek," *Cumhuriyet*, 16 January 1987. The phrase *sivil toplum* ("civil society") made an effective double entendre under the circumstances. The word *sivil* could be taken in its literal meaning *civilian* by those unfamiliar with the sociological term. Cf. Reinhard Bendix, *Kings or People: Power and the Mandate to Rule.* (Berkeley: University of California Press, 1980), p. 523: "Civil society refers to all institutions in which individuals can pursue common interests without detailed direction or interference from the government."

[15]Inter alia, *Milliyet*, 15 January 1987; the headline stretched across eight columns.

government by pulling the army back into the barracks.

Soon, however, the issue of fundamentalism again drew public attention away from all other political considerations, and Özal's pronouncements on civil society were temporarily obscured. A few days after Özal's interview was published, the press revealed a report on fundamentalist activities, which was prepared by the armed forces and presented directly to the National Security Council as the army's warning to reactionary movements. The report, in fact, had been presented to the National Security Council, but the prime minister had not subsequently brought it to the cabinet for discussion. Did the prime minister wish to distance himself and his government from an internal security issue that normally came under the purview of the presidency? Or did he feel uncomfortable bringing this particular issue for discussion among the ANAP politicians, a significant proportion of whom represented traditionalist groups and religious conservatives? The press claimed the ANAP had been thrown into a state of disarray over the issue of religion in public life, whereas the president had acted decisively in condemning reactionary movements and the public manifestations of religious posturing they engineered.[16]

Özal seemed to be in a difficult spot. As prime minister he could not risk creating the impression that he was at odds with the National Security Council. He could also not afford to share the National Security Council's strictly secularist stand, a position that he had eschewed a few days before ("there is presently no danger of fundamentalism"), possibly in anticipation of the developments to come. He hurriedly called a news conference in which he stressed that there were no major differences between the president and himself and that they shared the same concern about the "potential danger of fundamentalism." He added, however, that it was normal to have some differences of opinion, since "it is not possible for both of us to hold exactly the same views on every single issue." Were that the case, he told the reporters, "then you would claim, like others do, that we [the ANAP government] are an extension of the military rule."[17]

Most opposition leaders and the bulk of the press (ranging from left of center to moderate right) were convinced that the armed forces were unhappy with the government's equivocal position on fundamentalism, thus fueling speculations of a military intervention. When asked if the report given to the National Security Council reflected any restlessness on the part of the armed forces, Özal replied that the military felt uneasy only over the issue of fundamentalism and "nothing else." The statement, possibly meant to be preemptive, was a clever means of diverting attention from perceived strains between the military and the government by bringing the focus back to the issue of fundamentalism as if it were a problem the government and the military both faced.

The real challenge to the military came in the form of demands for a

---

[16]*Milliyet*, 15 January 1987.
[17]*Nokta* (Istanbul weekly), 5 April 1987.

constitutional amendment to remove the bans on former politicians. Both Ecevit and Demirel had not only been fully engaged in political debates but had come to act like political leaders. Despite the bans, they had been speaking out in political rallies and ignoring attempts by the prosecutors to charge them with violating the law. With the European Parliament and the European Community (EC) Commission watching closely over human rights in Turkey, it would have been impolitic to press for their prosecution. Early in 1986, President Evren had agreed to the lifting of the ban on public speaking, but the ban on participation remained in force.

With Demirel functioning as the chairperson of the DYP in everything but name and Ecevit leading the new DSP, which was ostensibly headed by his wife, the constitutional bans had been reduced to mere technicalities. Public opinion strongly favored restoring full rights to the former politicians. Some members of the ruling ANAP also joined the opposition parties in calling for the complete lifting of the bans, despite the fact that this would strengthen the competitive ability of the opposition. President Evren soon signaled that he would not object to a constitutional change concerning this issue.

The president's position reflected a significant shift from his earlier stand as the unequivocal guardian of the 1982 Constitution. His agreement to an early constitutional change was interpreted as a retreat in the face of increasing political pressure. As a result, critics of the regime gained enough confidence to make further demands for change. The scope of political debates broadened throughout the first half of 1987, bringing further challenges to the guarantors of the regime. The SHP went so far as to declare its intention to bring a parliamentary motion to amend Provisional Article 15 of the Constitution which provided immunity to members of the National Security Council—that is, the military leadership that had assumed executive and legislative powers on 12 September 1980. Although no such motion was ever considered in the Parliament, the declaration itself was tantamount to a threat to hold the president and, among others, the chief of general staff, personally accountable and liable for their actions and decisions during the 1980-1983 period.

The prime minister's interference in the succession of the chief of general staff constituted a major setback for the military. The news of Özal's decision to overrule the recommendation of the senior military command and to nominate his own candidate, General Necdet Öztorun, to succeed General Üruğ came as a surprise on 30 June 1987. Although civilian governments had previously promoted their own candidates within the top military command, they had taken great pains to manipulate promotions and assignments in advance to secure a clear path for the promotion of their preferred nominees. Özal's sudden decision was unprecedented. Whatever the prime minister's hidden political agenda, if any, might have been,[18] the announcement of the decision was clearly intended to demonstrate the power of the government over the military. Procedures for the new appointment were completed with lightning speed, and the president signed all necessary decrees within twenty-four hours.

The president's position reflected the breakdown of the barrier between the state and the government, but it also pointed to the emerging distinction between the state and the military. The government's demonstrated show of strength in establishing political authority over the military, as well as the president's acquiescence, dispelled the mystique surrounding the military's omnipotence as an agent of the state. The role of the armed forces in Turkish society and within the governmental structure of the republic—once considered taboo subjects—were now debated openly.

The notion that the armed forces were protectors of democracy was effectively challenged by convincing arguments to the contrary, pointing to the fact that praetorian guardianship could only impede the development of civil-societal institutions essential for obtaining a functioning democratic system. As one observer put it bluntly in a newspaper article, "It is impossible to establish a pluralist democracy, in the Western sense of the term, under the leadership of the armed forces, with their norms and behavioral patterns [imposed on the system.] Secondly, leaving them outside of any supervision may lead democracy to experience serious bottlenecks in the future."[19]

Because it had been tacitly agreed that political authority would not interfere with matters relating to the internal organization and funding requirements of the military, none of these issues—including the defense budget—had been debated in the Parliament since the 1960 military intervention. These taboos were also broken by the Özal administration, which in the summer of 1987 took the initiative in reviewing the country's defense funds and brought into public discussion resource requirements for professionalizing the army.

As if to cut the military down to size, a few months later Özal declared his plan to make the chief of general staff report to the defense minister, citing the example of Western democracies. He promised to obtain the necessary constitutional amendment to effect the change if his party returned to the Parliament with a two-thirds majority after the elections. What appeared to be a campaign promise was interpreted as a major operation toward domesticating the army within the governmental structure.[20] Although

---

[18] Three interpretations, not mutually exclusive, appeared in the press: (1) Özal had wished to block General Üruğ's carefully planned schedule of promotions that would bring his protégés to the top positions for the remainder of the century; (2) Özal had objected to General Necdet Öztorun in particular because the latter was known as an uncompromising Atatürkist and an expert in economic affairs who would not agree with Özal's policies; (3) General Öztorun had failed to provide timely information to the government about an attack by insurgents in the southeast.

[19] *Nokta*, 16 August 1987.

[20] A report in *Milliyet*, 12 October 1988, illustrated how the defense minister had taken on

Özal's plan was not implemented after his party gained less than a two-thirds majority in the Parliament, both the government and the defense ministry assumed greater authority over defense requirements, and the military budget was openly discussed. An interesting development was the formation of a public relations department in the Office of the General Staff soon after military issue came under public scrutiny.

In their aggressive drive to extend the influence of politics over matters of state, politicians met less with resistance than with recognition. The military and the president assumed a conciliatory tone on the issue of constitutional change. The president, in fact, acknowledged in a public speech that his powers as president were limited now that "a Parliament was formed, and a new government established."[21]

Civilianization

President Evren's willingness to allow a shrinkage of the state sphere and a corresponding augmentation of the political sphere was reinforced by the views expressed the day after the president's speech by the chief of general staff, who saw nothing sacrosanct about the bans on the politicians. "Perhaps we were mistaken in imposing these bans," admitted General Üruğ, who also said he felt uneasy about the president being drawn into polemics and warned against turning the constitutional issue into a crisis at a time when Turkey was facing dangerous challenges in the region.[22] The message was clear: The presidency would remain uncompromised by politics even if politics were allowed to challenge the presidency, and the military would retain responsibility (through the National Security Council) over security issues even after it returned to the barracks.

The issue of the constitutional amendment was eventually settled by a decision to submit it to public referendum. Not having the amendment voted on in the Parliament was a face-saving device for Prime Minister Özal, who cherished neither the idea of mobilizing his party's parliamentary majority to oppose the amendment nor of having seasoned politicians with grass-roots support join the opposition against his ANAP. Before the referendum, however, he campaigned against the amendment. After the amendment passed by the barest margin, Demirel and Ecevit–the very politicians the military had singled out as being the chief culprits in allowing the country to slide into anarchy in the late 1970s–assumed leadership of their respective political parties. Even the leaders of the former Islamicist

---

the responsibility to provide public explanation of the government's decision to cut the share of defense in the national budget and to discontinue housing construction for the military. A year later, the foreign minister declared that his ministry substantially differed from the Office of the General Staff regarding reduction in conventional forces; *Hürriyet* (Istanbul daily), 18 December 1989.

[21] *Milliyet*, 13 May 1987.

[22] *Haftaya Bakış*, 3-9 May 1987.

and ultranationalist parties, both of whom had criminal charges pressed against them after the 1980 coup, reemerged in the political arena.

In the meantime, the Özal government had begun to pursue a strategy of gradually curtailing the influence of the military on public policy. Despite the tacit agreement of cooperation between the president and the prime minister, the latter gradually came to act independently of the former, with a view to distancing himself and his party from the military leadership. The government began to ignore many of the regulations promulgated during the military regime and in other cases introduced new legislation to replace the draconian measures of the military era. New laws were enacted that severely restricted, but nevertheless allowed, collective bargaining and strikes, public meetings and demonstrations, the right to form associations and to make collective petitions–all of which had been made illegal in 1980. Moreover, the maximum period of detention of suspects prior to arraignment was reduced from 90 to 15 days, all but one of the labor unions were allowed to operate (the exception was the Confederation of Revolutionary Labor Unions, which was under indictment), and restrictions on forming new political parties were lifted. The government also replaced the military liaison appointees in each ministry with civilian administrators, and the death sentences passed by the military courts ceased to be implemented because the Parliament would no longer give the required approval. With the martial law in the last four provinces due to expire in July 1987, even so committed an antimilitarist as Cindoruk could bring himself to say, "The army has withdrawn from politics."[23]

The Özal government even came to ignore a key constitutional provision that affected parliamentary deputies. The Constitution put severe restrictions on the movement of parliamentary deputies from one party to another. Accordingly, any deputy who resigned from a party to join another would face loss of parliamentary membership by a vote of the absolute majority of the Parliament; nor could such a deputy be nominated as a candidate in the following elections by the central bodies of any party existing at the time of the deputy's resignation. The frequent and easy transfer of deputies among political parties had made it difficult to obtain stable majority governments prior to 1980, leading to disruption, immobilism, and a continued search for viable new coalitions. When transfers began in 1987, Prime Minister Özal did not threaten to use the ANAP's parliamentary majority to discourage deputies from changing parties or to remove from the Parliament those who had switched sides.

The government, meanwhile, continued to extend its authority into areas involving internal security. After the termination of martial law in the remaining provinces, the government announced the creation of a regional governorship with extraordinary powers to coordinate and im-

---

[23]*Milliyet*, 10 February 1988.

plement counterinsurgency measures against separatist guerrillas in eight southeastern provinces. A decree law empowered the Council of Ministers to arbitrate conflicts arising from the governor's exercise of the extraordinary powers vested in him, except for those that depended upon judicial decisions or military law. The government appointed a civil servant as governor to serve under the authority of the Ministry of the Interior Affairs. Another decree gave the prime minister unprecedented powers over the recruitment and personnel policies of the National Intelligence Agency (MIT). Although in principle the MIT had been attached to the prime minister (not the prime ministry), it was headed by a uniformed general appointed by the National Security Council and thus had a close connection to the Office of the General Staff. The agency, moreover, was claimed to have been virtually free of any supervision by governmental authority and had a past record of being selective in passing information to civilian governments.[24] The government's sudden decree, aiming to establish teams of experts within the organization to furnish intelligence reports directly to the prime minister, took the public by surprise: Was the MIT also being civilianized? This question could not be resolved quickly, but it remained a significant item on the agenda for national debate, thus bringing one more taboo subject into public discussion.

The MIT issue was temporarily eclipsed by several developments following the 29 November 1987 general elections. The opposition leaders and deputies failed to show due respect to the president when he addressed the first session of the new Parliament, whereas the ANAP deputies greeted him with a standing ovation. Shortly after this display of appreciation by the governing party, however, the state protocol was altered, elevating the prime minister over members of the Presidential Council (which was composed of four generals who, together with Evren, had conducted the 1980 military intervention and who now acted in an advisory capacity to President Evren). The change reflected symbolicly the increasing power of politics over the state to the extent of giving precedence to the elected chief executive over the constitutionally appointed guardians of the state. The military did not react: When asked what he thought about the change in the protocol, the new chief of general staff replied somewhat obliquely, "That is a political question."[25]

A month later, public opinion was stirred with the news of a secret MIT report that had been leaked to the press. The so-called report–which was worthy of the boulevard press and equally unconvincing–contained allegations, among others, of a sexual liaison between the former chief of general staff and a popular singer. Several commentators assessed the

---

[24]Several former prime ministers have asserted that the MIT deliberately withheld information from them. Demirel in particular complained that the MIT had kept him deliberately in the dark while military interventions were planned and twice executed against his government.

[25]*Milliyet*, 10 February 1988.

surfacing of this report as part of a plot to discredit the MIT, with a view to weakening its resistance to political control. Others viewed it as part of a vindictive effort to denigrate General Üruğ, who was held in high esteem even among antimilitarists. Whatever its circumstances, the report drew a sharp reaction from the president and the chief of general staff, as well as from military leaders, and public prosecutors initiated criminal a investigation.

Within two weeks, the prime minister's office said changes were not sought in the law governing the MIT, whose chief would remain a uniformed general. Provisions would be made to allow the chief a longer term in office to ensure administrative continuity and effectiveness. Concerning the speculations as to whether the MIT would be civilianized, sources at the prime ministry responded that it was a mistake to make a distinction between civilians and the military as far as the state's intelligence services were concerned.

It seemed as if the prime minister had backed down under pressure. The response from his office, calculated to appease the president and military leaders, stood in sharp contrast with the civilianization rhetoric of politicians, which essentially dwelt on the distinction between civilians and the military. But this time it proved difficult to appease them. With the president's term expiring the following year, a conspiracy was suspected to compromise the military's prestige and thereby pave the way for Özal's civilian presidency.

Meanwhile, Özal had made public his desire to change the procedures for presidential elections (from parliamentary to popular vote) and the length of the president's term in office (from one seven-year term to a maximum of two five-year terms). These proposals, which would have entailed yet another constitutional amendment, thinly disguised a wish to create a presidency resembling the U.S. model–that is, having a chief executive with a mandate from the people. Özal's obsession with the presidency lent credence to the conspiracy theory. The president felt obliged once more to state categorically that normal procedures were followed in reaching and implementing the decisions regarding military promotions and the state protocol; yet at the same time he sharply warned against the use of the term "civilianization" as a political slogan.

It soon turned out, however, that the government's plans for reorganizing the MIT had not been abandoned but were temporarily shelved to avoid further tensions. When cornered by the press in mid-June 1988, the prime minister said that the law governing the MIT could be reviewed and changed in the future but the government was occupied with other issues at present. Any such review, he added, had nothing to do with civilianization: The MIT might or might not eventually be headed by a person with a military background. The whole issue came full circle three months later, when Adnan Kahveci, then minister of state, applauded public discussion and criticism of the MIT within the context of Turkey's contemporary

democratic order and said that changing times dictated making adjustments in the management and operations of the MIT. The question of a
civilian chief for the MIT remained open until after the presidential elections in October 1989. Soon after the elections, it was taken up again by
members of the new cabinet, who brought this issue–along with the proposal to place the chief of general staff under the defense minister–to the
attention of the civilian president. Nothing came from that initiative.

Although the ANAP government seemed to have established control
over the sphere of politics, lingering doubts remained as to whether and
for how long the military might remain passive while being placed in
a position increasingly subservient to political authority. These doubts
resulted in part from a deeply seated perception that the Turkish military
would not willingly concede its time-honored role as the protector of the
state from internal as well as external threats. A large segment of public
opinion sincerely believed that the military would not accept a loss of
influence or of prestige. This stemmed in part from the perception that the
military would not remain a passive spectator while the ANAP gradually
dismantled many of the safety valves placed by the military to perpetuate
Turkey's state tradition.[26]

A pivotal issue was the divergence between the ANAP's relaxed attitude
toward religion and the strongly Atatürkian orientation of the military.
The ANAP's unwillingness to uphold Atatürk's secularist principles in
all areas of social life was viewed by the party's critics as an example
of reckless and irresponsible behavior that would engender yet another
military coup. Various theories also came to rise explaining the military's
cooperation rather than its perceived impatience with the government.
Some believed that despite appearances, the military continued to wield
power over the government behind closed doors. Others believed, to
the contrary, that the military's influence over the government had been
compromised by President Evren's cooperation with Prime Minister Özal
and by his failure to defend the prestige of the military. A third theory
was that the military had been weakened by the infiltration of religious
activists in the lower ranks and therefore lacked the strength to stand up
against political authority.

Contradictory perceptions notwithstanding, public opinion remained
obsessed with a possible renewed military intervention in the political
sphere. The president's public support of pluralist democracy, and his oc-
casional remarks on how the military had saved the country from anarchy
and chaos, were interpreted as carrots and sticks offered by the true source
of power during an extended period of transition. For example, one such
remark by the president in April 1988, to the effect that the armed forces
would again save the country from terrorism and anarchy, was widely interpreted as constituting a warning. Yet in 1988, the opposition no longer

---

[26]Concerning the safety valves in question, see Metin Heper, *The State Tradition in Turkey*
(Walkington, England: Eothen Press, 1985).

felt it had to mince its words in publicly criticizing the president for such blatant interference in the political arena. Even some leading industrialists stated that military intervention was not necessary or wholesome for the country's development. In the face of strong public reaction, the president retreated, saying that there was no danger of military intervention and that his remarks were aimed at reminding the public of the achievements of the 1980 intervention in establishing a peaceful social order.

The view that the military had become increasingly unwilling to intervene in politics gained credence in December 1990. When he disagreed with the policy pursued by President Özal in the Gulf War, Chief of General Staff Necip Torumtay resigned "over a matter of principle," instead of sending a memorandum to the president, as had been the earlier practice.

Conclusion

As the foregoing discussion suggests, the recent Turkish case is in many ways atypical of transitions from military rule and contrasts with the two preceding transitions, which displayed uncommon characteristics as well. Prior to the 1980s, Turkish transitions were characterized more as a contest between the sphere of politics and that of the state than as a passage from military to civilian rule. Both the 1960-1961 and 1971-1973 interventions were meant and perceived to be temporary suspensions of the political process. Because in both cases the military intervened on behalf of the state in coalition with civilian state elites, a military-civilian cleavage did not come into sharp focus prior to 1980. The transitions following these interventions were marked by a quick comeback of political actors and their eventual, but temporary, victory in gaining the upper hand and rendering the state elites ineffectual.

Unlike the earlier interventions, in 1980 the military executed the coup and implemented its program without having any partners among the intelligentsia, the civil bureaucracy, or the professional community. Although when the 1980 coup occurred the majority of the population was relieved that political conflict and violence were brought to an end, for the first time in Turkish history the military appeared as an isolated stratum rather than as part of the country's elite coalition. Its failure to bring political leaders to consensus ended the military's long-standing role as a moderating force among the elites. The military ceased to be viewed as an impartial arbiter after all the existing parties were closed in 1981. As a result, demilitarization and civilianization became key issues.

These issues were gradually resolved within a framework of a threeway contest that developed among the military, the ruling ANAP, and the opposition. Prime Minister Özal's ability to maintain a division of labor with the military mitigated the danger of confrontation, as had the military's earlier acceptance of his party's victory at the polls.

Also, a working relationship between the president and the political executive at the top made it easier for the military to withdraw into the barracks. Assured of its continued influence at the highest level, the military gradually relaxed its control over the civilian regime and devolved its powers to the political authority. The pressures from abroad as well as from the bulk of the intelligentsia and politicians also played an important role in this devolution.

Other factors also contributed to a smooth demilitarization and civilianization. One of these was prime ministers' exclusive focus on economic issues. Özal's notion of "the state for the people" gained currency in an environment in which private initiative was encouraged and government controls were lifted. Economic policies offered a convenient means for placing political priorities ahead of statist considerations without coming into an ideological conflict with the state.

A second factor was the extension of the laissez-faire approach to public debates on highly sensitive issues, such as the role of religion in public life. As a result, the people came to prefer pluralism as a comfortable alternative to ideological conflict. Age-old taboos were broken in an atmosphere that allowed increased freedom of criticism and debate, and the Özal government gradually, but firmly and deliberately, brought issues such as military appropriations, promotions, and strategy under public scrutiny–in part to diminish the influence of the military.

The third factor was the appearance of a cleavage in the state sphere itself. The presidency became distinguished from the military, as the latter gradually assumed a more professional role and avoided (probably in some instances with considerable restraint) being drawn into conflicts within the political sphere. President Evren, in turn, took on an increasingly conciliatory tone in response to criticism leveled at him or the military and eventually stressed the civilian character of his office.

Civilianization of politics was fully realized in 1989, with the election of the first civilian president since the 1950s. Özal's presidency also marked the end of the distinction between the state elites and political elites, possibly bridging the deep cultural cleavage that caused military interventions to occur in the first place. In an increasingly pluralist Turkey, democracy no longer merely represents the ideology of the state but is taken by many to be a positive contemporary value.

4

Democratization of the Constitutional and Legal Framework

Ergun Özbudun

In this chapter I briefly analyze significant constitutional changes that have taken place since the retransition to democracy, either by way of formal constitutional amendments or through the evolution of the 1982 Constitution. Also relevant are the changes in the Criminal Code (particularly the amendments to Articles 141, 142, and 163) and Turkey's signing and ratification of certain international conventions on the protection of human rights.

Constitutional Amendments

Of the three major political parties in Turkey, the Motherland Party (ANAP) seems to be the most comfortable with the 1982 Constitution, although it has indicated that it was not against making constitutional amendments. As prime minister (1983-1989), Turgut Özal often expressed the view that the new institutions created by the 1982 Constitution should be given a chance to function for some time before amendments could be seriously considered. Also contributing to this position was his desire to avoid an open confrontation with President Kenan Evren, who had declared himself the "guarantor" of the 1982 Constitution.

Consequently, the constitutional amendments realized or considered by the ANAP government (1983-1991) were relatively minor. Although at times Özal spoke of far-reaching changes, such as having the president be elected directly by the people or drawing up a radically different and much shorter constitution essentially limited to a bill of rights, neither project was pursued with any determined effort. Özal favored making the Constitution more flexible by broadening the scope of constitutional referenda, which was consistent with his preference for a more majoritarian type of democracy. Of his many constitutional projects, this is the only one that came to fruition.

Indeed, among the several amendments to the 1982 Constitution, which were introduced in 1987, the most important one was the change in the amendment procedure itself. The original version of the 1982 Constitution (Article 175) required a qualified majority of two-thirds of the full membership of the Turkish Grand National Assembly (TGNA) in order to adopt a constitutional change. The president had the power to send the amending bill back to the assembly for reconsideration. If the TGNA readopted the bill by the same majority, then the president also had the power to submit it to a popular referendum. Furthermore, during a six-year period following the reintroduction of civilian politics (6 December 1983-6 December 1989), the president had even broader powers regarding constitutional amendments: If the president returned an amending bill to the assembly for reconsideration, the assembly could override the president's veto only by a three-fourths majority of its full membership (Provisional Article 9). This provision was evidently designed to increase President Evren's control over constitutional amendments.

The essence of the change brought to the amendment procedure in 1987 was to make constitutional change somewhat easier. The new Article 175 provides for two different methods of amendment. One requires a less stringent majority for the adoption of constitutional changes: If the TGNA passed an amendment by a majority greater than three-fifths but less than two-thirds of its full membership, such a bill could become a constitutional amendment, provided that it was approved by a popular referendum. In such cases, constitutional referendum is mandatory if the president does not return the bill to the assembly for reconsideration. If he does so, then the amendment procedure becomes identical to the second method: If a proposed amendment is adopted by the assembly by a two-thirds majority either at its first deliberation or upon its being returned by the president, the president has the power to submit it to a referendum. In this case, referendum is optional. In referenda, a simple majority of the total number of valid votes cast is sufficient for amendment.

The changes made in Article 175 did not entirely satisfy Özal, who favored further changes in the amendment procedure in order to make the Constitution even more flexible. A year later he suggested that the minimum number of parliamentary votes required for the passage of the amendment bill could be lowered from its present level of 270 (three-fifths of the full membership of the TGNA) to 250 or even to 226 (that is, the absolute majority of its full membership), since in either case the amendment would be based on the choices made by a majority of the people's representatives.[1]

---

[1] *Güneş* (Istanbul daily), 25 August 1988.

At the time the amendment procedure was changed, the ANAP lacked the necessary two-thirds majority in the TGNA. The major opposition party, the Social Democratic Populist Party (SHP), was opposed to facilitating constitutional amendments and voted against it in the TGNA. The deputies from the True Path Party (DYP), however, supported the change–albeit somewhat reluctantly–since the ANAP insisted on changing the amendment procedure as a precondition for submitting to a referendum the lifting of the ban on former political leaders. During the TGNA debates on constitutional amendment the SHP spokepersons argued that under the present electoral system, a party with about 35 percent of the popular vote could obtain a three-fifths majority in the Parliament, in which case a party representing a minority of the electorate could initiate constitutional change without having to seek a broader consensus among political parties. Both the SHP and the DYP deputies also expressed doubt as to the appropriateness of referendum as a means of constitutional amendment, since in referendum campaigns, legal-constitutional arguments were likely to be obscured and demagogic appeals could easily prevail. In the end, Article 175 was amended by 284 votes, with 84 negative votes cast by deputies from the SHP and the Democratic Left Party (DSP).[2]

Two relatively minor and less controversial constitutional amendments adopted by the same act concerned the voting age and the number of deputies in the Parliament. Article 67 of the Constitution was changed to lower the voting age from twenty-one to nineteen. The amended text of the Constitution states, "Every Turkish citizen who becomes twenty years of age during the year of election or referendum, regardless of the month and day of his or her birth, has the right to participate in elections or referenda." Thus, under the circumstances referred to by the Constitution, one can obtain one's right to vote even before turning twenty. The lowering of the voting age reflected a consensus among political parties and in the country at large, although it fell somewhat short of the legal age of majority (eighteen years of age). The second change was an amendment to Article 75 of the Constitution whereby the number of deputies was increased from 400 to 450. This may have been designed to increase the chances of the ANAP deputies being reelected in the approaching general elections.

The most controversial and hotly debated amendment was the repeal of the Provisional Article 4, which had banned political activities of former party leaders. Although none of the political parties represented in the TGNA favored continuing the ban, the ANAP insisted that the repeal should be submitted to a popular referendum. The three opposition parties (SHP, DYP, and DSP), however, argued that the ban should be repealed by the Parliament alone and that a referendum was both unnecessary and undemocratic. The fundamental political rights of individuals, the opposition insisted, should not be put to the test in a referendum. At the

---

[2]*TBMM Tutanak Dergisi* (Minutes of the TGNA Debates), 13 May 1987 and 14 May 1987.

end, however, the DYP deputies, anxious to see an end to the ban, joined the ANAP majority to vote for the repeal of the ban conditional upon its approval by a popular referendum.

The text adopted by the TGNA immediately created a major constitutional issue. Ninety opposition deputies brought a suit before the Constitutional Court, arguing that the Constitution could be amended only in accordance with the amendment procedure in force at the time of the amendment. The TGNA, they argued, completed the amendment process by voting for the repeal of the ban by more than a two-thirds majority. However, the TGNA had no power to add an additional requirement to the amendment procedure in force at the time of its vote on the proposed amendment. It could not, therefore, place further conditions on the repeal enacted.

This argument carried a certain legal weight. However, under Article 148 of the Constitution, the review powers of the Constitutional Court with respect to constitutional amendments are limited to procedural grounds; the court cannot exercise substantive review over constitutional amendments. Furthermore, the Constitution limited the scope of such procedural review to three points: whether the amendment proposal was signed by the requisite number of deputies (one-third of the full membership of the TGNA), whether the amendment proposal was debated twice in the TGNA and not once in accordance with the "urgent procedure" clause, and whether the requisite number of deputies had voted in favor of the amendment. It was no surprise, therefore, that the Constitutional Court rejected the case in a ten-to-one decision, stating that the alleged irregularity was not related to the three points mentioned in the Constitution; hence, it was beyond the jurisdiction of the court to review the constitutionality of the amendment.[3] The referendum held on 6 September 1987 approved the repeal of the ban by a tiny majority (50.1 percent). Although all of the opposition parties supported the repeal in the election campaign, the ANAP opposed it.

In 1988, an attempt was made to change Article 127 of the Constitution through the new amendment procedure. Paragraph 3 of Article 127 stipulates that local elections be held every five years. The ANAP majority, anxious to have local elections earlier than the scheduled time, voted for a constitutional amendment empowering the TGNA to advance the date of local elections up to one year so that this time local elections could be held one year earlier. [4] However, since the two opposition parties were against the amendment, the amendment proposal was adopted by only

---

[3]Court decision of 18 June 1987, *Resmi Gazete* (Official Gazette), 4 September 1987, pp. 22-34.

[4]Earlier, the ANAP majority attempted to advance the date of local elections through ordinary legislation (Law No. 3,420, dated 31 March 1988). The Constitutional Court found it unconstitutional, however, in view of the explicit provision of Article 127 of the Constitution cited above (Constitutional Court decision of 14 June 1988, *Resmi Gazete*, 14 July 1988, pp. 23-69).

282 votes–that is, with more than a three-fifths but less than a two-thirds majority. Therefore, in accordance with the new amendment procedure adopted in 1987, the amendment was automatically submitted to a popular referendum, which was held on 25 September 1988 and resulted in the rejection of the proposed amendment by a 65 percent majority.

Evolutionary Change of the Constitution

In analyzing constitutional changes, a distinction could be made between constitutional amendment and the evolutionary change of a constitution. The latter, more than the former, has characterized constitutional change in Turkey since 1983. The main line of evolution has been the strengthening of the parliamentary character of the governmental system. At the time of its adoption, the 1982 Constitution established a mixed, or hybrid, system of government that combined presidential and parliamentary features. Indeed, the Constitution gave the president important autonomous powers that can be used independently of the Council of Ministers–that is, without requiring the countersignatures of the prime minister and the ministers concerned. Yet, it did not go so far as to adopt a presidential system. The system of government remained essentially parliamentary, in the sense that the executive branch maintained a dual structure, with a president who is not politically responsible to the legislature and a Council of Ministers that is politically responsible to it.[5]

Metin Heper has clearly shown how political power gradually but markedly shifted from the president to the prime minister between 1983 and 1989. Initially, Özal dealt rather cautiously with Evren, limiting himself mostly to matters of economic policy and giving the impression that foreign affairs and security issues were the proper domain of the president. In time, however, Özal became much more assertive; at the same time, he avoided an open confrontation with the president.[6] A significant example of this new assertiveness was seen in the appointment of General Necip Torumtay, as discussed in Chapter 3. This move was widely seen both as a sign of the growing power of the government vis-à-vis the president and as a manifestation of increasing civilian control over the military. Following his election as president in 1989, however, Özal appeared to reverse the process he had initiated and to seek consolidation of political influence in the presidency, at least as long as the ANAP governments were in power. Özal's tendency toward an active presidency seems to have been muted after the formation of the DYP-SHP coalition government

---

[5]For details, see Ergun Özbudun, "The Status of the President of the Republic Under the Turkish Constitution of 1982: Presidentialism or Parliamentarism?" in *State, Democracy and the Military: Turkey in the 1980s,* Metin Heper and Ahmet Evin, eds. (Berlin: Walter de Gruyter, 1988), pp. 37-45.

[6]Metin Heper, "Executive in the Third Turkish Republic, 1982-1989," *Governance* 3 (1990): 299-319.

(led by Süleyman Demirel) following the October 1991 general elections; after that, the cohabitation between Özal and Demirel developed along genuinely parliamentary lines.

Such a gradual shift of power in favor of the prime minister and the Council of Ministers was to be expected. Although the 1982 Constitution consciously sought to create a presidency that would be an impartial symbol of national unity and a guardian of national interest (as opposed to more particularistic interests represented by political parties), the differentiation between the role of the president and that of the politically active and responsible part of the executive is less a matter of constitutional choice than of political circumstances. The distinction that was initially observed between the political spheres of Evren and Özal was essentially dictated by the exigencies of the transition from military to civilian rule and by the fact that Evren became president as the candidate of the military.

Changes in the Criminal Code and Other Laws Concerning Human Rights

Substantive changes made more recently in the criminal law resulted in the removal of the most severe restrictions that had been placed upon individual freedoms since the early Republican period. The Anti-Terror Act (no. 3,713), adopted on 12 April 1991, brought about a number of improvements in the field of human rights, including the commutation of pending death sentences and the conditional release of tens of thousands of prisoners. The most significant effect of this Act was the abolishment of Articles 141, 142, and 163 of the Criminal Code, which had created a category dubbed in Turkish as "crimes of thought." Article 141 banned associations with the purpose of establishing Communist, anarchist, dictatorial, or racist regimes or of "destroying or weakening national sentiments." Article 142 made punishable all acts of propaganda with the purposes stated in Article 141. Article 163 banned associational and propaganda activities aiming to transform the secular nature of the state and to change its basic social, economic, political, or legal order in conformity with religious principles and beliefs.

The repeal of these articles has largely abolished the category "crimes of thought" in Turkish criminal law. Under Article 1 of the Anti-Terror Act, for any such act to be punished, it has to be perpetrated by means of "coercion, force and violence, intimidation, duress or threat." The crimes in question are now defined, in conformity with the practices of other democratic countries, in terms of *methods* by which they are committed, not of their *aims* or the values against which they are committed.

Since the adoption of the Anti-Terror Act, the only remaining crime of thought is separatist propaganda under Article 8 of the new law. However, a more precise definition of separatism has been introduced, and the penalties provided are much milder (two to five years of imprisonment, compared with five to ten years under the previous law).

An equally significant change brought about by the Anti-Terror Act is the repeal of the Act (no. 2,932) on the use of languages other than Turkish. The latter law, passed by the National Security Council (1980-1983), had clearly aimed to ban public use of the Kurdish language. With its repeal, not only verbal but also all written and recorded expressions in Kurdish became free.

Turkey, a member of the Council of Europe, was among the original signatories to the Convention for the Protection of Human Rights and Fundamental Freedoms (4 November 1950) and its Additional Protocol (20 March 1952). However, until recently, Turkey had not recognized the competence of the European Commission of Human Rights to hear individual complaints against it. The competence of the commission was finally recognized in April 1987 by a declaration of the Turkish government enabling any person, non-governmental organization, or group of people to petition the commission for any alleged violation of their rights, provided that all domestic remedies have been exhausted and that the petition is filed within six months of the date on which the final decision was taken, as stipulated in Article 26 of the convention.

Turkey has also become a party to the Council of Europe Convention and the United Nations Convention for the Prevention of Torture and Inhuman Treatment. Turkey was the first member state to ratify, on 26 February 1988, the European Convention for the Prevention of Torture and Inhuman or Degrading Treatment or Punishment, dated 26 November 1987. This convention establishes a European Committee for the Prevention of Torture and Inhuman or Degrading Treatment or Punishment. The committee, by means of visits, examines the treatment of persons deprived of their liberty, with a view to strengthening such persons' protection from torture and from inhuman or degrading treatment or punishment.

The United Nations Convention Against Torture and Other Cruel, Inhuman or Degrading Treatment or Punishment, adopted by the General Assembly on 10 December 1984, was also approved for ratification by the TGNA on 29 April 1988. This convention defines torture and requires the signatory states to take effective legislative, administrative, judicial, or other measures to prevent acts of torture in any territory under their jurisdiction. More recently (8 January 1990), Turkey also recognized the compulsory jurisdiction of the European Court of Human Rights and signed the Paris Charter for a New Europe (21 November 1990), adopted within the framework of the Conference for Security and Cooperation in Europe.

Conclusion

A point emphasized in Chapter 2 was the need for the institutionalization of norms and behavior patterns suitable for a smoothly running democracy in order to prevent the regime from drifting once more into some version of authoritarianism. It was also argued that in a democracy, consensus must be formed on procedural rules rather than on some substantive issues. On both counts, constitutional politics assumes critical importance in the consolidation of democracy in Turkey, for it is in this area that institutionalization is most clearly needed as a countervailing force of stability against pressures stemming from rapid social and political changes.

Although all major political parties in Turkey are strongly committed to a democratic regime, there appears to be a strong need for further agreement among these parties on the procedural rules of democracy. In the post-1983 period, whenever their interests conflicted–such as regarding the lifting of the ban on the pre-1980 politicians or changing the date of local elections – protracted struggles took place among the political parties. In the process, the relations became strained, and progress toward democratization was achieved, but with great difficulty.

Political parties could readily agree among themselves only when a particular arrangement would benefit them all, such as lowering the voting age or increasing the total number of deputies serving in the Parliament. Not unexpectedly under those circumstances democratization took place more easily. Also favorable to democratization were the smooth evolution of relations between Evren and Özal, and the pressures that came from the international environment. The latter contributed especially to the enhancement of human rights in Turkey.

5

Evolution of the Electoral Process

İlter Turan

Turkey experienced comprehensive legal and political changes during the military intervention in its political system in the 1980-1983 period. The military leadership was interested in building a political infrastructure that would help the political system become immune to the turbulence and volatility it had experienced in the pre-1980 era.[1]

The Legacy of the 1980 Military Intervention

Shaping the System Through Electoral Laws

Although they blamed the previous civilian governments for their inability to address such critical problems as a stagnating economy and civil disorder, members of the National Security Council focused on two main factors that had rendered political authority ineffectual in the pre-1980 period: the fragmentation of the party system and the growing importance of small parties in forming coalition governments.[2] They clearly preferred a two-party system consisting of a moderate center-right and a moderate center-left party. To achieve this end, three instruments of electoral engineering were used: cut-off provisions, redistricting, and mandatory voting.

Two separate cut-off provisions were included in the new laws. At the national level, a party was required to obtain 10 percent of the valid votes cast in order to place deputies in the national legislature. This high percentage reflected the concern that unless voting for small parties were rendered clearly unlikely to produce electoral success, votes in the national elections might continue to be broadly dispersed. At the district level, the

---

[1] İlter Turan, "Political Parties and the Party System in Post-1983 Turkey," in *State, Democracy and the Military: Turkey in the 1980s*, Metin Heper and Ahmet Evin, eds. (Berlin: Walter de Gruyter, 1988), p. 63.

[2] İlter Turan, "The Limits of Electoral Engineering," *International Newsletter*, Comparative Representation and Electoral Systems Study Group 2 (1987): 1

electoral quotient was adopted as the cut-off point. The electoral quotient is defined as the number that is obtained when the total number of votes cast in a district is divided by the number of deputies who will be elected to represent it. A party would be required to achieve the electoral quotient as a minimum in a district before qualifying to be included in the allocation of seats in that district. Initially, the districts had between three and seven representatives, rendering the cut-off point at almost 15 percent, even in the largest constituencies. Currently, this threshhold varies between 20 and 25 percent.

Historically, electoral districts in Turkey have corresponded to the administrative division of the country into provinces. Until recently, this meant that provinces that contained metropolitan areas were represented by a very large number of deputies. In 1983, a ceiling of seven deputies per electoral district was introduced, which necessitated the subdivision of large electoral districts into smaller units. In 1987, this limit was reduced to six, further raising the electoral quotient.

Finally, voting was rendered mandatory with two expectations. First, it was thought that a high voter turnout in the referendum to be held for the ratification of the new Constitution would serve to legitimize it while simultaneously preempting nonvoting as a means of protest. Also, the legal obligation to vote was anticipated to encourage the moderate voters—who might have shied away from the ballot box during the turbulent 1970s–to go to the polls, thereby helping to strengthen the political center.

Elections and Voters

On 6 November 1983, the elections were held that marked the passage from military rule to civilian politics. Because only three parties were allowed to compete in the elections (the Motherland Party [ANAP], National Democracy Party, and the Populist Party), it was impossible to test reliably the effects of electoral engineering on the party system. Yet to the extent that all three parties fulfilled the national cut-off requirement, it appeared that one intended consequence of the electoral constraints did not completely work. One party had indeed captured the majority of seats, but this was due to its superior electoral position than to the peculiarities of the electoral system.[3] Regarding how the electorate voted, Üstün Ergüder and Richard I. Hofferbert, using aggregate data, have explored the question of whether the 1983 election results constituted a simple replica of the old system of party preferences.[4] They identified three underlying dimensions along which the votes were split. The first of these was the center-periphery cleavage, in which the center was used to describe

---

[3]I have described the restrictions on the parties and the electoral process in my "Political Parties and the Party System in Post-1983 Turkey," pp. 68-72.

[4]Üstün Ergüder and Richard I. Hofferbert,"The 1983 General Elections in Turkey: Continuity or Change in Voting Patterns?" in State, Democracy and the Military: Turkey in the 1980s, Evin and Heper, eds., pp. 89-98.

the more modern and market-oriented segments of the electorate.[5] The second cleavage was the rather familiar left-right dichotomy found in all modern political systems[6] A third cleavage pertained to "system" versus "anti-system parties."[7] Noting that the results of one election would hardly produce sufficient evidence to judge whether the changed political environment of the post-1980 period had brought about a realignment in voting patterns or a new configuration of cleavages among the parties, the authors nevertheless offered some observations.

It appeared that the ANAP was not "the reincarnation of any single preexisting partisan entity." It was closer to the center in the center-periphery dimension: It was moderately on the right, yet it was also linked somewhat strongly with the anti-system dimension of the 1960s and 1970s.[8] The authors suggested that the absence of an acceptable center may have pushed some voters to the edges of the system and that the ANAP as a moderate-centrist force may have been instrumental in bringing these voters back into mainstream politics.[9] The Populist Party obtained its support from the left. The National Democracy Party drew moderate support from the periphery and from the right but not from among the supporters of the anti-system parties of the pre-1980 period.

Since the 1983 elections, the party system in Turkey has undergone major transformations. All of the parliamentary parties of 1983, with the exception of the ANAP, have departed from the Turkish political scene.[10]

The Changing Environment: Elections and Voters

Competitive politics were restored with the general elections of 1983. Four months later, in March 1984, local elections took place in which parties other than the three represented in the national legislature were allowed to compete. The results indicated that the ANAP continued to enjoy a high degree of support among the electorate, whereas a new set of parties had replaced those the military leadership had favored. The emergent anomaly of the coexistence of parliamentary parties without a credible electoral base and mass-supported parties without parliamentary representation was resolved only gradually. A reconciliation in the form of a merger between parliamentary and external parties proved possible because each side needed the other: Mass-based parties wanted to be represented in the legislature, and the deputies needed a constituency to represent. As a result, the new parties and elements–including some deputies–from the

---

[5]Ibid., p. 91.

[6]Ibid., p. 92

[7]Ibid., p. 93

[8]Ibid., p. 97

[9]Ibid.

[10]For a summary of this transformation, see Turan, "Political Parties and the Party System in Post-1983 Turkey."

parties that had been allowed to take part in the 1983 general elections joined forces to form new organizations in order to achieve both a more powerful electoral base and parliamentary representation.[11]

The Use of Electoral Laws as a Political Instrument

By the mid-1980s, the ANAP began to feel the decline of its popular support base, an experience shared by governing parties at the midterm of their rule. The consolidation of increasingly effective political parties, with improved linkages to their electoral bases, further undermined the ANAP's standing vis-à-vis the electorate.

The response of the ANAP to a perceived significant decline in its electoral support included frequent manipulation of electoral laws. Two strategies, which were contradictory in many ways, were pursued to perpetuate the ANAP's dominant position in the political system. First, provisions of various laws dealing with elections were modified so as to split the votes of the opposition among several parties. Also adopted were measures to encourage the emergence of political parties that appeared likely to take away votes from the major opposition parties. For example, an act passed in July 1986 relaxed the rules of admissibility of political parties to national elections, as well as their access to the use of public radio and television, on a one-time-only basis, with a view to encouraging the fragmentation of opposition. At the same time, however, majoritarian features of the electoral system were strengthened at the expense of small parties by means, for example, of reducing the number of seats available for distribution according to proportional representation.

The by-elections of 28 September 1986 nevertheless indicated that the ANAP was no longer assured of victory. Although by-elections in eleven districts could hardly be termed a nationally representative sample, a comparison of their results with those of the 1983 general elections and the 1984 local elections in the same districts clearly indicated that the electoral fortunes of the governing party had unmistakably taken a turn for the worse.[12]

Sensing that its electoral standing might decline further, in 1987 the ANAP decided to move the general elections one year ahead. Several other factors contributed to this decision. One was the clamoring of the opposition parties, which had been increasingly questioning the ANAP government's legitimacy; they argued that because the ANAP had been elected in quasicompetitive elections under the watchful eye of the National Security Council, it could not be considered truly representative. It made sense for the ANAP to hasten to prove its popular backing while it was still assured of a victory at the polls. Meanwhile, the referendum of 6

---

[11] Ibid.

[12] The intricacies of the electoral system make it virtually impossible to make meaningful predictions about how the shift in votes would have influenced the distribution of seats in the Parliament if these elections were general elections.

September 1987 approved the repeal of the bans on former political leaders, who were impatient to return to the Parliament. Pressures mounted on behalf of the reenfranchised politicians constituted a second reason why the government, which had campaigned against the repeal, would choose to be seen as the proponent of an election in which all actors would freely participate. The third factor was the government's apparent inability to control galloping inflation. The ANAP, aware that the needed austerity measures would be unpopular with the voters, wanted a new lease on life as quickly as possible so it could move on with the adoption of such measures.

A new law that moved the general elections a year ahead was enacted in early September 1987. Some articles of this legislation, which designated 1 November 1987 as the date of the general elections, were challenged in the Constitutional Court. The Social Democratic Populist Party (SHP), which initiated the judicial review procedures, objected, among others, to Article 8, which made it mandatory for the central bodies of political parties to draw up the list of candidates for each district as they saw fit, without the scrutiny or guidance of the High Board of Elections. Confining political parties to only one method of determining candidates, the Social Democrats argued, did not conform with democratic principles.

As the Constitutional Court proceeded to examine the case, preparations for the elections had to be made under the existing law; therefore, the central bodies of the political parties went on to designate their candidates. This undertaking created intense pressures on the leaders of political parties, since not all aspirants could be accommodated with a favorable place on the ballot. The opposition leaders felt the pressure more acutely than did then prime minister Turgut Özal, who enjoyed exceptional prestige as party leader and could count on members of his party to defer to his judgments and decisions even if they did not fully agree with him. His task was made easier by the fact that most of the ANAP's incumbent deputies could be placed in electable spots on the ballot. And since ANAP was expected to win, he was in a position to offer other rewards to those aspirants who would not be elected.

In the cases of both the SHP and the True Path Party (DYP), the incumbents were deputies who had transferred to their current party from one of the military-favored parties that had competed in the 1983 general elections. Therefore, grass-roots party organizations had been looking forward to a primary election as a way of displacing them. In both cases, the party leadership, which was mandated by law to determine the candidates, prepared lists the rank and file considered to be unrepresentative and insufficiently responsive to their preferences. In the case of the DYP, Süleyman Demirel, who had assumed the party's leadership after his political rights were restored, enjoyed sufficient charisma and power that the tensions his decisions generated could be somewhat contained. For the SHP, the internally divisive tendencies were more severe. Its leader,

Erdal İnönü, was not a charismatic politician, and his decisions triggered serious challenges and acrimonious debate. Moreover, because the party was expected to do well in the forthcoming elections, the competition for electable spots on the ballot was intense; failure prompted bitterness and recriminations.

After the ordeal was over, the list of candidates finalized, and the campaign beginning to build up momentum, the Constitutional Court rendered its decision. The court ruled that it was not in keeping with the principles of democracy, as defined in the Constitution, to make it mandatory for the central bodies of political parties to determine candidates.[13] Since the elections were scheduled to take place only three weeks after this decision was announced, and because political parties would have insufficient time to prepare new lists of candidates by using other, more democratic methods–including intra-party primaries–the court's decision had the practical effect of forcing a postponement of the elections.

The Özal government responded to this critical situation by passing a new law on 17 October 1987, moving the date of the elections to 29 November 1987 and redefining the ways by which candidates would be determined. The method already used in drawing up the ballots was allowed, but it was no longer the exclusive way. Both opposition parties proceeded to hold primaries in most of the electoral districts. There was considerable change in the list of candidates when the process was completed.

Early on, the ANAP also chose to strengthen the majoritarian features of the electoral system in anticipation of the benefits it might enjoy. A series of changes introduced in the Political Parties Law and in the Law on the Election of Deputies, beginning in March 1986, made it possible for political parties to nominate a district-level candidate in districts that were entitled to five or more candidates. The district-level candidate was assigned one of the seats allocated to a district, resulting in a reduction in the number of seats available for distribution according to proportional representation and in a concurrent raising of the electoral quotient. The party that obtained the majority or the plurality of the vote in a district would win the district-level seat.

Further changes were made in 1986 and 1987, and an electoral system that was considerably different from the one used in 1983 was applied in 1987.[14] Among the 104 districts that existed at the time of the 29 November 1987 general elections, 46 qualified to have a district-level candidate. In 1991, the number of districts was increased to 107, resulting in a decrease of the district-level seats to 44.

Table 5.1 shows the distortions caused by the existing electoral system, which favored the major political parties in the 1987 and 1991 elections.

---

[13] Decision no. 1,987/27, dated 9 October 1987.

[14] For details, see Hikmet Sami Türk, "YSK Karar ve Sonuçları, 1-2," *Cumhuriyet* (Istanbul Daily), 3 and 4 October 1987.

The system clearly worked against small parties, mainly as a result of the cut-off provisions. Furthermore, as Table 5.2 makes clear, the winner was favored more than the losers. The introduction of the district-level candidate system, which raised the district-level threshold, reinforced the anti-small party bias, but it had little impact on those parties that gained access to the Parliament, because the winning candidate in each district did not necessarily belong to the party that captured the highest number of votes nationwide.

Table 5.1: Distribution of Votes and Seats in the Post-1980 General Elections

	1983		1987		1991	
Parties	Votes (%)	Seats	Votes (%)	Seats	Votes (%)	Seats
ANAP	45.6	211	36.3	297	23.9	115
Populist	30.8	117	-	-	-	-
Nationalist Democracy	23.6	71	-	-	-	-
SHP	-	-	24.8	99	20.7	88
DYP	-	-	23.9	59	27.3	178
Democratic Left	-	-	-	-	11.0	7
Prosperity (Alliance)	-	-	-	-	16.6	62

Note: Percentages of the general vote is adjusted to reflect the distribution of the vote only among political parties that have won seats in the legislature. Percentages contain rounding errors (total number of seats).

It is evident that the ANAP reaped benefits from its successful strategy of changing electoral laws. The effects of the first strategy, dispersing the votes of the opposition, cannot be measured because the extent to which the changes in the electoral laws influence voting behavior cannot be isolated when aggregate data are used. Concerning the second strategy of strengthening the majoritarian features of electoral laws, there is convincing evidence that it has helped the government party significantly. But

Table 5.2: Differences Between Votes and Seats in the 1983, 1987, and 1991 General Elections (percentages)

Parties	1983 Difference	1987 Difference	1991 Difference
Winner	+ 7.2	+ 19.6	+ 12.1
Next-highest-vote getter	- 1.6	- 8.9	+ 1.6
Lowest vote getter	- 5.8	- 10.8	+ 9.4

Table 5.3: The Pro-Motherland Party Vote in General Elections, 1983-1991

Elections	Percentage of Votes
1983 general elections	45.1
1984 local elections	41.5
1986 by-elections	31.0
1987 general elections	36.3
1991 general elections	23.9

more important, the ANAP frequently meddled with electoral and political parties' laws (which also deal with such other matters as the allocation of television time and the extension of government funding to political parties); it changed these laws at whim and succeeded in turning the tables against the opposition. Although there was no question about the legality of these changes, they appear to be dysfunctional in respect to the stability of a competitive political system if they are used often as a political weapon to advance party interests.

The Changing Turkish Voter

If one traces the percentage of the vote captured by the ANAP (the only party that has been in existence since the restoration of competitive politics in 1983) in different elections over an eight-year period, one cannot help but notice the mobility of the Turkish voter or the fluidity of the votes cast (Table 5.3). The flux in the preferences of Turkish voters should not be surprising for several reasons. First, we may recall that many new parties entered politics and the electoral scene after the the 1983 elections. It is understandable that some citizens changed their votes when configuration of political parties was offered.

Second, since the return to competitive politics in 1983, a new generation has entered political life. Those who come of voting age do not necessarily replicate the voting patterns of those who had previously reached that status. Their life experiences, values, and political socialization differ from those of their elders, and these differences are reflected in their political and, specifically, their electoral behavior.

Third, the 1987 elections were the first fully open elections following the 1980 military intervention. All aspiring actors tried to see what chance they had of placing deputies in the legislature in the new electoral environment. Votes were dispersed, and only three parties were able to place deputies in the legislature.[15] In the interim—that is, until early elections were called

---

[15]Turan, "Political Parties and the Party System in Post-1983 Turkey," p. 80. For a more comprehensive study and discussion of the period of transition to democratic politics and its implications for political parties and voters, see also İlter Turan, "Cyclical Democracy: The Turkish Case," Paper delivered at the Annual Meeting of the Midwest Political Science

for 20 October 1991–efforts to forge new political alliances and coalitions were conducted by all political parties. Such efforts continued until the last minute in the case of the three right-wing parties (the Prosperity Party, the Nationalist Work Party, and the Reformist Democracy Party), which managed to produce one ticket under the Prosperity Party label that received nearly 17 percent of the vote and sixty-two parliamentary seats. This alliance of parties helped each individual party to exceed both the national and the district-level thresholds. Those deputies who were affiliated with the junior partners of this electoral alliance have since left the Prosperity Party to return to their "homes."

The realignment of political actors, including Turkish political parties and voters, is partly the consequence of economic and social changes. It has been confounded, however, by the disruption caused by the 1980 military intervention, which attempted to abolish an entire party system and replace it with one of its own creation, as well as by both the unusually strong majoritarian features of the electoral system and the frequency with which changes have been introduced in the electoral and other related laws. Further volatility in voting behavior can be expected until an electoral system is devised on the basis of mutual consensus among major Turkish political parties.

Toward a More Democratic Electoral System

One of the major indicators of the presence of an operating democratic system in a country is the change of government by means of free elections. The elections of 20 October 1991 marked the end of ANAP rule that had been uninterrupted since 1983. Although no party won a majority of the seats in the Parliament, the DYP, having emerged as the plurality party, formed a coalition government with the SHP.

The new government that took office in late November 1991 announced that full democratization of the political system had the highest priority on its agenda, although it has not articulated the specific steps it is prepared to take in this regard. One of its goals, the government stated, was to devise a new electoral system with a view to ensuring a more equitable distribution of parliamentary seats among major contenders. It can be safely assumed that in planning the system, an effort will be made to consult all major political parties, be they in the government or opposition. But whether the end product will reflect a genuine consensus among the major parties remains to be seen. The government also seems determined to review the existing legislation with a view to cleansing it of features that contradict the principles of democracy and human rights as defined in the Universal Declaration of Human Rights, the Helsinki Accords, and the Paris Charter. Many, but not all, such features were introduced during the 1980-1983

Association, Chicago, Illinois, 11-14 April 1984.

military rule. Some of the restrictive legislation was inherited from earlier regimes that placed a premium on national unity over individual liberty, but some restrictive clauses were incorporated into the 1982 Constitution. Those in the latter category cannot be easily removed unless a consensus is reached between the government and the opposition parties on what is to be changed and how that change is to occur. There is little obstacle, however, to the government's ability to amend laws and to introduce changes that would render the existing restrictions in the Constitution ineffectual.

The process of retransition to democracy has now been broadened to achieve full-fledged democratization of the political system. The focus is no longer exclusively on removing the constrains imposed by the military leaders of the 1980 coup; it is now expanding the freedoms and liberties accorded Turkish citizens thus far. The transformation of the political system that began under the ANAP government appears likely to continue in a systematic and sustained way, as evidenced thus far by the pronounced commitment to this objective by the governing as well as major opposition parties.

Conclusion

The new military interventionists opted for a two-party system, which they tried to bring about by introducing to the electoral system cut-off provisions, redistricting, and mandatory voting. The cut-off provisions did not have the intended impact; in the 1983 general elections, three parties returned candidates to the Parliament.

We cannot say that retransition to democracy either proceeded evenly under the ANAP government or was an integrated process. The changes introduced during the ANAP years did not necessarily further democratize political life; rather, they were measures to buttress the electoral chances of the governing party. In addition to strengthening the majoritarian aspect of the electoral system, the ANAP also attempted to manipulate electoral laws in the wake of its dwindling fortunes at the polls.

The post-1991 general election period seems to herald a new era in Turkey's electoral politics. The DYP-SHP coalition has promised to introduce a new electoral system on a par democratically with such systems in the established democracies in the West and to do this through a consensual process.

The Turkish voter has become more sophisticated than has usually been recognized by electoral analysts. The voter is no longer likely to support any political party to the bitter end. Few voters appear to be responsive to purely ideological appeals. Many do not seem to value the confrontational approach to politics that characterized pre-1980 politics in Turkey. Thus, although in the years to come we can expect a further democratization of the electoral process, the electorate's particular attitude may reduce tensions generated by political competition, which have sometimes been so intense that they could not be accommodated by ordinary politics.

PART THREE

Economic Transformation and Governmental Change

6

Liberalization of the Economy

Rüşdü Saracoğlu

Since 1980, Turkey has continually pursued adjustment policies simultaneously with a set of major reforms, albeit with varying intensities at different
times. Its policies, structural reforms, successes, and setbacks, as well as
its economic performance under the program, are detailed in various IMF-
World Bank documents.[1] Condensing that history into a brief chapter
is impossible. Consequently, the account here is limited to a number of
policies and structural reforms that lie at the heart of Turkey's adjustment
strategy. The purpose behind concentrating on a few policies is to bring
them into sharper focus, although the omission of some significant, but
relatively minor, details is likely to detract from a complete picture.

Background

Since the establishment of the Republic of Turkey in 1923, the government has always played a significant role in economic activity. Although
Turkey's founders tried to experiment with liberal economic policies immediately following the republic's formation, the experiment was short-
lived, owing in part to international economic developments that led to the
Great Depression. The Turkish government reacted to these developments
by discontinuing liberal economic policies and reinstituting protectionist
ones. Initially, the government viewed its protectionist policies as temporary measures designed to isolate Turkey from the harmful impact of the
Great Depression and of trade cycles. However, these protectionist policies

---

[1]In particular, international financial statistics and various board documents. Also see
Tosun Arıcanlı and Dani Rodrik, *The Political Economy of Turkey: Debt, Adjustment and Sus-
tainability* (London: Macmillan, 1990); Merih Celasun and Dani Rodrik, *Debt, Adjustment and
Growth: Turkey* (Chicago: University of Chicago Press, 1989); Peter Wolff, *Stabilisation Policy
and Structural Adjustment in Turkey, 1980-1985* (Berlin: German Development Institute, 1987);
Tevfik Nas and Mehmet Odekon, eds., *Liberalization and the Turkish Economy* (Westport, Conn.:
Greenwood Press, 1988).

proved to be more in accord with the general philosophy of the Turkish state tradition,[2] and the temporary measures became permanent.

Under protectionist economic policies, the state was assigned to be the driving force of the economy. The government created state economic enterprises (SEEs) to solve critical supply problems and accelerate industrialization. Initially few in number and operating in critical sectors, these SEEs proliferated rapidly and accounted for a major share of domestic production. With the advent of economic planning in the 1960s, the SEEs gained even more prominence as vehicles of industrialization and accelerated capital formation. Import substitution, a major objective of the economic policy, was adopted–with some political overtones–to assure Turkey's economic independence.

All economic policy instruments were used to support import- substitution. Licensing requirements, quotas, tariffs, and other levies rendered the trade regime excessively restrictive. The payments regime was also extremely conservative, with surrender requirements on external receipts, foreign exchange allocation schemes, and voluminous and complex foreign exchange regulations. The financial system was repressed and highly regulated to assure financial support for import-substitution activities. Nevertheless, by means of these policies the SEEs were able to deliver what was expected of them, and Turkey maintained moderately high growth rates throughout much of the 1960s and early 1970s–notwithstanding a balance-of-payments crisis in 1969, which resulted in even further tightening of the trade regime.

In the wake of the first round of oil price increases, the Turkish economy remained healthy, despite some underlying weaknesses. During the 1968-1973 period, real GNP increased at a rate of about 7 percent per annum. The current account of the balance of payments improved steadily and recorded a surplus for three successive years between 1971 and 1973. The current account improvement took place despite the worsening of the trade balance. Extremely buoyant workers' remittances played a crucial role in financing the trade deficit. The improvements in the current account, combined with a continuing surplus in the capital account, led to a rapid accumulation of foreign exchange reserves. By the end of 1973, Turkey's gross international reserves stood at US$2 billion–an amount equivalent to more than 12 months of imports. At the end of 1973, the total external debt–excluding International Monetary Fund (IMF) purchases–was under US$3 billion, of which only 8 percent was short term. Moreover, the debt-service ratio stood at a low 5 percent.

---

[2]See inter alia Şerif Mardin, "Turkey: The Transformation of an Economic Code," in *The Political Economy of Income Distribution in Turkey*, Ergun Özbudun and Aydın Ulusan, eds. (New York: Holmes and Meier, 1980); and Metin Heper, "The State and Interest Groups with Special Reference to Turkey," in *Strong State and Economic Interest Groups: The Post-1980 Turkish Experience*, Metin Heper, ed. (Berlin: Walter de Gruyter, 1991).

On the monetary side, during the period 1968-1973, both reserve money and M2 (cash in circulation, check deposits, and time deposits) expanded at an annual rate of about 25 percent. The rate of inflation, however, averaged only 13 percent, owing chiefly to GNP growth (7 percent) and the continuing monetization of the economy (3.5 percent per annum). The further expansion of the world trade volume from the beginning of the 1960s until the oil shock of 1973-1974 also had a positive impact on the internal development of the Turkish economy. Public-sector finances remained the weakest aspect of the financial environment. Revenues, with a tax burden of 15 percent of GNP, were inadequate to cover expenditures. Therefore, the public sector ran sizable deficits, forcing successive governments to resort to Central Bank financing.

In 1974, oil price increases and the resulting acceleration in the rate of inflation in industrialized countries led to a sharp and sudden deterioration in Turkey's terms of trade. Although the cost of Turkish imports increased rapidly, the onset of recession in the industrialized countries, coupled with Turkey's lack of domestic reorientation policies, resulted in a stagnation of exports. The current account of the balance of payments recorded ever-increasing deficits that climbed to over US$3 billion by 1977. In tandem with current account deficits, external indebtedness rose rapidly and stood at more than US$11 billion in 1977, 54 percent of which was short-term debt.

Although the deterioration of the economic environment originated in the external sector, the failure to adopt adjustment policies in time contributed significantly to this deterioration. Particularly important in this respect were the continuation of import-substitution policies, which necessitated an overvalued exchange rate for the Turkish lira, and of the aggressive public investment program, which led to a worsening of public-sector finances. The public-sector deficit rose to 6 percent of GNP by 1977. Part of this deficit was financed through domestic borrowing. In an attempt to keep the cost of servicing the public debt low, interest rates were kept depressed; with accelerating inflation, real interest rates became negative.

The government began to redress the deteriorating economic situation in late 1977. It implemented a number of measures designed to improve the balance of payments and entered into negotiations with the IMF and foreign creditors. As a result of these negotiations, a stabilization program was developed that formed the basis of a two-year standby arrangement, which went into effect in April 1978. However, the severity of the economic crisis rendered the program inadequate. Although some impovements took place in the current account, this was achieved through a drastic curtailment of imports and only a minor increase in exports. Moreover, the public-sector finances continued to deteriorate, mostly because of the increased operating losses of the SEEs.

The negotiations with foreign creditors also proved disappointing. After entering into a standby arrangement with the IMF, the Turkish government started debt rescheduling negotiations with commercial banks and the member countries of the Organization for Economic Cooperation and Development (OECD) consortium for Turkey. The Turks tried to convince the creditors that their foreign debt should become payable after ten years, but they met with strong resistance. Finaly, an agreement was reached, with maturities ranging from five to eight years and a new money facility of US$407 million. However, the effectiveness of the OECD countries' loan commitments was limited, because the OECD imposed special conditions on the use of credits.[3]

By the end of 1979, Turkey was in the midst of a severe foreign exchange crisis. The country was unable to import even essential items such as crude oil. Inflation had accelerated, and unemployment was widespread and increasing. During the years in which the crisis increased (1973-1979), the growth of GNP was on average of 4.4 percent. The public-sector deficits expanded rapidly, from under 2 percent of GNP in 1974 to over 8 percent in 1979, and they averaged 4.5 percent during the period 1974-1979. The government financed these deficits increasingly through the Central Bank. The inflation rate followed a similar course, averaging 34 percent per annum during the period 1974-1979. Moreover, interest rates became substantially negative in real terms, because they were not adjusted to changing conditions.

The inflationary environment also resulted in progressively excessive wage settlements. On many occasions, collective bargaining resulted in wage and benefit increases in excess of 100 percent. These wage increases further undermined the SEEs' finances and were then reflected as increases in the public-sector borrowing requirement. The competitiveness of exports eroded further. Thus, Turkey faced the second round of oil price increases with an extremely weak economy, a grossly overvalued exchange rate, virtually no foreign exchange reserves, highly negative real interest rates, a very high rate of inflation, widespread unemployment, stagnant output, and an external debt in excess of US$13.5 billion—more than a quarter of which was short term.

Economic Stabilization

Faced with the most severe economic crisis in the history of the Turkish Republic, the government finally became convinced of the need to undertake fundamental reforms that would alter the structure of the Turkish economy. On 24 January 1980, the government initiated a major change in the orientation of structural adjustment measures. Simultaneously, it entered into negotiations with both the IMF and official and private creditors. Negotiations with the IMF resulted in a three-year standby arrangement in

---

[3] At that time, the OECD member countries that took part in the consortium compelled Turkey to use these credits primarily against its imports of the goods originating from their countries.

June 1980. Later in 1980, this agreement and, more important, the strength of the underlying economic program helped to convince the OECD governments to postpone principal and interest payments due between 1980 and 1983 for ten years. Eventually, in 1981 commercial banks agreed to extend maturities of the rescheduled bank debts from seven to ten years.

The adjustment program was based on principles of a free-market economy. Import substitution was discarded as the basic strategy for economic growth. Instead, the government adopted an outward-oriented growth strategy based on export promotion. With the change in economic philosophy came additional measures that focused on the role of the exchange and interest rates as tools of economic policy. The government reevaluated the economic function of the SEEs, together with their pricing policies. However, the most urgent task facing the government was the stabilization of the economy–a task it accomplished relatively quickly because of its efficient use of every policy instrument at its disposal. Particularly important in this regard was the efficient and flexible use of the exchange and interest rates in a mutually supportive manner.

Until 24 January 1980, use of the exchange rate as a flexible instument of economic policy was impossible due to its politically sensitive nature. Consequently, governments had been reluctant to take appropriate action on the exchange rate until the excessive overvaluation of the domestic currency and the ensuing balance-of-payments problems forced them to act. Naturally, excessive overvaluation necessitated a larger devaluation, which compounded the government's political problem. After 24 January 1980, the government, in an attempt to maintain external competitiveness and to depoliticize the exchange rate, began to undertake smaller devaluations more frequently. It increased the frequency of these mini-devaluations continuoually until May 1981, when the Central Bank implemented daily exchange rate adjustments.

The government used the exchange rate to restrict domestic demand and thus to take the pressure off of prices. It also used it, however, to change relative prices and thereby encourage a shift in production away from the domestic market toward exports. Indeed, the flexible exchange rate policy that was adopted and the ensuing gradual real depreciation of the Turkish lira provided the greatest incentive for Turkish exporters while simultaneously helping to contain imports.

Since January 1980, the Turkish lira has been depreciated continually against major currencies to offset relative price developments and to maintain the competitiveness of Turkish exports. The real effective exchange rate depreciated by about 29 percent in 1980, 6 percent in 1981, 13 percent in 1982, 6 percent in 1983 and 1984, 12 percent in 1986, and 4 percent in 1987 and 1988; it appreciated by 1 percent in 1985, 10 percent in 1989, and 35 percent in 1990. The rate displayed wide swings in the short run, owing to fluctuations in international financial markets and, at times, to concern for the inflationary consequences.

The second instrument that was used effectively for stabilization purposes was the interest rate. Until June 1980, the Central Bank directly determined deposit rates and, to a large extent, the lending rates of the banking system. During the 1970s, only modest increases were granted, and with the acceleration of inflation rates, interest rates became increasingly negative in real terms. The velocity of circulation increased, and the role of the banking system in financial intermediation began to be undermined with the emergence of nonbank financial institutions (brokerage firms) which were not subject to interest rate regulations. In response to these developments–in particular to arrest the increase in the velocity of circulation–the government liberalized interest rates in July 1980. Initially, the banks decided to act in unison through a "gentlemen's agreement" and to limit the increase in interest rates. However, the competitive pressures from within the banking system and from other sources led to sharp increases in deposit rates by January 1981.

The increase in interest rates led to a very rapid rise in the demand for money and consequently reduced the pressure on prices to increase. More important, the increase in the demand for money allowed a sharp increase in bank credit, which was necessary to finance increased economic activity and exports, without rekindling inflationary pressures. During 1981 and 1982, broad money and quasimonetary aggregates increased rapidly, while at the same time the rate of inflation came down significantly.

A massive flow of funds to the banking sector followed the liberalization of interest rates. The realistic interest rate policy, combined with a similar exchange rate policy, reversed the outflow of capital. The government felt that because of the volatile nature of capital flows and the revealed inability of governments to prevent such flows through regulation, the best solution was to provide a confident environment and to assure a rate of return for such funds that was sufficiently high in view of international interest rates and the perceived element of risk.

Although interest rate policy played a major role in the stabilization of the economy and was perhaps the single-most-important factor in lowering the rate of inflation, the system of free interest rates did not work well. The competition for deposits was excessive, and real interest rates climbed to overly high levels on both deposits and credits, exacerbating financial difficulties. Banks were forced to roll over their credits and capitalize interest payments. In mid-1982, a number of nonbank financial intermediaries went bankrupt.[4] These events forced the government to reconsider its interest rate policy, and it decided to bring the rates under control once again.

---

[4]In 1982, several of Turkey's smaller banks tried to attract funds by selling certificates of deposits and bonds to brokers at higher rates than those offered by the large banks. When some of those smaller banks' clients defaulted on loan payments, this market collapsed, and the small banks could not honor their deposit obligations and had to be rescued by the authorities. Most of the brokers went bankrupt.

Another problem created by interest rate liberalization was that it made conducting monetary policy very difficult. From the start of the program, monetary policy was assigned a prominent role in stabilizing the economy. Monetary policy was conducted through quantitative limits on Central Bank credit, derived from broad money targets. These targets and the limits on Central Bank credit constituted the performance criteria under the standby arrangement with the IMF. With the liberalization of interest rates, the reserve money multiplier tended to increase beyond projections due to a shift from currency to deposits and to increased efficiency in the use of reserves by commercial banks, thus leading to monetary growth in excess of programmed rates.

The prevailing external environment must also be taken into account when evaluating the Turkish adjustment program. In 1980, oil prices more than doubled, resulting in a severe deterioration in the terms of trade. At the same time, interest rates in international financial markets reached unprecedented highs. The unfavorable economic environment in the industrialized countries and the significant shrinkage in the volume of world trade during the 1980-1982 period rendered an export-based growth strategy much more difficult to implement. Turkey was able to expand its exports rapidly partly because of appropriate policies and partly because of its proximity to the Middle Eastern markets. Since 1983, however, the economic recovery in the industrialized countries and a more favorable economic environment have not been reflected in Turkey's export performance. In response to the success of Turkey's export drive–because of their own economic policies devised independently of the IMF proposals–several European countries and, more recently, the United States have imposed quantitative restrictions on imports from Turkey, particularly on those commodities such as textiles with which Turkey is internationally competitive. The impact of these restrictions has been significant.[5]

As mentioned earlier, on the strength of the underlying economic program, Turkey was able to convince the OECD goverments to reschedule its debt. Naturally, regardless of how carefully devised the program was, the country's adjustment efforts would not have been successful without the necessary balance-of-payments financing. Both the IMF and the World Bank provided sizable assistance in support of the program. The IMF approved a three-year standby arrangement in the amount of SDR (Special Drawing Rights) 1,250 million in June 1980, followed in 1983 and 1984 by two one-year arrangements, both in the amount of SDR 225 million. The World Bank provided US$1,600 million through five structural adjustment loans between 1980 and 1985 in support of wide-ranging structural reforms–from rationalization of industrial production to public finance and from external debt-management systems to financial-sector restructuring.

---

[5] The IMF has not protested, possibly because the issue did not concern the general equilibrium of the economy.

Turkey also received assistance in the form of debt relief and debt rescheduling from the OECD consortium and private creditors. Under the OECD agreement, US$3 billion in principal and interest was rescheduled and a more favorable repayment scheme was adopted. This was soon followed by the rescheduling of commercial claims under similar conditions. Overall, Turkey received over US$6 billion in debt relief, which was crucial in reducing the need for foreign exchange at the start of stabilization, and provided much-needed breathing space for the economy.

Structural Adjustment

The aims of the 1980 adjustment program were to achieve both the goal of stabilizing the economy and the long-term objective of restructuring it to assure steady growth under the principles of a free-market economy. To accomplish the latter, over the years the government undertook a number of reforms, with major implications for economic management and the structure of the economy.

Because the most important aspect of the 1980 stabilization package was a greater reliance on the market mechanism, applying this principle to the determination of key economic prices–including commodity prices, interest rates, wages and exchange rates–was only natural. The government removed almost all controls on various commodity prices by abolishing the Price Control Commission and liberalizing the determination of private-sector commodity prices. More important, the new economic policy involved a significant adjustment of the public-sector prices (immediate increases ranging from 100 percent to 400 percent), and the number of subsidized basic commodities subject to price controls was reduced drastically. The SEEs producing nonbasic commodities were instructed to base their prices on commercial principles.

New measures opened the SEEs to competition and simultaneously freed their managers to adopt pricing policies based on commercial principles. The managers were allowed to pursue independent strategies in administrative, financial, and operational matters and to be flexible in determining wages and salaries. Decisions on investment expenditures were constrained by the ability to finance these expenditures. Personnel expenditures were reduced by restricting new positions. New personnel could, however, be hired on a contractual basis, allowing the SEEs to compete with the private sector for skilled people.

The government also reformed agricultural pricing policies. With few exceptions, price controls on agricultural products were gradually lifted, and most goods were eventually taken off the control list. The prices of those few items that were still controlled were determined by taking into consideration factors such as the world prices, input prices, stability of products' prices, producers' incomes, domestic inflation, and the like.

In determining the support prices for exportable products, world prices played a key role, whereas domestic demand and relative productivity factors were significant for products that were consumed domestically. The subsidies of agricultural inputs have also been gradually reduced.

These reforms significantly improved the SEEs' financial position. Their expenditures rose less than their revenues, resulting in substantial profits for the first time in a long while. The SEE borrowing requirements fell in proportion to GNP, and the share of Central Bank borrowing and budgetary transfers fell significantly, although foreign and other domestic borrowing has increased in recent years.

A second area of reform pertaining to trade policies was the liberalization of exports and imports. This move was extremely significant in view of Turkey's historical experience with an excessively restrictive trade regime. Because the adjustmet program emphasized export promotion, policies needed to promote exports were implemented rapidly. Initially, to give momentum to export activities, the government offered exporters a number of incentives in addition to a realistic exchange rate policy. Exporters were given generous tax rebates and had access to preferential credit through the Central Bank. The Central Bank also extended credit to activities that supported exports and to export-related investments. Moreover, exporters were allowed to import raw materials and semifinished products without paying customs duties.

As export activity gained momentum in 1981, the government provided additional incentives for exporters of industrial goods and, to promote exports in general, granted further tax rebates. In response to the incentive schemes, exports increased rapidly through 1982 but stagnated in 1983 due to a change in policy emphasis on export promotion away from direct subsidies and toward a more aggressive use of the exchange rate policy. The government gradually lowered tax rebates, and in January 1985, the Central Bank discontinued the preferential export credit facility and replaced it with an alternative facility in which the interest rate was no longer subsidized but was lower than commercial bank rates.

Policies aimed at export promotion were effective not only in increasing the volume of exports but also in shifting exports toward manufactured goods. The share of manufactured goods rose from 35 percent in 1980 to 75 percent in 1985 and 78 percent in 1991. Markets also diversified. Although Turkish exports to traditional markets, such as Europe, expanded somewhat, the major market penetration was achieved in the Middle East and North Africa.

On the import side, adjustment policies aimed at a less restrictive import regime by permitting a much larger number of items to be imported legally. The government expected competition from the enlarged flow of imports to reduce oligopolistic and monopolistic tendencies, especially in small domestic markets. In the first year of the program, import guarantee deposit rates were reduced. Around one hundred items were transferred from Liberalization List II to the less restrictive Liberalization List I, and stamp duty charges on imports were reduced from a maximum of 25 percent to 1 percent.

In January 1981, the government abolished global quotas and transferred goods subject to quotas to liberilization lists. The liberalization policy continued in 1982, with the transfer of two hundred more items from List II to List I. Also, some items were transferred to a new list called the "Fund List." Starting in 1983, all import transactions had to be made in convertible foreign currencies, and the import guarantee deposit rates were lowered again, this time from 20 percent to 15 percent for importers and from 10 percent to 7.5 percent for industrialists. Notwithstanding this gradual liberalization, the operational principle remained that if an item was not on the list, its importation was prohibited.

The major move toward import liberalization came in 1984. The government changed the operational principle to one of a negative list under which if an item was not on the Prohibited List, it could be imported. The 1984 import regime classified imports under (1) the prohibited list, (2) imports subject to approval or license, (3) the liberalization list, (4) the Fund List.

A comparison of the 1984 import program with that of 1983 reveals the dramatic effect of the policy change. In one year, the number of liberalized items had increased from 1,000 to 2,500, and the Prohibited List had shrunk from 1,800 items to 459 items. The Approval List (formerly Liberalization List II) had been reduced from 1,300 items to 1,000 items. The number of items contained in the Fund List had increased from 40 to 100, some of which were consumer goods included in the list to prevent price increases because of supply bottlenecks. In May 1985, goods formerly included in the prohibited list were transferred to the License List, excluding narcotics, weapons, and related goods.

Another significant aspect of the 1984 import regime was the reduction in tariffs and other levies on imports. Since 5 December 1985, the right to import from public institutions and export trading companies (with exports exceeding 50 million dollars over a year) in countries in which foreign trade is state controlled had been extended from special public companies to encompass companies holding investment certificates. Hence, under this program the government achieved substantial liberalization of imports. Although this led inevitably to a higher import bill, economic benefits resulting from a more liberal trade regime easily justified the move. Particularly since 1984, Turkish producers, faced with foreign competition, have taken measures to rationalize and streamline their operations, thereby improving the quality of their products.

As indicated earlier, the monetary policy was assigned a pivotal role in the stabilization program. During the implementation stage, the fragility and the results of decades of financial repression of Turkish financial markets became painfully clear. Negative real rates, credit rationing, lack of competition, excessively high intermediation costs, and lack of diversity of financial institutions and instruments were all part of the scene. Financial markets were almost completely dominated by commercial banks and were protected by, and accustomed to, nonprice competition.

The need for financial reforms became critical when the financial system was severely shocked by the widespread failures of brokerage firms, which adversely affected the liquidity position and the health of the entire banking system. In 1982, the transition to positive real interest rates proved to be harder than expected for Turkish financial markets.

The financial reforms had two objectives. First, the country had to develop adequate monetary policy instruments and to improve the effectiveness of the existing instruments. Second, the allocational and operational efficiency of the money and capital markets had to be improved drastically.

Historically, bank credits have been kept in check by controlling the size and composition of the banking system's assets. New policies, however, were directed at exercising monetary control through the banks' liabilities. With this new philosophy in mind, the Central Bank initiated changes in the management of commercial banks' required reserves and liquidity. Reserve ratios had been unified and simplified in 1983. A complex, tiered system of reserve ratios for preferential credits had been either abolished or streamlined, compliance periods had been reduced, access to the discount window had been restricted, and the scope of preferential credit facilities had been narrowed. In April 1986, as part of its program of extending the instruments of monetary policy, the Central Bank organized an interbank market that functioned similarly to the U.S. Federal Funds market, and the first open market operations were conducted in February 1987.

The government enacted a new banking law with extended provisions on capital requirements, contingency reserves for problem loans, a new deposit insurance scheme, unified accounting and reporting standards, and external auditing requirements. The Central Bank instituted a new bank supervision system. All these innovations were expected to make the banking sector, and competition in the banking sector, financially healthier, and foreign commercial banks were allowed to enter the market.

After the collapse of the brokerage firms, as noted above, the government had to restore people's confidence in the financial markets. Furthermore, to provide risk capital and long-term funds for the financially weakened Turkish industry, it needed to develop capital markets. The Capital Markets Board, established in 1981, assumed the responsibility of safeguarding the capital markets. After a slow start, and despite the high and variable inflation rate, corporations made increasing use of the corporate bond market, indicating that the crisis of confidence was over and that the capital markets would eventually be able to channel long-term funds to Turkish industry and bring healthy competition to the banking sector. To foster further development of equity markets, the Istanbul stock exchange was reorganized as a modern stock exchange.

New and successful financial instruments have been introduced in both money and capital markets. Revenue sharing certificates issued by the Mass Housing and Public Participation Agency[6] have been well received by savers. Financial deepening continued with the successful introduction of weekly auctions of Treasury securities in money markets with various maturities.

Although the developments in new institutions and instruments in Turkish financial markets were modest in comparison to those in developed markets, they were impressive when we remember that Turkey reached this stage from the brink of a recent financial collapse. Turkey's financial industry was now likely to be the economy's fastest-growing sector.

Because most sections of the Turkish economy were undergoing a thorough structural change, the country's tax system had to be improved. Rising inflation had increased marginal tax rates that, in turn, had adversely affected the work and saving habits of wage earners. An antiquated and weak tax collection administration had further exacerbated the problems, as tax collections were delayed and tax evasion became a common practice. To improve the tax system's equity and efficiency, in 1981 the authorities launched a major tax reform as part of the comprehensive structural adjustment program.

The most important feature of income tax reform involved the adjustments in the tax brackets of corporations and individuals. Personal income tax brackets were initially adjusted upward, and marginal rates were restructured that provided for a gradual reduction of all rates over the next four years. Corporate income tax was unified. New taxes were introduced to broaden the revenue base. The government introduced tax rebates to individuals whose wages and salaries were subject to withholding tax in order to offset the increased tax rates and to induce compliance among business taxpayers through collection of receipts by wage earners so they could qualify for tax rebates.

In January 1985, Turkey instituted by far the most comprehensive tax reform in its history in an attempt to broaden the tax base and introduced a 10 percent value added tax (VAT). The VAT substituted for various production taxes and other duties that had been imposed at various rates on certain groups of commodities and services. The implementation of the VAT has been very successful, even though there were some operational problems at the outset, as expected. Proceeds from the VAT have far exceeded expectations in the following years.

---

[6]This organization was set up in 1986 to promote public housing and to carry out privatization. In 1990, the first of these functions was transferred to the newly founded Mass Housing Agency.

Conclusion

The economic program has resulted in a remarkable improvement in Turkey's economic situation. The most striking feature of the recovery has been the dramatic growth in exports of goods and services. This rapid growth has been at the heart of the outward-looking, export-led growth strategy that has been in effect since 1980. A realistic exchange rate policy, with the ensuing gradual depreciation of the Turkish lira, has been the major cause of this favorable outcome. Improvements in Turkey's external performance helped restore the country's creditworthiness. In addition to the increase in the total volume of exports, the commodity composition of exports changed in favor of industrial goods.

The performance of Turkish exports becomes even more notable if we consider the slowdown in world trade during the 1980s. Under the unfavorable conditions of economic recession and protectionist barriers, particularly in the industrialized countries, Turkey initiated a dynamic trade policy and successfully penetrated the Middle Eastern and North African markets. Within this group exports to Iran and Iraq recorded the sharpest growth for some time.

In addition to the efforts to increase exports, Turkey has fundamentally altered and liberalized its import regime, particularly since January 1984, with a view to opening up the economy to international competition. With the exception of a slight decline in 1982 and 1986, Turkey's imports have increased throughout the decade, although at a lower rate than exports. These increases in imports provided the necessary inputs to the country's industrial modernization.

7

Privatization of the State Economic Enterprises

Selim İlkin

Early Privatization Attempts (1933-1980)

Privatization appeared early on the political agenda of Republican Turkey.[1] Its history dates back to the establishment of the state economic enterprises (SEEs) in the 1930s. The charter of Sümerbank, a textiles conglomerate founded in 1933, set forth the principle that it would sell all or part of its shares to persons and corporations when necessary. In the same year, the Supreme Economic Council (*Âli İktisat Meclisi*) recommended that all industrial enterprises should be made the property of the general public or the private sector after they took firm root and became profitable. The difficulties experienced by the SEEs in their early years, the hardships of World War II, and–perhaps most important–the politically weak position of Turkish business circles prevented the implementation of these principles.[2]

However, an intensive debate over privatization took place in the post-war years, when Turkey adopted a multiparty system. The program of the Democratic Party (DP), founded in 1946, articulated the principle that private enterprise and capital constituted the foundations of economic life. This program, moreover, set forth the policy that those state enterprises that remained outside the clearly defined boundaries of state involvement would be transferred to the private sector under suitable conditions.[3]

---

[1] Privatization is the transfer of assets owned by the public sector to the private sector. It may also involve a reshuffling of the entire or upper echelons of management as well as the labor force, leading to a radical change in the behavior of the firm.

[2] Selahattin Özmen, *Türkiye'de ve Dünya'da KİT'lerin Özelleştirilmesi* (Istanbul: n.p., 1987), pp. 48-50.

[3] Tarık Zafer Tunaya, *Türkiye'de Siyasi Partiler, 1859-1952* (Istanbul: Doğan Kardeş, 1952), pp. 668-669.

The SEEs were one of the main issues taken up by the Turkish Economic Congress of 1948. Focusing on this issue within the framework of étatism, the congress observed that the SEEs, which were initially meant to be transitory instruments for providing an industrial base, had acquired a permanent place in the system. The congress also deplored the way in which the SEEs were conceived and felt they would not lead to the development of individualistic capitalism or of state capitalism. It noted that an economic system that heavily favored the state sector would detract from the democratic system based on competitive politics that was being established, since individual freedoms would be curtailed while the means of livelihood remained essentially in the hands of the government.

During the 1950s, some work was done toward privatization. However, the transfer of the major SEEs, such as Sümerbank, Etibank (a mining and metallurgy conglomerate), and the Turkish Sugar Factories Corporation, to the private sector could not be realized.[4] Only a small number of enterprises that had symbolic significance could be turned over to the private sector because of the weakness of the private sector, the less than satisfatory management patterns of the companies in question, and the lack of a capital market. The government also realized that the direct and indirect benefits provided by the SEEs could be used for distributing such rewards as jobs and product allocations.[5] The government not only did not sell these enterprises, but it established new ones.

Turkey adopted centralized planning under the 1961 Constitution. During the 1960s, various select committees were formed to reorgarnize the SEEs. Although some of the reports prepared by these committees included proposals for the "liquidation" of the SEEs (or their subsidiaries), no effective action was undertaken.[6] During the planned period, most discussions concerning the issue focused not on privatization but on the relative size of the public versus the private sector. The SEEs continued to pose major problems, but the idea of privatization was shelved.[7]

Privatization During the 1980s

In 1980, Turkey signed a standby agreement with the International Monetary Fund (IMF) and began to implement a stabilization program that entailed a major policy shift. This program emphasized the market forces and

---

[4]Memduh Yaşa, *İktisadi Meselelerimiz* (Istanbul: n.p., 1966), pp. 49-60.

[5]"Sümerbank, Etibank ve T. Şeker Fabrikaları A.Ş. Fabrikalarından Bazılarının Görüşme Protokolları," typescript, Ankara, 1951; Muhlis Ete, *State Exploitation in Turkey* (Ankara: n.p., 1951).

[6]Coşkun Can Aktan, *Kamu İktisadi Teşekkülleri ve Özelleştirme* (İzmir: n.p., 1987), pp. 43-94; M. Berra Altıntaş, *Kamu İktisadi Teşebbüslerinin Özelleştirilmesi ve Özelleştirmenin Sermaye Piyasasına Etkileri* (Ankara: Sermaye Piyasası Kurulu, 1981), pp. 35-49.

[7]Bertil Walstedt, *State Manufacturing Enterprises in a Mixed Economy: The Turkish Case* (Washington, D.C.: World Bank, 1989).

called for diminishing the size of the public sector.[8] The policy package included privatization. [9]

However, it was during the 1983 general elections that the idea of privatization once again appeared on the political agenda. Turgut Özal, who earlier had played a critical role in the formulation of the 1980 stabilization program and who–except for a short period–carried out that program as deputy prime minister during the interregnum (1980-1983), founded the Motherland Party (ANAP) and ran in the 1983 elections, which the ANAP won.

The main points of the ANAP program were as follows: (1) The stabilisation measures adopted in 1980 were to be maintained; (2) the economic growth policy was to be based upon the entrepreneurial spirit of individuals; and (3) the state was not to engage in commerce and industry. In those exceptional cases in which the state would establish industrial facilities in the economically backward regions, these were eventually to be transferred to the people. It was also stipulated that all SEEs would be transferred to the people in due course.[10]

Once it was in power, one of the policy measures the ANAP introduced was that of issuing revenue-sharing certificates. Against these certificates, the state was to borrow from the public by keeping the ownership of such infrastructural facilities as the Bosporus Bridge and Keban Dam as collateral.

On 28 February 1988, the Mass Housing and Public Participation Agency (Toplu Konut ve Kamu Ortaklığı İdaresi: [TKKOİ]), an agency under the Prime Ministry, was created by an act of Parliament. The same act empowered the agency to complete and carry out transactions concerning revenue-sharing certificates and stocks. The discussion of the bill leading to this act involved harsh exchanges between the ANAP deputies and opposition deputies in the Parliament. The ANAP emphasized the importance of the bill as an instrument for increasing revenues. Prime Minister Özal said: "We shall encourage voluntary savings . . . . The bridge stands there and our unemployed people merely look at it. That is not acceptable. We shall sell this Bridge as well as others. We shall build new ones. They will continue to serve this country."[11] The ANAP deputies suggested that the revenue-sharing policy was instrumental in "spreading the ownership of the industry to the masses."

Opposition deputies objected to the sale of these facilities which, had been "established with the savings of the people." They were vehemently

---

[8]Peter Wolff, *Stabilisation Policy and Structural Adjustment in Turkey, 1980-85* (Berlin: German Development Institute, 1987).

[9]World Bank, "Turkey: Industrialization and Trade Strategy," Washington, D.C.: World Bank, 1982, p. 28.

[10]Anavatan Partisi, "Anavatan Partisi Programı," Ankara, 1983; Anavatan Partisi, "Seçim Beyannamesi," Ankara, 1983; Anavatan Partisi, "Genel Ekonomi Sorunları: Turgut Özal'ın Görüşleri," Ankara, 1983.

[11]TBMM, *Tutanak Dergisi* (Ankara: TBMM, 1984), pp. 226 and 183.

against their sale on such grounds as social justice, equality, and the like, and argued that it would be impossible for the lower and middle classes to buy revenue-sharing certificates, since these people were barely able to make ends meet because of high rates of inflation. The deputies pointed out that foreign capital would become the most likely buyer, as a result of which key sectors of the economy would come under foreign control. Although all opposition parties stood against the project, the Social Democratic Populist Party (SHP) went so far as to declare that it would renationalize the privatized firms when it came to power.[12]

At a press conference on 15 August 1986, Prime Minister Özal further elaborated his party's policies concerning privatization: "In the model we adopt, the worker is the owner of the company; he also shares in the profits and has a say in its management. . . . Thus, the company would operate more efficiently, and both the enterprise and the employees would benefit from it . . . . Another advantage of this practice is that it would spread the ownership of capital to wide segments of society, and in the process would enhance general welfare."[13] He went on to indicate that the stocks held by the employees of the SEEs would give them a permanent revenue. The state would not leave the employees to fend for themselves. The state would make efforts to ensure that the enterprises were succesfully run, and it would support them by providing credits and competent managers.

The procedure to be followed in privatization was to review and evaluate the activities of the SEEs and to determine the priorities as well as forms of sale. This demanding job, for which a World Bank loan was obtained, was assigned to the Morgan Guarantee Trust. This bank prepared a "master plan," which analyzed the salability of thirty-two SEEs and their subsidiaries. The plan classified the SEEs in terms of how easily they could be privatized, order in which they should to be put up for sale, and whether the entire firm or just part of its shares should be sold.[14]

Shortly after the guidelines were determined, the government swiftly forced through the Parliament a bill that concerned the implementation phase. During deliberations on this bill, which empowered TKKOİ to implement privatization procedures, heated debates took place again in the Parliament. Criticisms focused on the bill's lack of clarity as to whom the stocks were to be sold and how. In the case of sale, it was pointed out, it was not clear whether the employees of the companies would be granted the right of first refusal and what the principles would be that governed the right of first refusal. Moreover, who among the general public would be offered the shares? Lack of an antimonopoly provision putting a maximum on the number of shares that could be bought by individual

---

[12]Ibid., p. 177.

[13]"Başbakan Turgut Özal'ın Konuşma, Mesaj, Beyanat ve Mülâkatları," Ankara, Anavatan Partisi, 1984, pp. 736-773.

[14]The Morgan Guarantee Trust, "Privatization Master Plan", Ankara, State Planning Organization, June 1986.

persons or corporations, and the ambiguity as to whether foreign capital were to be involved in privatization, constituted two other major points raised during of the debates.[15] The SHP deputies opposed the entire bill. The law, however, was duly enacted.

The fact that definitive guidelines were not laid down led to the spread of discouraging rumors among the public. A survey by the Union of Chambers and Stock Exchanges of Turkey (TOBB), the organization that most widely represents the business community, showed that employers favored the transfer of management to the private sector and the spreading of the equity shares first to the employees and then to the general public.[16]

The government proceeded to contact certain firms, mostly foreign, and and asked them to prepare "feasibility" studies investigating in greater detail which SEEs should be sold first in the latter half of 1986. A number of companies, all located in small towns and most of which were in the process of building their plants, were sold to the private sector on the condition that the buyers would complete the projects and bring the plans into use. Major privatizations were scheduled for 1987.[17]

The timetable for these privatizations was announced in early April 1987. Yet, large-scale privatizations did not begin for quite some time because the sales of some public sector minority shares in private joint-stock companies in late August 1987 were followed by major falls in stock prices. This development revealed that the size of the capital market was not large enough for large-scale privatization. It also became clear that the privatization strategy had not been carefully drawn up and that setbacks were caused by insufficient preparations.

Yet, in late October 1987, a huge advertisement and promotion campaign was launched. It was announced that some SEEs were to be sold immediately. The main theme of the campaign was reflected in Prime Minister Özal's words: "The general public's participation in ownership will strengthen democracy; this is economic democracy; it will be the greatest economic reform in Turkey." The campaign displayed specially made photographs and films depicting typical representatives of lower-income and middle-income groups, with the following statement by Özal as a caption: "This is the first time in this country that our people are offered such an opportunity! Now, all of my citizens can have a share in Turkey's riches, by holding capital ownership and getting their share from profits."[18]

During this campaign, it became apparent that there was no agreement in the government circles on the main objectives behind the privatization efforts. In the case of sales to employees, it was not clear as to whom, at what price, and with what considerations sales would be made and how the enterprises so sold would be managed. All political parties regarded

---

[15]TBMM, *Tutanak Dergisi* (Ankara: TBMM, 1986), pp. 311-338, 326, 390-425, 442-445.

[16]*Cumhuriyet* (Istanbul daily), 13 November 1985, and 25 July 1986.

[17]"Anavatan Partisi İcraatı," Ankara, 1987, p. 62.

[18]*Tercüman* (Istanbul daily), 23 August 1987.

this campaign as sheer political propaganda by the ANAP, in anticipation of the next general elections scheduled to take place in late November.

The government, in fact, postponed actual privatization, first until after the elections and then until after the new cabinet was formed. The ongoing stock exchange crisis gave the government the necessary excuse. Thus, privatization was put off until 1988.

A decree law, passed in early 1988, introduced major changes concerning the management and operations of the SEEs. The decree prohibited the appointment of new personnel in the SEEs. The government aimed at gradually liquidating the tenured personnel. Also, the public enterprises and establishments had to transfer their equity shares to those enterprises or their subsidiaries that had been engaged in the same type of activities in the past ten years.

These provisions, it was argued, were made in order to prepare the SEEs for privatization. In addition, some guidelines for privatization were prepared. An external auditing system using international firms was adopted. Although the establishment of a support fund for privatization and for underwriting dividends was contemplated, no action was taken.

The government continued its attempts at privatization despite arguments by influential persons in the private sector, leading journalists, and academics that adequate preparations had not been made.[19] Even the economic measures package of 4 February 1988, and its adverse effects on the capital market, did not prevent the government from going ahead with major privatization efforts.

The First Experiment: TELETAŞ

The first large-scale privatization was carried out in February 1988, following an extensive advertising campaign. TELETAŞ was chosen for this purpose possibly because this enterprise, which was in the lowest ranks of the first-priority category in the Morgan Guarantee Trust's master plan, could be attractive to the general public because it was a highly profitable but relatively small-scale high-technology venture.

The Post, Telephone, and Telegraph Agency (PTT) (TELETAŞ's chief customer) held 40 percent of its shares, a foreign shareholder held 39 percent, and a number of domestic shareholders held the remaining 21 percent. In the course of the privatization, PTT shares were transferred to the TKKOİ. The plan was to put up for sale slightly over half of the shares held by the TKKOİ–that is, to offer 22 percent of the total shares to private individuals, leaving 18 percent in the hands of the public sector.[20]

It soon became apparent that as a result of this offering, a foreign firm would emerge as the largest shareholder of TELETAŞ. A measure was

[19] *Cumhuriyet*, 22 January 1988.
[20] "TELETAŞ Hisse Senetlerinin Halka Arzı," Ankara, 1988, typescript.

introduced to prevent the control of management by foreign interests: The TKKOİ was to retain its influence in management through a right of veto– that is, by preserving the golden share until stocks it held were reduced below 3 percent.

Through a revalorization, 5.4 billion liras worth of shares, corresponding to the 22 percent of the total, were to be privatized. Of this, a 3-billion-lira portion was earmarked for TELETAŞ and PTT employees, of whom 70 percent were willing to buy shares. They were to obtain their shares by making payments from their salaries, premiums, and the like, within three years. A 1-billion-lira portion was to be sold to Turkish workers abroad, against payment in foreign currency. The remaining 11.4 billion in lira shares was to be sold directly to the general public through those banks that had extensive branch office chains and through intermediary financial institutions.[21] Initially, an attempt was made to conduct sales outside of the stock exchange. It was assumed that demand for smaller denominations would be enhanced if the demand for stocks exceeded the supply. Dividends were guaranteed for the first two years.

The demand, it turned out, was indeed mostly for stocks in smaller denominations: 45,000 persons bought shares.[22] As a result, TELETAŞ emerged as the industrial enterprise with the greatest number of shareholders of all companies in Turkey.

A survey conducted by İNTERLİNK, Inc., of bank branches in large cities provided data concerning the new TELETAŞ shareholders. Sixty percent had previously bought similar financial instruments. Of the 40 percent who bought stocks for the first time, 30 percent were self-employed, 21 percent were civil servants, and 13 per cent were pensioners; others were housewives, students, and the like. The survey indicated that 48 percent of shareholders perceived privatization as opening the enterprises to the public, and a mere 18 percent viewed it as "spreading the capital to the masses."[23]

The TELETAŞ experience provoked extensive debate. Criticism was focused on the fact that the TELETAŞ management remained unchanged after privatization; in fact, the sale of shares did not truly lead to privatization since the "captain" had not changed and the general public had a limited role in the process.[24] These reactions led the minister of state in charge of privatization to make the following statement: "TELETAŞ is not, of course, a typical example of privatization. The state does not hold many shares in this enterprise. We shall also privatize those enterprises where the state holds majority shares. We shall, for example, privatize

---

[21]*Güneş* (Istanbul daily), 8 January 1988.

[22]*Dünya* (Istanbul daily), 21 March 1988.

[23]İNTERLİNK A. Ş., "TELETAŞ Özelleştirme Sonrası Alıcılar Nezdinde Yoklama," April 1988, typescript.

[24]*Milliyet* (Istanbul daily), 28 February 1988.

Ereğli [Steel Mills], too."[25]

Meanwhile, the prices of the TELETAŞ shares declined soon after they were quoted in the stock exchange. The TKKOİ and some of the state banks made support purchases. Those purchases, however, were discontinued when it became apparent that the general downward trend in the stock exchange would continue. Neither dividends nor free-of-charge shares distributed to the shareholders could reverse the downward trend in the price of the shares.[26] At the end of the first seven months, the price of shares declined from 5,000 liras to 2,700 liras.

Those in capital market circles admitted that TELETAŞ's sale was ill-timed and that it had adverse effects on the stock exchange. However, the same circles also considered this operation a success, arguing that the decline in the prices of the TELETAŞ shares was less than that in the general level of stock prices. The relatively better performance of the TELETAŞ shares might have been the result of guaranteed dividends and the distribution of bonus shares, free of charge, to the shareholders. The effect of these sweeteners, which potentially distorted the market, was not addressed. As for the shareholders, they were only concerned with the losses they experienced in seven months and were deeply disappointed by this turn of events.[27]

The Search for a New Privatization Strategy

The TELETAŞ experience showed that some changes were necessary in the privatization strategy. A major stumbling block was the fact that the stock exchange was still in its infancy. A high inflation rate coupled with the measures taken to slow it down, such as high interest rates, had added to the problems of the stock exchange. As indicated by the Capital Markets Board chairman in June 1988, the capital market was still not "ready for privatization."[28]

In view of the constraints imposed on privatization by the shallowness of the Istanbul Stock Exchange, the government began to develop a new policy that also envisaged the sale of the SEE shares to domestic or foreign companies. The former emphasis on the sale to the general public, made popular under the slogan of extending property ownership to the masses, was clearly waning, whereas other objectives of privatization–mainly the development of a free-market economy and increased efficiency–now dominated discussions.[29] The new approach was explained as follows: "It is

---

[25] *Cumhuriyet,* 9 March 1988.

[26] *Dünya,* 14 March 1988; *Tercüman,* 16 April 1988.

[27] *Financial Times,* 23 May 1988.

[28] *Dünya,* 20 June 1988.

[29] The post-1988 policy concerning privatization is elaborated in Sven B. Kjellström, "Privatization in Turkey," World Bank Working Paper, Washington, D.C. November, 1990; Cevat Karataş, *Privatization in Britain and Turkey* (Istanbul: Istanbul Chamber of Commerce, 1990);

wrong to offer to the general public 100 percent of the SEE shares. A complete sale to the public may seem politically appropriate. But, a complete sale in small denominations will cause management [and thus efficiency] problems. There must [also] be a locomotive shareholder."[30]

Block sales to both local and foreign companies were also contemplated. The TKKOİ made an intensive effort to sell in block a package that included small cement factories belonging to ÇİTOSAN, as well as Boğaziçi Taşımacılık and USAŞ, two companies that provide air transportation and services to airlines, respectively.

During the second half of the 1988, the TKKOİ opted to shift privatization efforts abroad. A Turkey Fund was established, designed as an intermediary in the sale of Turkish securities abroad. It was to offer SEE stocks to foreign investors and to invigorate the privatization program, in particular, by the sale of the shares of the companies to be privatized.[31]

Although block sales of shares to local and foreign companies would have solved the management problems of these companies, the questions of whether the public would continue to buy shares and under which conditions the public would remain engaged in privatization went unanswered. The objective of the spreading the SEE shares to the masses became emphasized less and less.

Then, beginning in 1991–the year that witnessed more public sector borrowing as a percentage of GNP than had occurred since 1978-1980–the main objective of privatization has shifted altogether from attaining allocative or managerial efficiency to alleviating public-sector deficits.[32] President Özal went on record, saying that it was time for the government "to relieve the nation from the SEEs plague," reflecting the new perception of the problem shared by the government and business circles alike.[33]

The coalition government of the True Path Party (DYP) and the Social Democratic Populist Party (SHP), which was formed following the October 1991 general elections, announced a two-step program concerning the SEEs. First, the SEEs that did not provide essential public services would be rehabilitated; then, when favorable conditions were achieved, they would be privatized.[34]

Ziya Öniş, "Privatization and the Logic of Coalition Building: A Comparative Study of State Divestiture in the United Kingdom and Turkey," *Comparative Political Studies* 24 (1991): 231-253.

[30]*Hürriyet*, 11 July 1988.

[31]*Milliyet*, 7 September 1988.

[32]Türkiye Sanayiciler ve İşadamları Derneği, *Türkiye'de Özelleştirme Uygulamaları* (Istanbul: TÜSİAD, 1992).

[33]*Dünya*, 6 December 1991.

[34]*Cumhuriyet*, 20 January 1992.

Conclusion

The post-1983 strategy for privatization was less than coherent. The intentions and expectations of the various groups involved varied greatly. The criteria by which privatization deals are judged include total funds involved in the sale, equity prices, expected returns, and the quality of management. The groups involved in privatization–political leaders, bureaucrats, private-sector players–never formed similar views on virtually any of these issues.

Domestic venture capital personnel were mainly interested in providing management services and in obtaining profits from such services without committing to a sizable capital investment. The general public, the ultimate supplier of funds, was not much attracted by privatization because the prospects for large dividends were uncertain and the average Turkish investor was not used to taking risks. In any case, all along the general public was bombarded with the virtues of the "real return" it could expect to obtain from virtually risk-free investments, such as deposit accounts in banks and government bonds.

The government has not displayed a consistent sense of purpose and direction. At times, it said that funds raised by the state would be recycled into new public investments. This required an overestimation of the value of fixed capital to be transferred. At other times, the impression was given that the government simply wanted to get rid of the SEEs altogether, for political or financial reasons. This, in turn, necessitated an underestimation of the sale value. More recently macroeconomic considerations came to the fore. The inefficient operation of the SEEs is perceived to be one of the major stumbling blocks in the efforts to stem inflation.

The frequent reversal in the overall policy was paralleled by a desire for a quick fix. This tendency resulted in setting into motion initiatives that were not well planned, which in turn contributed to frequent changes in the measures adopted.

Also unfortunate was the impression given all along that the state would not cease to meddle in the management of the privatized enterprises. This was sufficient to arouse suspicion in a country in which many people have been critical of the SEE system from the start because of the enterprises' vulnerability to political manipulation by the government.

In early 1992, the DYP-SHP coalition claimed its objective was to liquidate as many SEEs as possible in the shortest time possible. It remains to be seen whether the government will learn from past experience and move systematically to achieve its objectives. Turkey's progress toward achieving a full-fledged liberal-democratic state will be served to the extent that the government can successfully pursue its stated program and priorities in this critical area.

8

Decentralization of Government

Ersin Kalaycıoğlu

Decentralization took a prominent place in the Turkish political agenda after 1980, marking a significant departure from the deeply rooted tradition that had existed since the Ottoman period of upholding the power of central authority. Since 1980, successive governments have shown a preference for decentralization, particularly by means of restructuring the metropolitan municipalities.[1] The post-1983 Motherland Party (ANAP) governments not only underscored decentralization in their programs, but also reaffirmed, as often as they could, their dedication to the cause of decentralizing of government in general. Then Prime Minister Turgut Özal, various ministers of his cabinets, and the ANAP mayors of major Turkish cities repeatedly argued that ANAP's decentralization policy had the objective of further democratizing the Turkish political system.

Types of Decentralization

One meaning of decentralization is that the people of a locality will be "self-governing through political institutions which have their roots within the territory for which they have jurisdiction. They will not be administered by the agents of a superior government but will be governed by the institutions that are founded on the politics of the area."[2] Decentralization in this sense refers to self-government, or local democracy.

Local self-government rests on the assumption that "decisions made by a local authority are made by people who, in general, will be affected by the

---

[1]Metin Heper, ed. *Dilemmas of Decentralization: Municipal Government in Turkey* (Bonn: Friedrich-Ebert-Stiftung, 1986), p. 93; Ayşe Öncü, "The Potentials and Limitations of Local Government Reform in Solving Urban Problems: The Case of Istanbul," in Heper, pp. 68-76; and Metin Heper, ed. *Democracy and Local Government: Istanbul in the 1980s* (Walkington, England: Eothen Press, 1987), pp. 4-8.

[2]B. C. Smith, *Decentralisation: The Territorial Dimension of the State* (London: George Allen & Unwin, 1985), p. 18.

outcome. People care about what happens to them and their neighbours."[3] Hence, to the extent that it fosters self-government, decentralization enables people to grapple with those issues that are closest to home. Since the times of Alexis de Tocqueville, town and council meetings were assumed to bring politics within the reach of the people and to teach people how to use and enjoy their own power and liberty.[4] Thus, local government not only enabled people to make decisions that reflected local choices on local issues, but it also educated people in how to become "good citizens" in a democracy. Moreover, it has been posited that democratic local government "induces wider support of and understanding for the system as a whole."[5] Consequently, at least one student of local government has contended that "in one sense local democracy is only national democracy translated to the local level with modifications necessitated by the different scale of operations, the different context and its subordinate position."[6]

Decentralization, however, does not always mean self-government, or local democracy. There is little democratization, for instance, in the case of deconcentration of authority, where decentralization consists of only a limited delegation of authority to the local branches of the central bureaucracy. The appointed officials of the central government continue to possess the authority to make binding decisions.

Furthermore, some democracies may place a strong emphasis on centralization: "Territorial interests may be classed among those sectional interests which are seen as incompatible with society's 'general will' represented by the nation's legislature. Sovereignty may be regarded as unified, not dispersed."[7] In fact, this has been the case in Turkey. Every Turkish Constitution has clearly stated that the members of the Turkish Grand National Assembly (TGNA) are representatives of the entire Turkish nation.

In this chapter, I use the term *decentralization* to mean the devolution of power by the central government to local administration. Thus, local self-government, rather than deconcentration, is emphasized as the essence of decentralization.

Local Government in Turkey

Bureaucratic Tutelage

The 1982 Turkish Constitution stipulates that in terms of its establishment and functions, public administration constitutes a unified whole and

[3]Peter G. Richards, *The Local Government System* (London: George Allen & Unwin, 1983), p. 174.

[4]H. Maddick, *Democracy, Decentralisation and Development* (Bombay: Asia Publishing House, 1963), pp. 59, 106.

[5]Richards, *The Local Government System*, p. 175.

[6]Jeffrey Stanyer, *Understanding Local Government* (Guildford: Martin Robertson, 1976), p. 265.

[7]Smith, *Decentralisation*, p. 19.

is regulated by law (Article 123). Article 127 of the Constitution further designates that the central administration has the legal authority to practice administrative tutelage over government.

However, local autonomy and decisionmaking capabilities were increased in the early part of the 1980s, first by means of laws promulgated by the National Security Council (NSC) during the 1980-1983 period and chiefly by means of decree laws thereafter. The fact that most of the important changes affecting municipalities were introduced by executive decrees or regulations reflected the significantly subordinate status of the legislative branch as compared with that of the executive branch. One piece of legislation (Act 3030 of 1984), which introduced an innovative two-tiered metropolitan municipal system, stands alone as a singular example of a law concerning local government that was promulgated by the TGNA during this period.[8] There is no evidence that any steps taken toward decentralization after 1984 were the result of the active support of a legislative majority. As an example of decentralization by executive decree, the Turkish case may be said to resemble more a process of deconcentration than devolution of authority.[9]

Indeed, the local government system of the Turkish provinces is still closely connected with the center. The mayors and municipal councils are popularly elected, as they had been in the pre-1980 period; however, municipalities remain subject to close supervision and control by the central bureaucracy, except in the case of real estate development where they are empowered to make binding decisions.

The center's continued tutelage of local government is reflected in various practices. Inspectors of the Ministry of Interior Affairs investigate every operation and action of municipalities. Municipalities must obtain the endorsement of provincial governors before they can submit their budgets to the Ministry of Interior Affairs and their budgets are then incorporated into that ministry's budget. Any actions by municipalities that fall into the policy domains of cabinet ministries, such as Reconstruction and Settlement, and Health and Social Security, require prior endorsement

---

[8]Ersin Kalaycıoğlu, "Türk Yasama Sistemi ve Siyasal Temsil," in *Türk Siyasal Hayatının Gelişimi*, Ersin Kalaycıoğlu and Ali Yaşar Sarıbay, eds. (Istanbul: Beta Publications, 1986); and Ersin Kalaycıoğlu, "The 1983 Parliament in Turkey: Changes and Continuities," in *State, Democracy and the Military: Turkey in the 1980s*, Metin Heper and Ahmet Evin, eds. (Berlin: Walter de Gruyter, 1988), pp. 61-62.

[9]The metropolitan and district mayors are now popularly elected; however, the metropolitan mayor represents a higher level of authority. The district mayors are members of the metropolitan city council, whereas the metropolitan mayor acts as the head of that legislative body. The district mayors also have a popularly elected district-level municipal council; they have the authority to decide on details of city planning and zoning, although the guidelines are determined by the metropolitan municipality. Decisions of the district municipalities may be rescinded by the metropolitan council. The metropolitan mayor also enjoys veto power over the decisions of the metropolitan council. The district municipalities provide such basic services as firefighting, garbage collection, sewerage, and the like; the metropolitan municipality plays a coordinating role in these services.

from those ministries. Cabinet approval is necessary to change the names of settlements within the boundaries of municipalities. Moreover, decisions by municipalities concerning some personnel matters must also be approved by the cabinet.

The introduction of a metropolitan model of municipality for the major provincial capitals was the most significant innovation introduced by the ANAP governments. Yet the extent of the center's administrative tutelage of the metropolitan municipalities was not significantly reduced after the adoption of the two-tiered system. Provincial governors are still empowered to make changes in the budgets of the district or metropolitan municipalities; the secretary-general of a metropolitan municipality can only be appointed with the approval of the Minister of Interior Affairs; and the salaries and wages of certain types of municipal employees must be the approved by both the State Personnel Office and the Ministry of Finance. Finally, metropolitan or district municipalities can establish new service units only with Ministry of Interior Affairs approval of the municipal council decisions to that effect. On certain matters, municipalities are even required to seek the approval of the Council of Ministers.

In October 1988, the government promulgated a decree law, enabling even provincial governors to remove duly elected mayors from office. Although this decree was annulled by the Constitutional Court after an appeal was made by the Social Democratic Populist Party, the very fact that it was introduced clearly reflected the government's intention to impose as much central control over the local government as possible.[10]

Political Party Control

As the foregoing makes clear, the governing parties in Turkey are able to wield a considerable amount of influence over local government by means of bureaucratic tutelage. The governing party can also influence local government through its members of the Provincial Council and the Provincial Standing Committee, as well as through the governor.

The governor is an agent of the central government. He cannot be affiliated with any political party. However, the governor's appointment is determined by the governing political party elites. Although they may try to be impartial and stand above party politics in their provinces, there is no evidence that all governors show the same degree of prudence.

Another factor that blurs the distinction between local and central government is the definite slant to consider local politics in Turkey as if they were an integral part of national politics. Whenever local elections are held, their results are immediately compared in the media with those of the previous national legislative elections by political and academic observers alike. The "localness" of the local elections is often cast in doubt by

[10]Mümtaz Soysal, "Kararnamenin Düşündürdükleri," *Milliyet* (Istanbul daily), 11 October 1988.

a system in which major mayoral seats are distributed among the country's leading political parties in the same way legislative seats are distributed in the national elections. Party leaders are highly instrumental in deciding who will be candidates for the seats of metropolitan and district mayors. In the final analysis, the two-tiered municipal system that was to have stood in the way of any single party gaining monopolistic control over various levels of local government was helpful neither in promoting decentralization nor in preventing government parties from attempting to establish such monopolistic controls by tampering with the rules of the game or through recruitment procedures. Prior to the local elections of 26 March 1989, for example, the ANAP leadership attempted to devise an electoral system to enable ANAP to control a disproportionate number of mayoral seats in comparison to the votes it would receive in the elections. Although these electoral arrangements introduced by the ANAP were overruled by the courts, this attempt was a sign of the ANAP leaders' continued preference to prolong the tutelage system.

Financial Resources

In 1981, a new law (Act 2464) was adopted by the NSC, which gave the municipalities other than the metropolitan ones new sources of stable income. Between 1982 and 1984, 5 percent, and later up to 8.5 percent, of the national tax revenues were allocated to the municipalities.[11] One percent of that amount was earmarked for provincial administrations between 1982 and 1984[12] and 1.2 percent thereafter.[13] Municipalites were authorized to require the beneficiaries of the newly installed water supply projects to participate in their financing. Cost sharing of municipal investments by the local communities was preserved. The new law also authorized the municipalities to collect new taxes, including those from the residents of neighboring areas outside the municipal boundaries who benefited from municipal services. The overall consequence of the new law was to increase the revenues of the municipalities by almost threefold from 1981 to 1984,[14] and the municipalities' share of the state's tax revenues rose by 313.6 percent between 1980 and 1990.[15]

Act 2464 brought a solution to the severe financial problems of some municipalities. Because the newly allocated funds were distributed among the municipalites according to their communal sizes, the least populous municipalities, and the resort areas with seasonally fluctuating popula-

[11] Halil Nadaroğlu and Ruşen Keleş, "The Past and Present of Intergovernmental Fiscal Relations: The Case of Turkey," in *Fiscal Relations between Central and Local Governments*, Nadaroğlu and Keleş, eds. (Istanbul: Marmara University Publication, 1991), p. 67.

[12] İlhan Özer, "Türkiye'de Mahalli İdarelerin Mali Kaynakları ile İlgili Son Gelişmeler," *İller ve Belediyeler*, nos. 475-476 (1985): 213.

[13] Nadaroğlu and Keleş, "The Past and Present of Intergovernmental Fiscal Relations," p. 67.

[14] Ibid., p. 148.

[15] Ibid., p. 74.

tions, such as Istanbul's Adalar municipality, were unable to benefit from the provisions of the new law.[16]

Metropolitan municipalities were entitled to 3 percent of the national taxes collected within their boundaries. They were also to receive 50 percent of the fees levied for the provision of such services as electricity, natural gas, and garbage collection. Municipalities were also given the right to launch business ventures, but there has been no evidence that they have been able to raise significant revenues from such sources (Table 8.1).

The financial resources of the local governments in Turkey still depend largely upon the central government. In 1986, about 38 percent of the municipal revenues consisted of transfers from the national budget, which accounted for 49 percent of the resources of the Istanbul metropolitan municipality municipalities resources and 46 percent of those of İzmir.

Financial autonomy of the municipalities is still a distant goal. Table 8.1 indicates that municipalities have started to raise some of their own revenues, but it is too early to judge whether they will become self-sufficient even in the longrun. Still, municipalities, especially the metropolitan ones, have been able to spend more–including expenditures on investments– with a view to addressing major ailments of the cities (Tables 8.1 and 8.2).

Not only were the municipalities able to expand their service areas and make new investments, but their per capita expenditures and resources increased dramatically after 1984 (Table 8.1). However, it was chiefly the metropolitan municipalities that recorded such increases. For instance, the Ankara metropolitan municipality increased its investments close to twenty times from 1981 (TL3,956 million) to 1986 (TL70,265 million), at current prices. The expenditures of the Istanbul metropolitan and district municipalities accounted for 42 per cent of the 1986 national total. As Table 8.2 indicates, investments and other expenditures rose sharply after the ANAP government began to implement its decentralization policies.

The ANAP governments were mainly concerned with increased services by municipalities, especially in the metropolitan cities. Consequently, the municipalities were given some flexibility in spending their funds. In spite of the fact that they were still under the budgetary control of the central government, they were able to allocate large amounts of financial resources to major infrastructural and recreational projects. In early 1992, the same trends persisted in municipalities controlled by the Social Democratic Populist Party and the True Path Party.

Yet, it is hard to determine the extent to which resource allocation decisions were autonomously made by local authorities. It is also difficult to identify the level of the local government at which decisions were made to spend funds. However, a partial answer can be derived from a study I conducted of the relations between the district and metropolitan mayors

---

[16]Yılmaz Esmer, "Allocation of Resources," in *Local Government in Turkey: Governing Greater Istanbul*, Metin Heper, ed. (London: Routledge, 1989), pp. 52-60.

Table 8.1: Municipal Expenditures and Revenues (in million Turkish Liras)

	YEARS					
	1981	1982	1983	1984	1985	1986
Type of						
Expenditures						
Current	55,617	65,477	99,927	148,702	289,675	472,688
Investment	17,295	22,320	40,595	61,269	177,217	568,092
Capital Formation						
and Transfer	10,027	15,753	20,810	29,116	87,831	192,832
TOTALS	82,939	103,549	161,331	239,087	544,723	1,233,611
Per capita[a]	3,111	3,724	5,574	7,948	17,766	38,511
US$[b]	23.5	20.1	19.9	17.9	30.9	50.2
Municipal/						
Public (%)	5.47	6.46	6.17	6.32	10.28	14.84
Type of						
Revenues						
Taxes Collected						
Directly by Local						
Administration	-	10,380	17,799	31,281	50,239	79,800
Non-tax	30,637	40,055	69,842	106,888	281,356	682,402
Transfers						
from National						
Budget	46,162	40,846	61,028	104,419	223,128	471,409
TOTALS	76,799	91,282	150,649	242,588	554,723	1,233,611
Per Capita[a]	2,880	3,283	5,205	8,064	17,766	38,511
US $[b]	21.8	17.7	18.6	18.2	30.9	50.2
Municipal/						
Public (%)	5.29	6.26	6.47	8.50	12.04	17.24
Transfers/Total						
Revenue (%)	60.11	44.75	50.51	43.04	40.22	38.21

Note: Municipal/Public indicates the proportion of the total municipal funds or revenues to the total amount of public funds indicated in the consolidated budgets of the same year. Transfers/Total indicates the proportion of funds transferred from the national budget in the total municipal revenues. All figures for the years 1981 through 1984 reflect final accounts, and all figures for 1985 and 1986 are budget figures. The final accounts, however, indicate that those budgetary figures may be too optimistic: in 1984, 59.3 percent of the revenues of the Istanbul metropolitan municipality actually came from the national budget.

[a] Reported in Turkish Liras.

[b] Converted according to end of year US dollar parity of the Turkish lira.

Sources: Prime Ministry State Institute of Statistics, *Municipalities, Provincial and Village Administrations Budgets and Final Accounts 1987*, Ankara, 1987; and Ministry of Finance, *Annual Economic Report*, Ankara, 1987.

94

Table 8.2: Expenditures of the Ankara, Istanbul, and İzmir Metropolitan Municipalities (in million Turkish Liras)

Cities	Type of Expenditure					
	Current		Investment		Capital Formation and Transfer	
Ankara						
1981	3,956	(100)	1,708	(100)	985	(100)
1982	6,746	(079)	1,451	(067)	1,929	(155)
1983	10,139	(154)	6,337	(223)	2,981	(182)
1984	14,125	(147)	8,129	(196)	2,150	(090)
1985	45,357	(332)	28,957	(491)	8,672	(255)
1986	70,265	(384)	68,905	(873)	22,378	(491)
Istanbul						
1981	12,245	(100)	3,766	(100)	1,354	(100)
1982	13,714	(089)	4,683	(098)	2,573	(150)
1983	18,603	(092)	9,805	(157)	3,027	(135)
1984	28,116	(094)	17,966	(196)	2,304	(070)
1985	55,788	(132)	70,785	(544)	31,609	(676)
1986	100,239	(177)	338,865	(1946)	82,620	(1320)
İzmir						
1981	5,664	(100)	1,736	(100)	886	(100)
1982	3,923	(055)	3,234	(147)	1,350	(120)
1983	5,779	(061)	2,907	(101)	2,320	(158)
1984	6,887	(050)	4,229	(100)	2,241	(104)
1985	13,426	(069)	12,993	(217)	5,652	(185)
1986	20,351	(077)	33,688	(420)	8,979	(219)

Notes: All figures for the years 1981 through 1984 reflect final accounts, and all figures for 1985 and 1986 are budget figures. The figures in parentheses constitute an index, with 1981 taken as the base year, or 100. Index figures are corrected for annual inflation as measured by the wholesale price index.

Sources: Prime Ministry State Institute of Statistics. *Municipalities, Provincial and Village Administrations (Annual Statistics), 1986*, Ankara; and idem, *Statistical Pocket Book of Turkey 1988*.

of Istanbul.[17]

During the interviews for this study, whenever I asked the district mayors about the relations between their municipality and the metropolitan municipality, they almost unfailingly referred to their close and strong personal ties with Bedrettin Dalan, then metropolitan mayor of Istanbul. The formal relations between district and metropolitan municipalities seemed insignificant compared with the personal and informal contacts between the mayors. No binding norms seemed to regulate interaction between the metropolitan and the district mayors, a further indication of how little decentralization of local government has progressed within the metropolitan municipality system itself. The relationships between the central and municipal governments were no more institutionalized than those between the metropolitan and district municipalities.[18] Under these circumstances, the ANAP governments' interference in the affairs of local administrations continued unabated.[19]

In a complete reversal following the ANAP's defeat in the 26 March 1989 local elections, the central government launched a policy of recentralization. Between the March 1989 local elections and the October 1991 general elections, the ANAP governments further decreased the allocation of financial resources to the municipalities.[20]

Local Government Personnel

As a final indicator of the significance, or nonsignificance, of local governments in Turkey, a comparison between the number of local administration employees and central government personnel is presented in Table 8.3. Municipalities seemed to have experienced a large increase in the size of their bureaucracies in the post-1984 period. Table 8.3 includes figures compiled in 1985. By December 1987, the number of white-collar employees of the municipalities reached 103,141. This approximately 45 percent increase in the ranks of municipal white-collar employees was much greater than

---

[17]For the research design, data, setting, and other methodological aspects of the study, see Ersin Kalaycıoğlu, "Division of Responsibility," in *Local Government in Turkey: Governing Greater Istanbul*, Heper, ed., pp. 16-17.

[18]Ali Erkan Eke, "Anakent Yönetimi ve Yönetimlerarası İlişkiler: Batı Deneyimi ve Türkiye," *Amme İdaresi Dergisi* 18 (1985): 59-61; Michael N. Danielson and Ruşen Keleş, *The Politics of Rapid Urbanization: Government and Growth in Modern Turkey* (New York: Holmes & Meier, 1985), pp. 81-93.

[19]Events prior to the 1989 local elections indicated that the central government abided by the norms that often coexist with decentralization. The governmental decree (no. 336) enabled the Ministry of Interior Affairs to redraw the borders of municipalities with more than eighty thousand inhabitants. This measure was taken about nine months prior to the 1989 local elections, and it was an obvious example of gerrymandering. With the systematic addition and subtraction of certain villages or even districts from major municipalities, it was possible to enhance the chances of the government party winning more municipal contests than it otherwise could. For an elaboration, see Coşkun Kırca, "Belediye Sınırları," *Hürriyet* (Istanbul daily), 17 August 1988.

[20]Limitations imposed on municipal expenditures had begun in 1987, as is explained below, in the next section.

Table 8.3: Comparison of the Number of White Collar Employees of the
Central and Local Governments

	EMPLOYEES		EMPLOYMENT			
Type of Budget	Number	% of the Total	0-1 year	1-5 years	6-10 years	11+ years
General	758,129	60.7	56.5	55.9	59.0	64.0
Annexed	110,728	8.9	12.0	10.0	9.4	7.8
State economic enterprises	253,218	20.3	14.5	21.7	20.4	20.1
Special	55,892	4.5	4.1	5.3	5.3	3.6
Local government	70,856	5.7	12.9	7.1	5.9	4.5

Source: Turkish Republic, Prime Minister's Office, Directorate of State Personnel, The Results of the Survey of Public Employees, Ankara, 1986, p. 85.

the comparatively meager 20 percent increase in the white-collar workers employed by the central government during the same period.

In summary, although local government grew rapidly in terms of both budgetary capacity and number of employees, it remained dependent on the central government in respect to allocating resources and recruiting top level employees. In the past, the fluctuations in the numbers of local government personnel had been highly influenced by the central government.[21] Municipalities still must seek the approval of the central government to hire or terminate the employment of some high-level personnel.

Decentralization and Democracy

The recent restructuring of municipal government in Turkey has constituted a timid step toward decentralization in a highly centralized political system. As noted earlier, however, the authority given to municipalities after 1984 to make decisions on real estate development, planning, and construction represented a significant devolution of power from the center. As a result, the metropolitan municipalities and their mayors emerged as the most powerful and influential actors responsible for shaping the urban environment.[22] One consequence of the increased authority in this area and of full autonomy in issuing construction permits was the launching of macro projects for all the big cities in the nation.

[21] Tahir Aktan, "Mahalli İdarelerde Vesayet Denetimi," Amme İdaresi Dergisi 9 (1976): 3-24.
[22] Sema Köksal and Nihal Kara, Büyük Şehir Yönetimi: Etkin Yönetim mi? Yerelleşme mi? (Istanbul: Marmara University Publication, 1988), pp. 28-37.

An overall result was the soaring of municipal expenditures.[23] This was one of the causes of the galloping inflation, which reached 75 percent in 1989. Consequently, beginning in 1987, the central government began to seek ways and means to cap municipal expenditures, and it thereby intruded into the realm of local governments.

The central government increased its control over the municipalities for two other reasons as well. First, accusations of local government corruption emerged as standard news items in the daily newspapers. For instance, the ANAP mayors of Istanbul's Eminönü and Sarıyer districts were removed from office following such accusations by the ANAP government's minister of interior affairs.

Second, air, land, and water pollution became a major concern for the urban population, as more and more land was allocated by the municipalities for building construction. The municipalities got into the habit of issuing industrial and residential building permits without considering the environmental consequences.[24] The municipalities' cavalier attitude toward the rapid urban growth also prompted the central government to increase its tutelage over them.[25]

It is often suggested that decentralization contributes to democracy by enhancing political equality and participation through rendering the local authorities accountable and responsive to their constituents.[26] This does not seem to have been the case in Turkey. Rather the most well-organized local interests benefited the most from local politics. Decentralization in Turkey led to a subtle arrangement whereby landowners and construction companies came to wield greater influence on municipal decisionmaking, whereas the general public did not.[27]

It is uncertain whether decentralization or a stable national democracy comes first. In the West, stable national democracy seems to have preceded decentralization.[28] In Turkey, it is not yet clear that the process of transition to democracy has been completed and that a democratic form of government has been firmly consolidated at the national level. In the meantime, however, local government policies of the 1980s have opened up new channels for public participation,and although the organized local interests obtained the lead in issue management, the general public was not completely left out. Members of the general public began to make use of the new channels offered to them for voicing their problems and making demands for services. As Table 8.4 shows, the public's contact with the municipalities evinced an overall increase over a four-year period after

---

[23]Ibid., p. 30.
[24]Öncü, "The Potentials and Limitations of Local Government Reform in Solving Urban Problems," pp. 76-78.
[25]Ibid., pp. 78ff.
[26]See inter alia Smith, *Decentralisation*, pp. 23-30.
[27]Öncü, "The Potentials and Limitations of Local Government Reform in Solving Urban Problems," pp. 84-88.
[28]Smith, *Decentralisation*, p. 25.

Table 8.4: Demands for Service in Some Istanbul District Municipalities

	Number of Uses of Municipal Health Facilities	Number of Applications to the Council	Number of Complaints Made to the Municipal Police	Number of Cumulative Applications
Bakırköy				
1984	-	11,045	1,888	-
1985	-	22,058	2,026	-
1986	-	19,213	1,593	-
1987	-	32,105	894	-
Beşiktaş				
1984	536	-	-	7,547
1985	535	-	-	10,712
1986	857	-	-	13,057
1987	981	-	-	10,209
Şişli				
1984	3,627	-	-	-
1985	5,581	-	-	-
1986	7,918	-	-	-
1987	8,175	-	-	-
Üsküdar				
1984	-	20,326	-	-
1985	-	22,681	-	-
1986	-	48,957	-	-
1987	-	46,678	-	-

(-) No available data.
Sources: The 1987 Annual Reports on the Municipal Activities of the Bakırköy, Beşiktaş, Şişli, and Üsküdar municipalities.

the inception of the ANAP's decentralization strategy. For instance, in the district of Üsküdar, from 1984 to 1987, the number of applications to the Municipal Council more than doubled and in the district of Bakırköy they nearly tripled.

It may be suggested that public awareness of the new local administration and interest in its affairs have increased during the recent years.[29] A significant factor in this increased awareness is the primordial group ties of the rural migrant majorities of the metropolitan areas, which have contributed to the establishment of successful clientelistic linkages. New patron-client networks have fostered career patterns for the local political elites. Provision of a greater number of services through similar clientelistic

---

[29] Köksal and Kara, *Büyük Şehir Yönetimi*, pp. 17-23.

politics has also been expected from the district municipalities.[30] District mayors have been perceived by some as "super headmen"; they have been expected to cope with even the personal problems of the inhabitants of their districts.[31]

Local input in municipal government seems to have increased in terms of both funds raised locally and political representation of the local groups.[32] At the same time, people's expectations from the local government have increased commensurately. But there is little chance of these expectations being fulfilled, despite the recent attempts by the municipal governments to provide more varied and relatively more comprehensive service. Unfulfilled expectations are likely to cause alienation from the system and to result in protest behavior.[33]

Earlier optimistic evaluations of the Turkish decentralization of 1980s as a "liberal revolution"[34] need to be reconsidered. A modest step toward decentralization, taken in 1984, was a starting point for democratization in the localities. A recent study by Nihal Kara and Sema Köksal concludes that Istanbul's metropolitan model has encouraged participation in local politics, especially by the rural migrants.[35] However, the authors also hasten to add that the two-tiered system, with a very powerful metropolitan mayor at the helm of local government and his almighty "technocrat/bureaucrat" administration, has been beyond the reach of many local groups, as well as of the elected assemblypersons of the metropolitan city council and even the district mayors.[36]

Conclusion

Local governments in Turkey began to experience a severe challenge from the rapid social mobilization in the 1960s and 1970s. Municipal Act 1580, enacted in 1930, failed to equip municipal administrations with the means to cope with the challenges of social mobilization. Thus, new steps were taken in the 1980s to bolster the powers and the financial resources of the municipalities.

The foregoing analysis should make clear that decentralization policies of the 1980s were designed primarily to alleviate the financial burden of the municipalities; whatever limited progress was made toward decentralization was not made because the people demanded more say in the running of their local affairs. The decentralization policies of the ANAP govern-

---

[30]Ibid., pp. 17-33.

[31]Kalaycıoğlu, "Division of Responsibility," pp. 22-23.

[32]Köksal and Kara, *Büyük Şehir Yönetimi*, pp. 17-25; Esmer, "Allocation of Resources," pp. 52-60.

[33]This point is discussed at some length in Kalaycıoğlu, "Division of Responsibility," p. 14.

[34]Metin Heper, "Introduction," in *Local Government in Turkey*, Heper, ed., p. 1.

[35]Köksal and Kara, *Büyük Şehir Yönetimi*, pp. 23-25.

[36]Ibid., pp. 34-42.

ment, not unlike the preceding military NSC regime, emerged in line with the engrained state tradition in Turkey: The central political authorities perceived the municipal administrations as a drain on the national budget. Thereafter, they tried the best they could to make local governments financially self-sufficient.

Not unexpectedly, the ANAP leadership paid somewhat more attention to the implications of decentralization for democratization than had the military NSC. The ANAP governments' programs referred to decentralization of local government as a more sucessful way of satisfying the demands of the people and as a form of democratic participation by the people in local decisionmaking, although the latter interpretation was not adopted as an overriding objective.

All in all, central governments from 1980 to the present have tended to overlook democratization in formulating their policies in respect to local governments. The Turkish political system is still overwhelmingly centralist. Local politics still does not constitute an autonomous political domain in Turkey.

The measures toward decentralization taken by the NSC and the ANAP governments were rife with uncertainty. New and braver steps toward the delegation of power by the central government to local government need to follow if a meaningful form of decentralization of government is to be achieved in Turkey. Such steps are not likely to be taken unless there is strong demand for them from elements of civil society.

PART FOUR

International Dynamics and Domestic Politics

9

The European Community, the United States, the Middle East, and Turkey

Udo Steinbach

The student of Turkish foreign policy is struck by the extent of continuity with which that policy has been evolving since the inception of the Turkish Republic in 1923.[1] There are few ruptures, emotional reactions, volte-faces in terms of changing alliances, and military entanglements such as those that characterize the foreign policy of other states in the Middle East. The Turkish political elites were guided by the interests of the state, but they were hardly mistaken about the potentials at the state's disposal to further those interests or about the circumstances that determined the maneuvering space for Turkish governments to act in their regional and international milieus. Since 1983, Turkish foreign policy has been unfolding within the framework of three parameters: the political regime of the country, the experiences the republic has been drawing from the past, and the external political environment.

Formative Decades

Until Atatürk's death, his charismatic personality primarily set the course of Turkey's foreign policy, the basic slogan being "peace at home and peace in the world." This obviously reflected a lesson drawn from the Ottomans' permanent involvement in numerous wars and conflicts, which finally led to the downfall of the empire. Total independence, thus, was a logical aspiration for Turkey in its emergence as a nation-state. The international system, based on the equilibrium among the major European powers and on the absence of an external threat to Turkey's territorial in-

---

[1] For a comprehensive overview of many aspects of Turkish politics, see Klaus-Detlev Grothusen, ed., *Turkei: Südosteuropa-Handbuch, Volume IV*, (Göttingen: Vandenhoeck und Ruprecht, 1985).

tegrity, provided a favorable milieu in which Atatürk could uphold the principles of independence and peace until his death in 1938.

After World War II, the coordinates of Turkish foreign policy changed considerably. Given the new international system, characterized by the cold war and by direct Soviet pressure on Turkey, the Turks had to redefine their place in the world. They decided to enter into an alliance with the West for security reasons and eventually became a member of the North Atlantic Treaty Organization (NATO) in 1952. Significantly, these developments paralleled a change in Turkey's political regime. In 1945, a multiparty system was introduced. The Democratic Party, which came to power in 1950, began to liberalize the economy. By the beginning of the 1960s, ground was laid for closer relations between Turkey and the European Economic Community; an Association Agreement, signed in 1963, symbolized this new relationship.

A change in the overall constellation of Turkish foreign policy occurred again in the mid-1960s, triggered by the first Cyprus crisis, which erupted in 1963. Turkey felt the need to reconsider its international relations, particularly following the receipt of U.S. President Lyndon Johnson's notorious letter of 5 June 1964. This letter, which stated that "NATO allies have not had a chance to consider whether they have an obligation to protect Turkey against the Soviet Union if Turkey takes a step which results in Soviet intervention without the full consent and understanding of its NATO allies," made Turks realize that the way they conducted their foreign relations was no longer adequate to fully serve Turkey's national interests, particularly in light of the détente process that had begun to change the international climate.[2] As a consequence, the Turkish government embarked on a process of mending fences with the Soviet Union. Equally significant, it looked for ways to heal the rupture with the Arab states,[3] which had existed since Atatürk abolished the Caliphate and, in a dramatic gesture, took the country out of the Islamic orbit within which the Turks had played a leading role for centuries.

Also beginning in the early 1960s, along with ideological polarization and political fragmentation, Turkey's foreign policy became a matter of contention within domestic politics. The American arms embargo in the wake of the Cyprus crisis of summer 1974 came as a shock, much as Johnson's letter had ten years earlier. The embargo significantly influenced the debate over Turkey's foreign and security policies. The perception that the West treated Turkey not as an ally but as a developing country led for the first time to a widespread feeling that Turkey might indeed be a part of the Third World. This feeling was prevalent among the leftist circles, both inside and outside of the Republican People's Party (CHP). It was argued that Turkey should find its place among the Third-World countries

---

[2] The full text of Lyndon Johnson's letter is published in *The Middle East Journal* 20 (1966): p. 386.

[3] The only exception involved Turkey's warm relations with Iraq during the 1950s.

and demonstrate solidarity with them. At the same time, a debate was conducted within the CHP over a new defense concept advocating an independent security structure and calling for means to defend the country with its own resources.[4]

However, Turkey's maneuvering range turned out to be much more limited than the advocates of an independent foreign policy seem to have realized. A few symbolic gestures were made, but no substantial change occurred, except that Turkey became a full member of the Organization of the Islamic Conference (OIC) and in 1978 the Association Agreement with the European Community (EC) was frozen. The Turkish government made some overtures toward the Soviet Union and rhetorically claimed to base its security policy strictly on the principle of national interests. Prime Minister Bülent Ecevit's visit to Moscow in June 1978 became the litmus test of Soviet-Turkish relations; it became obvious that the basic parameters of Turkey's security policy had not changed.

Transition to the Third Turkish Republic

The 1980 military takeover ended what could be labeled an experimental phase in the conduct of Turkish foreign policy. Continuity rather than change was again the striking feature of the overall picture. Foreign policy had not been left out of the controversies among the various parties and groups. Although domestically the country was rapidly moving toward the brink of collapse, foreign policy–in its real conduct and not only as an issue of academic and ideological debates–continued to occupy an important place. The most significant achievement of the era between the mid-1960s and the end of the Second Republic was the adoption of a multidimensional foreign policy.

However, the 1980 military intervention did not ipso facto imply a major reshuffling of the country's external relations. Although Washington openly admitted that it was satisfied with the prospect of Turkey's return to greater stability, Moscow was apparently eager to maintain relations that were as normal as possible with a military regime that harshly persecuted the left as well as the extreme right. In any case, the leader of the military regime, General Kenan Evren, although making strong anti-Communist statements, refrained from accusing the Soviets of supporting subversion in Turkey.[5]

Although the constant debate with most of the European governments over human rights did not lead to a breakdown of relations, it nevertheless strained Turkey's relations with most members of the EC and contributed

---

[4]Udo Steinbach, "Perspektiven der türkischen Aussen- und Sichereitsopolitik," *Europa-Archiv*, 25 July 1978: 431-440.

[5]Udo Steinbach, "Die sowjetisch-turkischen Bezienhungen seit 1973," *Osteuropa* 34 (1984): 723-733.

to a renewed focus on Turkey's relationship with its Middle Eastern neighbors. Much more important were the business opportunities offered by some of the oil-exporting countries in the wake of oil price hikes following the fall of the Iranian monarchy and by Iran's and Iraq's need for goods in transit through Turkey after the outbreak of the Iran-Iraq War in September 1980.[6] Another contributing factor was the new regime's quest for recognition, which it could obtain more easily in the Middle East and in countries such as the People's Republic of China (where democratic principles were not highly respected) than elsewhere. In fact, Turkey's position in the region became such that it appeared at times as if Ankara would be able to mediate first in the Iran-Iraq War and then in the Gulf War. In the same vein, Turkey toned down its diplomatic relations with Israel (reducing them to an absolute minimum) and stepped up those with the Palestinian Liberation Organization (PLO), and President Evren became the chair of the Permanent Committee for Economy and Trade of the OIC (1984).[7]

Finally, the military's decision to continue pursuing the export-oriented economic policy launched in early 1980 had far-reaching significance. The custodians of Kemalism consented to an economic program that admittedly meant the end of étatism and the introduction of a market economy as the overall philosophy of economic growth. Although trying to eliminate the politicians of the previous regime by blaming them for the demise of the Second Republic, they appointed the architect of this economic policy, Turgut Özal, as deputy prime minister in charge of the economy.

In view of another attempt at competitive politics under the Third Republic, the change of economic policy was to have a number of significant implications. On the domestic level, economic liberalization further contributed to the erosion of the power and influence of the traditional bureaucratic elites, who had taken advantage of their position of patronage to bolster their own powers. The opening up of Turkey's economy also gave economic considerations far greater weight in foreign policymaking than they had enjoyed since the beginning of the republic. To put it simply, Turkey's approach to foreign policy became more pragmatic as economic interests, along with political and security interests, came to be considered essential elements in policy formulation.

---

[6]Erol Manisalı, ed., *Turkey's Place in Europe: Economic, Political and Cultural Dimensions* (Istanbul: Üç-er, 1989); Selim İlkin, "Turkey's Economic and Financial Relations with the Arab Middle East: The Recent Past and the Near Future," Paper presented at the Centre d'Etudes et de Recherches Internationales (CERI), Paris, 16 March 1990. For the earlier period, see Selim İlkin, "Turkey's Attempts to Approach the Islamic Countries after 1974," in *Die Türkei auf dem Weg in die EG*, Werner Gumpel, ed. (München: Oldenburg, 1979), pp. 217-235.

[7]"Turkey Scores High Points at Casablanca," *Briefing* (Ankara), 23 January 1984; "Istanbul Meeting Reaffirms Turkey's Leading Role," *Briefing*, 19 November 1984.

Toward a Multidimensional Foreign Policy

The return to competitive politics in 1983 did not lead to a far-reaching reorientation of Turkey's foreign policy. Although the basic aquis was preserved, a few significant accretions came into the picture, the most noteworthy of which was the application for full membership in the EC.

Turkey's relationship with the United States remained stable. For Washington, despite the changes in American-Soviet relations, Turkey continued to hold geostrategic importance. Before the Soviet Union disintegrated, Turkey was particularly important in the defense of NATO's southeastern flank. It maintained both intelligence-gathering bases, which monitored Soviet troop movements and communications, and major air fields on its soil. In turn, for Ankara, U.S. military and economic aid was essential for Turkey to maintain its military force and modernize its army. American aid also provided a sense of security against threats that could potentially originate in any of Turkey's neighboring states. When the Soviet Union began to collapse, Turkey's significance for the United States was questioned, but the Gulf War changed the entire situation. During that war, Turkey gave strong support to the allied forces led by the United States; it promptly complied with the UN resolutions and even let U.S. bomber aircraft operate from its soil.

However, at times relations with the United States faced difficulties.[8] One of the basic differences–although it was rarely voiced loudly by either side–stemmed from different interpretations of the nature of their alliance. With the deterioration of the overall situation for the West–especially in the Gulf area following the revolution in Iran, the Soviet invasion of Afghanistan, and the outbreak of the Iran-Iraq War–Washington counted on Ankara to let American operations be carried out from Turkey should the necessity arise. Until the Gulf War, however, all Turkish governments, even the military ones, made it clear that Turkey did not want to become involved in any contingency outside the NATO defense area.

There were also some issues to which Turkey reacted with sensitivity. These included congressional efforts to cut military assistance to Turkey, to link embursement of assistance to "progress" on the Cyprus issue, and to make April 24 a day of remembrance for the "Armenian genocide committed by the Ottoman government,"–behind all of which the Turkish government tended to see pressure by the Greek and Armenian lobbies in Washington to drive a wedge between the United States and Turkey.

By the end of the 1980s, the Turkish government appeared confident that it had bargaining chips when dealing with Washington. This was reflected in the dilatory way in which it treated the prolongation of the Defense and Economic Cooperation Agreement, which had expired in December 1985. The extension of the agreement to 1990 was ratified only when Washington, in a side letter, reaffirmed its pledge to seek every means to

---

[8]"Washington and Ankara–How Close?" *Briefing*, 28 March 1983.

fulfill its proposed annual military and financial aid budget for Turkey. By the early 1990s, Turkey was a valued U.S. ally.

Turkey's relationship with the Soviet Union stabilized and improved during the 1980s. The transition to a democratic system in Turkey nearly coincided with Mikhail Gorbachev's ascent to power in Moscow, and the overall reorientation of Soviet policy had an impact on the relationship. In the Turkish perception, the Soviet Union became increasingly predictable in its foreign relations and thereafter was considered less of a threat. Both sides obviously took pains to build each other's confidence, notably in the military field: Chiefs of staff exchanged official visits in 1985-1986,[9] and in April 1988, Turkish officers were invited to watch Soviet military maneuvers.[10] The "hardware" of the relationship lay with increasing economic cooperation. Given the precarious economic situation in the Soviet Union, the targets set in the Turkish-Soviet economic protocol seemed quite ambitious, calling for bilateral trade in 1988 close to US$700 million.[11]

On the political level, however, no change occurred. A number of issues that had been unresolved since the 1970s soured relations from time to time. Among these were the Cyprus question (Moscow supported the Greek claim for a withdrawal of Turkish troops from the island as a precondition for a settlement), the boundaries of the fishing zone in the Black Sea off the Turkish cost, and the fact that the Soviets tolerated the continuing repression of the Turkish minority in Bulgaria. Nevertheless, the opening of the border station at Sarp in September 1988, which had been closed since 1937, showed that both sides were resolved to go ahead with the normalization of relations. During the Azerbaijani crisis in early 1990, the Turkish government took pains not to appear involved in any way. Turkey's "careful policy" concerning Turkic republics in late 1991 and early 1992–an active policy of establishing communication with the independent republics while respecting the Russian Federation's sensibilities–further improved relations.

The most significant event in Turkey's international affairs after the return to democracy was its application for full membership in the EC in April 1987.[12] This reflected Ankara's resolve to define Turkey's place in the world in a clearer and more rational way than had been the case before. After having been forced to side closely with the United States in the climate of the cold war, and subsequently, in the 1970s, experimenting with new openings in its foreign relations, the Turkish government appeared to seek stability in accordance with the political, economic, and cultural policies it adopted under the Third Republic. It would be wrong to consider

[9] *Turkish Daily News*, 2-3 August 1986, 5 August 1986.

[10] *Arab News*, 23 August 1988.

[11] *Financial Times*, 14 July 1988.

[12] For the most comprehensive account on the subject, see Heinz Kramer, *Die Europäische Gemeinschaft und die Türkei: Entwicklung, Probleme und Perspektiven einer schwierigen Partnerschaft* (Baden-Baden: Nomos Verlagsgesellschaft, 1988); Ahmet Evin and Geoffrey Denton, eds., *Turkey and the European Community* (Opladen: Leske Verlag und Budrich, 1990).

this step as either an expression of opportunism or merely a matter of simple pragmatism aimed at having access to the financial benefits to be gained from the EC; nor was it triggered by a wish to counteract the Greek influence on the EC. This was a deliberate step taken on the basis of a widespread consensus among most of the political and social groups and a thorough economic restructuring, which has brought the country–from the viewpoint of economic policy–closer to the EC than ever before. As most of the elites saw it, membership in the EC would be the keystone to Turkey's becoming an integral part of Europe; it would be the crowning achievement of a process begun in the nineteenth century.

The freezing of relations with the EC by Prime Minister Bülent Ecevit in 1978 reflected the domestic quarrels, economic problems, and external ambiguities the country was experiencing at the time. It also turned out to be a serious mistake: Not only did the EC's southern enlargement complicate Turkey's access to the European market, but the decision dimmed the country's chances of eventually becoming a full member when it applied to the EC after the restoration of democracy. Given the frustrating discussions about the free movement of labor (which the government claims should have come into effect at the beginning of 1987), the prevailing skepticism and doubt concerning the state of Turkish democracy, the strong criticism of Turkey's human rights record, and the delay of the implementation of the fourth financial protocol (according to which the EC was to provide an economic aid package to Turkey), Turkey's efforts to become a full member of the EC were tantamount to undoing the Gordian knot. However, the application reflected the Turkish political elites' newly acquired self-confidence and their resolve not to be pushed around, especially by the Europeans, in an arrogant fashion. The basis for such confidence was not only Turkey's continuing contribution to the security of the West but also, more important, its economic performance since the early 1980s. Impressive figures of economic growth (around 7 percent), and of increasing foreign trade as of the early 1980s, made the new leadership optimistic and confident about the country's potential to achieve European economic standards and to become an attractive market for which industrialized countries would compete.

With the application for full membership in the EC, the ball had been passed to the Europeans' court. In Brussels, the application met with skepticism, if not uneasiness and covert resistance; it was found too early by the members of the community. In particular, the timing of the application seemed to cause irritation. Since Turkey's application for full membership in 1987, all of the implications of Turkey's application–political, economic, and, in particular, cultural (religious) aspects–has been debated at length. Ankara seems to have taken a realistic stand. Instead of expecting full membership in the near future, it appears the Turkish government would be satisfied if Brussels would reach a decision leaving open the possibility of full membership after a process of transition and adaptation of structures—a process that could extend into the early twenty-first century.

Given the centrality of this issue for Turkey's aims and ambitions in cultural, political, and economic spheres, the future of Turkey-EC relations will have considerable impact on its domestic and external policies. Although the report made public by the Commission of the European Communities in December 1989[13] was not completely negative, it left no doubt that the EC did not view Turkey as being ready to enter as a full member in the foreseeable future.

Meanwhile, in spite of the ongoing criticism of Turkey's human rights performance, most of the European countries normalized their relations with Ankara. This development clearly reflected the European preference to distinguish between EC relations with Turkey as a possible future member of the community and bilateral relations with Turkey, which were—especially economically—too important to allow European countries to base their individual relationships with Turkey exclusively on human rights considerations.

It is a valid observation that Turkey's rapprochement with the European Community by no means negatively affected its relations with its regional neighbors. As mentioned before, the "discovery" of the Middle East started in the 1960s. The reorientation was less a deliberate move than a reflection of Turkey's frustration over the failure of its post-World War II partners to respond positively to Turkish national interests, mainly in the case of the Cyprus issue. It may seem paradoxical that only after the takeover by the military junta, which claimed to be staunchly Kemalist, did cooperation with its Muslim neighbors become a stable component in Turkey's overall approach to foreign policy. West German President Richard von Weizäcker, the first European head of state to visit Turkey since the inception of the Third Republic, proposed in one of his speeches that Turkey could provide a bridge between Europe and the Middle East. Whether this is feasible remains to be seen, but economic considerations did play an important role in Turkey's increased relations with its Middle Eastern neighbors. Yet, President Evren's election as chair of the OIC—regardless of the relative importance of that office—was nevertheless a significant gesture that demonstrated the extent to which secular Turkey and the Islamic world had accepted one another. President Evren's acceptance of the chairmanship also paralleled the Kemalist military leaders' policy to use Islam as a bulwark against the left.

---

[13]Commission of the European Communities, "Commission Opinion on Turkey's Request for Accession to the Community," 20 December 1989.

Basic Coordinates of the Third Republic's Foreign Policy

The rationale behind the Third Turkish Republic's approach to foreign policy becomes clearer when it is examined in terms of the three basic coordinates outlined at the beginning of this Chapter. On the international level, the overall constellation was determined by the climate of détente between East and West, as well as by a remarkable global stability demonstrated impressively by the considerable progress in nuclear arms reduction. There was no longer an open threat from the Soviet Union and later, its successor states. On the regional level, for a number of reasons, the leaders of the Third Republic found it advantageous to go on with the process of normalization, and even to increase cooperation, with the regional states east and west of Turkey to the extent possible. This policy applied clearly to most of the Muslim states that provided business opportunities for Turkey during the 1980s. However, the notorious instability of the region, the ongoing conflicts, the hostility of Syria (which was manifested in the support lent by Damascus to the PKK [Workers' Party of Kurdistan] which was involved in separatist activities in Turkey), the adherence to the concept of laicism albeit a watered-down one, the Turkish elites' inability to manage their Middle Eastern relations, and similar factors set clear limits to the process of integrating Turkey into the region.[14]

The most dramatic attempt at creating a political environment in accordance with the priorities set by the new regime in Ankara was the effort undertaken by Turgut Özal, then prime minister, and his Greek counterpart, Andreas Papandreou, to normalize relations between their two countries in the aftermath of their well-publicized meeting at Davos in February 1988. Although the "spirit of Davos" turned out to be short-lived, at the time both sides thought that in the long run, a settlement of the dispute was in their mutual interest. Ankara was obviously strongly motivated to reach a settlement: As things stood in Brussels, the Greek government could block, through its veto, practically every move toward Turkey's becoming a full member of the EC.

Considering the foreign policy of the Third Republic in light of the second coordinate—that is, experience from the past—we must turn to Turkey's role in the Muslim world. Obviously, the lessons drawn by the bulk of the post-1980 Turkish political elites were different from those of the founder of the republic. This was only natural, given the difference in political circumstances. With the shock of the downfall of the Ottoman Empire, and confronted with the tasks of reversing the plans to divide Turkey among Western powers and then to establish a totally new state out of the shambles, Atatürk emphasized Turkish nationalism and secularism, with the consequences for the new state's foreign policy outlined above. In the post-1980 period, the Turkish Republic had established its distinct identity

---

[14] "A Question of Salesmanship," *Briefing*, 12 December 1983; "Özal's Visit: Will Damascus Change Its anti-Turkish Stand?" *Briefing*, 13 July 1987.

as a nation state; hence, it could easily reassess the past without undermining the very foundations of the republic and without abandoning crucial elements of the heritage of Kemal Atatürk.[15] Looking over the past one-and-a-half centuries of Turkish history, there can be little doubt that Turkey has shown a double face, one of which looked toward Europe.[16] When the modernization of the Ottoman Empire began in the early nineteenth century, it meant selective Europeanization. With the advent of the Kemalist revolution, it became outright Europeanization. Thus, Turkey has gradually become European in terms of the goals it has pursued, the basic political and societal concepts the elites have adopted, and the political system the Turks began to establish following World War II. It is, therefore, logical that an increasing part of the elite began to consider Turkey's membership in the EC as a final step in the long process of Europeanization.

The other face looked toward the Islamic East. Around fifty years after Atatürk's death, it was apparent that the country had become European only in a limited sense, contrary to what its founder had wished. Islam remained a force that constantly shaped Turkey's outer appearance, and it continued to be a strong element among the set of values that made up the identity of most of the Turks. Although "official" historians of the early Republican period found the roots of "Turkism" in a mythical era long before Turks had become Muslims, recently many Turkish social scientists have begun to study the extent to which the pre-Republican tradition, culture, and religion continued to have an impact on the political, social, and cultural attitudes and behavior of Turks. It became obvious that modern Turkey could not be totally dissasociated from its Ottoman predecessor.[17]

Also, the Turkish governments increasingly came to the realization that Turkey could not avoid taking part within the system of Islamic states. The economic advantages Turkish governments saw in dealing with their Muslim neighbors provided the initial incentive, or catalyst, for Turkey's closer relations with those countries; the real dynamics, however, lay deeper—possibly, in a tacit but irresistible desire to take advantage of the country's position to play a greater role in the region.

The lesson we learn from the past and the way we try to translate it into policy are closely connected with the third basic coordinate—that is, the nature of the political regime. What were the most significant features of the political regime of the Third Turkish Republic that influenced decisionmaking in the field of foreign policy?

---

[15]Semih Vaner, "Etat, société et parties politiques en Turquie depuis 1982," *Revue d'Etudes sur le Monde Méditerranéen et Musulman* 50 (1988): 87-107.

[16]Udo Steinbach, "Turkey-EEC Relations: Cultural Dimension," in *Turkey's Place in Europe*, Manisalı, ed., p. 13-24.

[17]This argument is illustrated in Şerif Mardin, "Freedom in an Ottoman Perspective," in *State, Democracy and the Military: Turkey in the 1980s*, Metin Heper and Ahmet Evin, eds. (Berlin: Walter de Gruyter, 1988), pp. 23-35.

First and foremost, the Third Republic turned out to be a pluralist regime, which gave adherents to various Weltanschauungs ample room to express themselves and to debate matters of foreign policy. Although the prime minister and the foreign minister made the final decisions, their decisions were based largely on inputs from many groups, such as political parties, professional groups, the military, and the like.

The vast majority of the political and social elites in the country were basically pro-Western, as reflected by the broad consensus behind Turkey's application for full membership in the EC. Others, who for political or ideological reasons advocated closer relations with either the former Soviet Union or the Islamic states at the expense of the West, constituted no more than marginal groups. Even if full membership could not be achieved, and even if NATO membership looked strategically less important by the end of the 1980s, it was hardly imaginable that a complete *renversement des alliances* would take place. It could be assumed that Ankara would continue to seek a modus vivendi with the West, which would be in the interest of Turkey.

The regime's approach to foreign policy was less ideological than that of its predecessors in the 1970s. The country's political and economic interests, rather than its ideological orientation, were of paramount importance for the regime. Attempts at diffusing the tensions with Greece, rather than placing priority on maintaining a firm position, constituted one example of flexibility and pragmatism, as did continued economic relations with Iran and Prime Minister Özal's trip to Damascus in July 1987 to seek rapprochement with Syria, with a view to diminishing Damascus's support of the Kurdish insurgents in the southeast.

The new pragmatism was perhaps most clearly reflected in Turkey's economic policy. Although adopted prior to the military intervention of 12 September 1980, liberal economic policies were followed by the military regime and staunchly pursued under the Third Republic. There is little doubt that the overall picture of Turkey's economy significantly improved after the étatist strategy was abandoned. The post-1980 economic measures made Turkey dive into the uncertain waters of the international markets, in which it has fared remarkably well, especially in terms of increasing exports and regaining creditworthiness. I must add that the tremendous structural changes made in the Turkish economy resulted in a greater compatibility with the economies of the EC member states and thus improved Turkey's prospects of achieving full membership.

The role of Kemalism as a state ideology also underwent change. Its interpretation among the political elites, and even among the staunch Kemalists in the military, became less rigid and more flexible.[18] Kemalism will undoubtedly remain the guiding ideology under the Third Republic, although there is no longer a single authoritative source to explain what

---

[18] Udo Steinbach, "Turkey's Third Republic," *Aussenpolitik* 39 (1988): 234-251.

precisely is to be understood by "Kemalism." Turkish nationalism remains firmly entrenched as a component of the identity of the overwhelming majority of the Turks; and secularism will remain the fundamental principle on which the polity is founded, despite the fact that Islam is becoming increasingly manifest. Finally, the Turkish elites will continue with the modernization of the country, more or less in line with European patterns.

Yet the Kemalist nature of Turkey no longer seems to clash with manifestations of traditional values in public life. The elites who represent the Kemalist concept of state and society, especially including the military, have taken a much more conciliatory tone in interpreting such concepts as modernism and secularism than their predecessors had taken in the past. Modernism no longer seems to be equated with slavish cultural and political imitation of the West, and secularism is no longer viewed as being tantamount to atheism. Instead, it is permissable today to search for a new, historically rooted sociocultural identity. The state elites accept the usefulness of traditional symbols insofar as these serve to strengthen national unity and social solidarity. In fact, the most visible change concerning the nature of the regime, compared with those of the First and Second Republics, is the role of Islam. As a religious and societal phenomenon, Islam has received unprecedented recognition since 1980. It has begun to permeate political and social life in Turkey to a greater extent than has been the case at any time since 1923. Islam has emerged in a dual role: It represents a crucial component of the new cohesion and consensus in society, and recourse to Islam is expected to help establish a broad and effective web of traditional social solidarity.

Conclusion

An examination of Turkey's foreign policy since the founding of the republic reveals that its scope has been consistently widened–from the remarkable isolation of the Atatürk era to the multidimensional and multifaceted policy under the Third Republic. There was hardly a region and an international issue to which post-1980 Turkey did not pay attention. Turkey showed an abiding interest in complex international negotiations, such as nuclear disarmament, multilateral and balanced force reductions, and the Conference on Security and Cooperation in Europe. Throughout the 1980s, Turkey's foreign policy was well adopted to the new trends in the international system, set in motion with Mikhail Gorbachev's initiation of a "new policy" in Moscow. The end of the Cold War gave Turkey greater space in which to maneuver and broader options in determining its relations with the superpowers. Its foreign policy also reflected the pluralistic nature of the Third Republic, as well as its emphasis on the country's economic interests and its recognition of Islam as an essential element of the societal fabric.

However, it cannot be said that the basic orientation of the country's foreign policy was radically altered under the Third Republic. After 1973, Turkey's foreign policy had undergone an experimental phase at both the international and the regional level, mainly because of the fluid and unstable domestic situation. In the more consensual and less polarized atmosphere of the Third Republic, coherence and stability were achieved, and Turkey's foreign policy came to be governed by long-term considerations and interests.

At the beginning of the 1990s, the main challenge to Turkey's foreign policy was that of reconciling various components into a stable and balanced network of international relations. Thus, there was a need for both flexibility and a clear definition of the country's place within the global system of political powers and ideological currents. The Turks had to make a clear-cut distinction between what was of primary importance–that is, of strategic value–to them in furthering their national interests and what was of secondary or tactical importance. They appeared to have been successful in making these distinctions and in developing a capability and readiness to compromise. Although Turkey's determination to enter the European club on the one hand, and its increased interaction with countries in the Islamic orbit on the other, occasionally threatened to cause friction, serious conflicts were avoided in the implementation of a multilateral foreign policy. Likewise, neither Iranian attempts to export fundamentalism nor Syrian assistance to the PKK insurgents were allowed to derail Turkey's pragmatic policy of pursuing its economic interests by seeking long-term influence in the region.

Turkey-EC relations constituted the most significant facet of Turkey's foreign policy, reflecting the multidimensional political and economic considerations of the Third Republic; this was comparable to the developments after World War II, when Turkey's alliances with the West (especially the United States) accelerated the process of political pluralization and eventually helped to establish a multiparty democracy. The rapprochement with the EC also had implications for Turkey's domestic policy. A broad spectrum of Turkish leaders came to realize that the country would have to live up to the European standards of democracy if it were to be seriously considered for full membership in the EC. Since 1983, a step-by-step democratization has been carried out, moving away from the type of "democracy" the military had in mind toward a genuine parliamentary system. Constant European pressure has even succeeded in drawing the attention of the Turkish leadership to the sensitive issue of human rights and in making the government publicly admit shortcomings and take measures to correct them.

Whereas the new pattern of its relationship with the EC increased Turkey's exposure to pressure in certain fields, the Turks, on their part, made deliberate efforts to avoid being pressured from outside. Although the rapid process of détente between the superpowers and later the disintegration of the Soviet Union created propitious conditions for Turkey, it was the Turkish government that took the initiative to enlarge its space of maneuver in the region.

Turkey can no longer be compared to a boat being thrown around by winds. Since the beginning of the 1980s Turkish leaders have managed–more effectively than their predecessors–to steer the course of the country within a complex international system.

By the early 1990s, the political system of the Third Republic clearly looked more stable than that of its predecessor, which crumbled just a decade ago under ideological confrontation, social unrest, economic failure, and the lack of even a minimal consensus among the leading politicians as to how to save the political regime. Beyond all differences among political parties over policies and Weltanschauung, there is now a widespread readiness to employ the democratic instruments offered by the Constitution to steer the course of the country and not to impose the rule of one group upon another at any cost. And a widespread consensus exists in respect to Turkey's foreign policy and its international position. Naturally, different political parties and interest groups have different priorities and ideas. But these differences relate primarily to particular policies governing the fulfillment of political, economic, and social functions; they do not constitute irreconcilable differences concerning the basic foundations of the polity and of society, such as those that led to fragmentation and polarization in the 1970s.

10

The Limits of International Influence for Democratization

Ali L. Karaosmanoğlu

Turkey's geopolitical situation raises the question as to the extent to which the country's democratic evolution might have been affected by external influences. How might a range of different influences have tended to offset or reinforce one another? Under which conditions, and to what extent, might external factors have promoted democracy in Turkey? In this Chapter I address these questions.

Historical Background

Ottoman Modernization

To many people, Turkey poses a paradox. Its sociopolitical and economic evolution has followed a different path from that of Europe. Turkey has been undergoing a process of Westernization since the eighteenth century; yet profound differences in religious ideology, culture, social-political systems, and statecraft have continued to separate the European and Ottoman worlds from one another.

Long before the Treaty of Westphalia (1648), when the European system was in an embryonic stage, the Ottoman Empire was an important factor in the European balance of power. Through its wars, alliances, and economic policies, it became significantly involved in the continent's international politics. The Ottoman state was formally included in the European state system by the Treaty of Paris in 1856: "That simple formality codified a century and a half of precedent, embedded in an even longer process."[1]

---

[1] Thomas Naff, "The Ottoman Empire and the European States System," in *The Expansion of International Society*, Hedley Bull and Adam Watson, eds. (London: Oxford University Press, 1984), p. 143.

At first, the Ottoman Empire was a dominant power; then the Treaty of Karlowitz (1699) marked a decisive turning point in the military balance between Europe and the Ottoman Empire. After that date, the Ottoman state adopted a balance-of-power diplomacy–not to expand its influence and control in the West but to slow down the pace of its own retreat. This policy was supported by European diplomacy, which tried to avert the creation in the East of a dangerous power vacuum that could result from the abrupt collapse of the empire. By the second half of the eighteenth century, the Ottoman Empire had become a weak state with shrinking territory, internal upheavals, and decaying institutions. In response, Ottoman statespersons sought to introduce a series of reforms to reinforce the balance-of-power policy. Thus, "reform became an element of policy in Ottoman relations with Europe."[2]

The military and political modernization was first initiated by the state as a measure of self-defense. Ottoman rulers "have judged that the only effective way of holding one's own against the West is to fight the West with Western weapons in the broadest sense of the word–a sense in which it covers Western ideas and institutions as well as Western makes of guns and bombs."[3]

The Ottomans' recognition of European military superiority as early as the end of the seventeenth century prepared the necessary psychological ground for the later cultural, administrative, and political borrowings from the West.[4] The spread of the modernization process to areas other than the military institutions was inevitable. The modern army needed officers trained in Westernized military schools, where to a certain extent they became familiar not only with new military techniques, but also with the Western way of life and Western culture and ideas. The rising costs of the new military corps and their administrative organization necessitated the establishment of an efficient taxation system. Political modernization led to the adoption of the constitutional monarchy proclaimed for a brief period in 1876 and reintroduced in 1908; it culminated in the establishment of the Turkish Republic in 1923 and the secularizing reforms of Atatürk.

Ottoman leaders were well aware of the close connection between domestic reform and foreign intervention.[5] They adopted secular laws and institutions in order to satisfy the European powers, which acted as protectors of the empire's non-Muslim subjects. For example, when confronted with the rebellion of Muhammed Ali of Egypt and his threatening military might, they felt it necessary to gain the sympathy and confidence of

---

[2]Ibid., p. 169.

[3]Arnold J. Toynbee, *Change and Habit: The Challenge of Our Time* (London: Oxford University Press, 1966), p. 154.

[4]Halil İnalcık, "The Nature of Traditional Society: [Turkey]," in *Political Modernization in Japan and Turkey*, Robert E. Ward and Dankwart A. Rustow, eds. (Princeton: Princeton University Press, 1964), p. 62.

[5]James P. Piscatori, *Islam in a World of Nation-States* (Cambridge: Cambridge University Press, 1986), p. 52.

the Western powers by initiating wide ranging administrative and social reforms in the late 1830s. For their part, the Western powers were also interested in supporting the Ottoman reforms. Modernization, they thought, would delay the Ottoman collapse and thereby help ensure the continued protection of their strategic and economic interests in the region.[6]

In order to reverse the process of disintegration, the Ottoman reformers adopted two categories of modernizing measures. One category consisted of strengthening the armed forces and recentralizing the government. The government assumed a series of new responsibilities in such fields as education, law, trade, taxation, and agriculture; earlier, most of these functions had been performed by local, communal, or religious institutions. Centralizing reforms were regarded as an essential means for effective control of the periphery. But the resulting authoritarian system of government led not only to the differentiation and centralization of administrative functions essential for political modernization but also to a kind of "enlightened despotism," which later became the main target of the rising intelligentsia.[7]

The second group of measures concerned the improvement of the status of both the Muslim and non-Muslim subjects of the empire in order to satisfy the demands for equality, land ownership, and the improvement of individuals' status before the state. At the outset, these two kinds of measures were considered necessary to ward off foreign encroachments. In time, they gradually evolved into two complementary, but at times contradictory, approaches to modernization, which continued to mark the process of democratization in Turkey.

Toward the Installation of Democracy

Following World War I, Turks fought against the Western occupation. The War of Independence (1919-1922), however, did not aim to distance Turkey from Western principles of government or from European economic and social systems.[8] On the contrary, it was a struggle to create a modern nation-state with a Western type of polity. The Republican reforms to establish such a polity were initiated and carried out under a mildly authoritarian single-party regime, whose leaders preferred to exercise "controlled political intimidation" rather than resorting to repression.[9] The Kemalist revolution which took on the characteristic of an elite movement, sought to suppress symbols and values of the Ottoman ancien regime.[10] There is no doubt, however, that the Kemalist movement paved the way–even if in a

---

[6]See İlkay Sunar, "Anthropologie politique et économique: L'Empire Ottoman et sa transformation," *Annales: Economies, Sociétés, Civilizations*, nos. 3-4 (1980): 566.

[7]See İnalcık, "The Nature of Traditional Society," p. 62.

[8]Mehmet Gönlübol, "A Short Appraisal of the Foreign Policy of the Turkish Republic, 1923-1973," *The Turkish Yearbook of International Relations* 7 (1974): p. 14.

[9]Şerif Mardin, "Ideology and Religion in the Turkish Revolution," *International Journal of Middle East Studies* 2 (1971): 198.

[10]Ibid., p. 199.

very indirect sense–for the later structural changes such as the gradual rise of a bourgeoisie, the emergence of a labor movement, the growth of municipal autonomy, the liberalization of the economy, and related political and economic processes.

The Republican People's Party (CHP), established in the early 1920s, dominated the political scene until 1945. Attemps were made in both the 1920s and the 1930s to introduce a multiparty system despite the adverse international climate of the interwar period, when dictatorships flourished and totalitarian ideologies, such as communism and national-socialism, became increasingly popular. In both cases, Turkey's experiments with democracy were short-lived. Turkey's transition to democracy in the years following World War II was motivated partly by foreign policy considerations.

The policy of strict neutrality during World War II saved Turkey from the scourge of war, but it created discontent among the allies and left Turkey vulnerable to Soviet territorial and ideological expansionism. Moscow did try to exploit Ankara's postwar isolation in a heavy-handed way by making territorial claims over Turkey. Faced with the Soviet threat, Turkey could no longer afford to remain neutral. It sought to establish closer ties with the West and to obtain much-needed economic and military assistance from the United States at a time when the Western bloc appeared to be increasingly concerned with promoting democracy as the mainstay of the "free world." Because authoritarianism was perceived to stand in the way of Turkey's joining the Western orbit, Ankara considered it vitally important to transform the regime toward a multiparty system.[11]

Geopolitical and Transnational Challenges

Geopolitics

Its geopolitical position creates remarkably unfavorable conditions for the consolidation of democracy in Turkey. Although Turkey is politically and militarily aligned with the West, it is geographically distant from Western Europe and shares frontiers with five authoritarian countries which at times attempt to destabilize their neighbors–including Turkey–in order to further their own ideological and territorial ambitions. Greece has been Turkey's only democratic neighbour since 1974, but, despite the recent signs of improvement in their relations, the lingering disputes between the two countries continue to create a climate of insecurity and hinder cooperation.

---

[11] Ferenc A. Vali, *Bridge Across the Bosporus: The Foreign Policy of Turkey* (Baltimore: Johns Hopkins University Press, 1971), p. 64. For the continuing convergence of the international and domestic factors, see Dankwart A. Rustow, "Turkey's Travails," *Foreign Affairs* 58 (1979): 87.

Despite its Western characteristics and orientation, Turkey also belongs to the Middle Eastern subsystem. Its diplomacy and security are closely affected by the developments in the region. But Turkey is a "heterogeneous" element in this subsystem by virtue of its secular polity, democratic regime, liberalizing economy, and Western ties; thus, it constitutes a target for subversion originating from Middle Eastern states as well as nonstate entities in the area. Although Turkey has pursued a policy of noninterference, at least until the recent Gulf War, some of its neighboring regimes have shown a persistent tendency to intervene in Turkey's domestic affairs. The most prominent examples are the statements made frequently by the Iranian and Libyan leaders and Iran's continual subversive broadcasting, which is beamed on Turkey. Another example is Syria's support of the Workers' Party of Kurdistan (PKK).

The present trends, which seem to point to a new period of détente, provide reason for optimism in respect to regional stability. Détente would undoubtedly decrease the possibility of war and provide suitable ground for the development of economic relations. But at the same time, it may enhance the likelihood of indirect, incremental, and low-intensity activities of a politico-military nature, which are difficult to deter. For example, during the first period of détente, in the 1960s and 1970s, Turkey experienced a rapid democratization of its political life, but it also had to cope with rising terrorism, which, among other things, twice brought about military takeovers and severely disrupted the process of democratization. Although the current transformations in the Eastern bloc have undoubtedly contributed to creating a favorable international environment for democratization, we must remember that rapid changes almost always lead to uncertainty and increased instability.

Terrorism

During the 1970s, Turkey suffered from an unprecedented degree of terrorism, which destabilized the polity and dealt a severe blow to the democratization process by undermining public confidence in democracy. Law and order came to a point of total collapse as the number of assassinations approached thirty a day. In addition to the extremists of the left and the right, the victims included moderate members of the Parliament, journalists, and university professors, as well as a former prime minister. Most people were relieved when the military took control of the government on 12 September 1980 to put an end to the rampant anarchy, and they believed that the military would establish law and order with a view to preserving the representational system in the long run.

Terrorism in Turkey, with its multiplicity of external connections, had a strong transnational aspect. The leftist terrorists adopted the propaganda themes broadcast in Turkish by Soviet-supported radio stations in Bulgaria and the former Democratic Republic of Germany. Moreover, evidence indicated that terrorism was being financed from abroad. The total spending for all terrorist activities from 1977 to 1980 was estimated at US$1,000 million,[12] a sum equal to the total U.S. and other NATO military aid to Turkey during the same period. Bank robberies committed by terrorist organizations could account for only a small fraction of this amount. Interception of arms shipments to Turkey from Bulgaria and Syria, as well as the training and logistic support given to some terrorist groups by the pro-Soviet elements of the Palestinian Liberation Organization (PLO) in Lebanon and Syria, pointed to the involvement of external actors. Evidence of Bulgarian and Syrian support was corroborated by the confessions of captured terrorists.[13]

Terrorism by the extreme nationalist right was another major factor contributing to political violence. Ultrarightists regarded themselves as the defenders of the state against communism, but their activities instead undermined the state authority, as well as the democratic institutions. According to a perceptive analyst, in the process of destabilizing Turkey, "Competitiveness between right and left became, in fact, cooperation. Both groups of terrorists drew support from the same shadowy sources."[14] The rightist terrorists, however, seemed to have obtained much less support from abroad than the leftists had.

The 1980 military intervention ended the widespread urban terrorism. But since 1984, Turkey has faced a new kind of insurgency by the PKK, concentrating on rural areas in the southeastern region. A secessionist Marxist organization, the PKK, has utilized very harsh methods to terrorize the civilian population and to show them that the government had no effective control in the region. Earlier, the PKK concentrated almost exclusively on civilian targets, but more recently it has conducted attacks on military personnel. PKK groups infiltrated Turkey mostly from Syria, after having been trained at camps in Syria and in the Syrian-controlled Bekaa Valley in Lebanon. Reports also indicate that the Secret Army of Liberation for Armenia (ASALA), the Armenian terrorist organization, has obtained refuge in Syria.[15] Despite complaints by the Turkish government, so far Damascus has shown no willingness to curb activities of these organizations.

The Iran-Iraq War also helped to increase subversive activities in the southeast. The PKK militants, taking advantage of the hostile parties'

---

[12]See Aydın Yalçın, "Terrorism: the Turkish Experience," Hearing before the Subcommittee on the Judiciary, the United States Senate, 25 June 1981, Serial no. J-97-43.

[13]Paul B. Henze, *Goal: Destabilization, Soviet Agitational Propaganda, Instability and Terrorism in NATO South* (Marina del Rey, Calif.: European American Institute for Security Research, 1981), pp. 15-47.

[14]Paul B. Henze, "Coping with Terrorism: What Do We Know? What Can Be Done?" Paper prepared for the conference convened by the Social and Economic Studies Foundation (Istanbul), Istanbul, 3-6 October 1982, p. 8.

[15]For the Lebanese and Syrian connections in question, see Michael M. Gunter "The Armenian Terrorist Campaign Against Turkey," *Orbis* 27 (1983): 447-477; and *Turkish Daily News* (Ankara), 24 October 1985 and 3 March 1986.

inability to control their frontier areas effectively, infiltrated Turkey especially from the Iraqi side. In order to put an end to such border violations, the Turkish armed forces undertook several military operations against the insurgents in Iraqi territory, initially with the express consent of the Iraqi government and later without it. In the aftermath of the Gulf War, a power vacuum was created in northern Iraq, which made it even easier for the PKK to stage new raids on Turkish military posts near the border. When Turkey responded with cross-border operations into northern Iraq, it was heavily criticized in the Western media.[16]

Turkey's response to the PKK activities complicated its relations with Western Europe, including the allied countries. Turkey was broadly criticized in Western Europe for resorting to heavy-handed tactics to deal with the PKK and was blamed, except in certain conservative circles, for suspending democratic principles and human rights while seeking to establish law and order. Turks, in turn, deplored the European's lack of understanding concerning the problems facing Turkey, and argued that the purpose of the measures taken after the 1980 military takeover was to pave the way for democracy by achieving law and order in the first place.

The sympathetic attitude toward the PKK in some European circles aroused indignation within Turkish public opinion. Turkey was quick to point out that PKK propaganda activities were supported by Communist and, to some extent, Socialist parties in some West European countries, where a number of organizations backed the PKK–including local Kurdish organizations.[17]

Armenian terrorists also constituted a serious threat. Armenian terrorist organizations concentrated their operations outside Turkey, targeting the lives and property of Turkish diplomats and officials. Over thirty Turkish diplomats have been assassinated abroad since 1973, and diplomatic missions have been targets of numerous bomb attacks. In addition, twelve persons were killed in two operations carried out in Turkey. The typical small Armenian community in Turkey, with only about sixty thousand people, does not pose any nationality problems and deplores these acts, which are planned and executed by external organizations.

Many Turks believe the Armenian terrorism, though in no way comparable to the PKK phenomenon,[18] nevertheless tended to drive a wedge between Turkey and its allies by exacerbating the inherited Western prejudice against the Turks. Their fears were justified to some extent in June 1987 when the European Parliament adopted a resolution that called on Turkey to recognize the "genocide" of the Armenian population by the Ottoman government during World War I. The Turkish Parliament passed

---

[16]*Briefing*, 21 October 1991, p. 15.

[17]For a long list of West European governments and organizations that tolerate or support the PKK, see *Briefing*, 4 July 1988, p. 47.

[18]Incomparably more people died in those incidents; the PKK incidents continue, whereas the Armenian activities seem to have lapsed during the recent years.

a strongly worded motion, condemning this resolution as "an open invitation to terrorism," and stating that it would only serve to affect adversely Turco-European relations. The Turkish indignation was directed against those who voted for the resolution in the European Parliament, not against the European Parliament itself or the center-right political groups who refused to take part in the debate and the voting on the resolution.

Religious Extremism

One of the major issues on Turkey's recent agenda has been the extent to which Islamic fundamentalism might pose a threat. This same concern has been shared by Turkey's Western allies. Would Turkey gradually fall into the hands of Islamic extremists? What was the impact of the Iranian Revolution on Turkey? What were the outside connections of the religious groups in Turkey? In this section I discuss mostly the latter of these questions.

One aspect of Islamic revival in Turkey was the activism of certain religious groups and sects and their alleged transnational links. There were reports that most of the sects had close connections with some Islamic states, in particular with the Muslim business groups in those countries.[19] It was even claimed that the U.S.-Saudi Arabian oil giant ARAMCO had been a major supporter of the Nakshibendi sect in Turkey and that many Islamic states in the region had made investments in Turkey with the aim of strengthening their ties with certain other religious groups.[20]

Another example of religious subversion originating from abroad was Iran's radio broadcasts in Turkish. On several occasions, Ayatollah Khomeini himself criticized Atatürk and his secular reforms and claimed that those who follow Atatürk could not be called Muslims, a view frequently repeated by the religious activists in Turkey. Nevertheless, Shia Ayatollahs gained only a limited influence in Turkey, where Islamic extremists are Sunni in orientation. Moreover, the Iranian regime lost much of its prestige in Turkey after its failure in the Iran-Iraq War. Fundamentalist movements gradually lost their appeal as examples of a reaction against Western cultural and economic penetration. The recent developments in Eastern Europe and the former Soviet Union constituted the greatest challenge to fundamentalism. Western ideas and values such as pluralism and democracy, condemned by the fundamentalists as "corrupt and dying," became increasingly popular.[21]

According to some observers, certain Western attitudes were prone to encourage Islamic fundamentalism by unconsciously justifying the Muslim believer's perception of the world and serving to reinforce basic political premises held by Muslims. The fundamentalist discourse rather

---

[19] *Briefing,* 20 October 1986, p. 11.

[20] Ibid.

[21] Amir Taheri, "Exit Communists and Khomeinists?" *The Times* (London), 22 December 1989.

simplistically postulates a Christian-Muslim dichotomy as the basis of its approach to world affairs. The West is seen as a hostile monolith that should be conquered or converted. The modern world, viewed as having been corrupted by Western values, has to be reshaped in accordance with the Koranic tenets. In the West, too, there is a growing tendency to view regional problems in the Middle East and the former Soviet Union from the perspective of a generalized Muslim-Christian conflict. This inclination also became increasingly obvious in Turkey's relations with Western Europe, where certain politicians–from the left as well as the right–have put forth religious incompatibility as an argument against Turkey's full membership in the EC.

The recent crisis in the Caucasus has provided another striking example of a biased approach by the Western media and governments. The developments between Armenia and Azerbaijan, and the eventual intervention of the Red Army in Baku, have generally been described in terms of a Christian-Muslim confrontation. The question of nationalities, self-determination, human rights, and, above all, the predominantly secular character of the Azerbaijani nationalist movement are completely ignored. Such biased Western approaches undermine the efforts by the secular Turkish intelligentsia, who attempt to present the West as a model of secular society to emulate.

The Domestic Context and Transnational Linkages

The Military

In Turkey, the armed forces have been an instrument of modernization, and among other things, modernization has implied an attempt to establish democracy. Consequently, although from time to time they had serious doubts about the intentions and abilities of the political elites, Turkish military leaders never changed their favorable attitude toward democracy: "Democracy for them remained an ultimate, if not an immediate, goal."[22]

The military was the first institution to undergo drastic reform in the nineteenth century. As expressed earlier, the Ottoman reform movement had two major aspects. It strove to increase the efficiency and power of the centralized state, and it was a liberal movement aiming to establish political equality and to improve individuals' status before the state. These two interlocking drives shaped the Turkish military's seemingly paradoxical, but in fact realistic, approach to democracy.

Also during the Republican period, the military acted as both the custodian of the state, protecting its territorial integrity and secular nature,

---

[22]Metin Heper, "The State, the Military, and Democracy in Turkey," *Jerusalem Journal of International Relations* 9 (1987): 54.

and as the defender of political democracy.[23] Turkish democracy came into existence with the implicit consent and support of the military in the 1940s. Since then, there have been three military interventions–in 1960-1961, 1971-1973, and 1980-1983. In none of these cases, however, did the military aim to establish a long-lasting authoritarian regime. Even the junta of 1960, renowned for its excesses–such as the execution of one prime minister and two ministers–adopted a constitution that emphasized basic rights and liberties before transferring power to civilians in 1961.

Most of Turkey's high-ranking officers have either visited or served in various NATO headquarters in Europe or in the United States. Such experiences abroad gave them an international outlook and contributed to their sense of professionalism. Although their priorities in interacting with their foreign colleagues were strategic and defense-oriented, their commitment to maintaining their country's ties with the West prevented them from overlooking Western views on regime problems in Turkey.

The Turkish military has been a highly professional institution that has placed an overriding emphasis on its external defense mission. Top commanders have never liked the involvement of officers in political matters to the detriment of their professional functions. Generals believed military intervention in politics undermined the professionalism of the armed forces, their tradition of hierarchy, and combat effectiveness.[24] The military's sensitivities in this respect were strongly reflected in General Kenan Evren's instructions to the armed forces on 10 October 1980, four weeks after the coup, when Evren pointed out that he and his colleagues had carried out the coup because there was utmost necessity for it and that officers should focus on their professional duties.[25] Its commitment to professionalism appears to be one of the reasons the Turkish military has disengaged itself from politics as quickly as possible following each intervention. Its professionalism and high level of discipline, moreover, have not favored the adoption of extremist ideologies among officers.

The Civilian Elites

Since 1983, Turkey has gone a long way toward consolidating democracy. Compared to most Western democracies, however, the Turkish system still suffers from certain restrictions on political and civil liberties. Although the leading politicians have been fully aware of the deficiencies of Turkish democracy, they have not utilized their parties' transnational

[23] Kemal H. Karpat "Turkish Democracy at an Impasse: Ideology, Party Politics and the Third Military Intervention," *International Journal of Turkish Studies* 2 (1981): 7.

[24] See İlter Turan, "Stability Versus Democracy: The Dilemmas of Turkish Politics," Paper prepared for submission to "Colloque sur les Groupes d'Interêt d'Europe du sud et leur Insertion dans la Communaute Européenne," Universite de Genève, April 1986; Heper, "The State, the Military, and Democracy in Turkey," pp. 59-60.

[25] Kenan Evren, *Kenan Evren'in Anıları*, vol. 2 (Istanbul: Milliyet Yayınları, 1990), pp. 208-213. Also see Nevzat Bölügiray, *Sokaktaki Asker* (Istanbul: Milliyet Yayınları, 1989), p. 17.

connections in order to accelerate the process of democratization. When talking to foreigners, the leaders have usually adopted a resentfully balanced tone, emphasizing not only the shortcomings but also the achievements of Turkey's democratic development. Although political leaders have urged Turkey to comply with the Western standards of democracy and human rights, they have carefully refrained from encouraging foreign governments, transnational groups, and international organizations to intervene in Turkey's domestic affairs. At times, they have even unequivocally discouraged them from doing so.

Süleyman Demirel's approach, for instance, has illustrated the attitude among the leading politicians. Demirel–a fierce critic of the military rule–said in an interview given to a daily newspaper in 1985, before his political rights had been restored: "In reality, there is no need for the West to defend democracy in Turkey. Turkey will set up and preserve its own democracy. . . . They should not applaud or criticize us. They should just let us do things our own way. Turkey is able to solve its own problems."[26]

There were various reasons for the politicians' reluctance to make use of transnational linkages, even though such linkages have been useful for the promotion of democracy and human rights in Turkey. First, Turkish and West European political parties stand somewhat apart from each other. There are profound differences in their historical origins and the interests they represent. In Europe, socioeconomic cleavages, and the ideologies based on them, dominate political conflicts; parties generally represent different social and economic groups.

In Turkey, party politics originated principally from a center-periphery cleavage. Only recently did politics in Turkey begin to acquire overtones of socioeconomic cleavages. Under Bülent Ecevit's leadership, the CHP to a certain extent adopted a Western European model of social democracy. Ecevit established close links with the Social Democratic and Socialist parties in Europe and gained membership in the Socialist International for his party. But the CHP could not completely eliminate its elitist and bureaucratic-reformist tradition, which, to some extent, was inherited by the Social Democratic Populist Party after 1985.

Two other factors have contributed to the unwillingness of politicians to seek West European interference in favor of democracy and human rights in Turkey. The first is the belief held by some that Turkish terrorist groups have had the backing of certain West European governments and organizations. Second, there is widespread disappointment within public opinion that neither the adoption of liberal values nor the rise of secularism in Turkey seemed to have changed the inherited prejudice of Western Europeans toward the Turks. These two factors, reinforcing each other, largely decreased the credibility of any European attempt to influence the process of democratization in Turkey.

---

[26] *Turkish Daily News*, 24 March 1985, p. 5.

Labor leaders, on the other hand, appeared to be willing to further their interests by making effective use of their transnational linkages. The example was DISK, a Marxist federation of trade unions, which had been very active in Turkish politics in the 1960s and 1970s, although it was not the largest labor organization in the country. It was a member of the Communist-oriented World Federation of Labor Unions and was actively supported by its counterparts in Europe. DISK was closed and its leadership prosecuted after the 1980 military intervention.

TÜRK-İŞ, which is a member of the International Confederation of Free Labor Unions (ICFLU), has been the most influential labor organization in Turkey. TÜRK-İŞ has often urged the government to take steps to ameliorate the plight of the workers and to lift the restrictions on trade union activities. It also warned from time to time that if the government failed to make any serious initiatives, it would bring its case to such fora as the ICFLU and the UN International Labor Organization (ILO). With encouragement from TÜRK-İŞ, for instance, hundreds of Turkish workers sent cables of protest to the ILO General Assembly session in June 1988, complaining about restrictions on trade union activity.[27]

The most efficient linkages were those established between the extreme left in Turkey and supporters in Eastern and Western Europe. The extreme leftist solidarity has recently been demonstrated by a number of Communist parliamentarians from various West European countries who protested, on a number of occasions in the courts of law and in front of the prime minister's residence, against the detention and trial of two leaders of the outlawed United Communist Party.[28]

The West and Democratic Consolidation

Achieving integration with Europe has continued to be Turkey's long-term objective, because Europe has always been the single-most-important point of reference for Turkish policymakers. Connections with the Middle East have never been considered a serious alternative to those with Western Europe. It is true that both regions have played an important and even a complementary role in respect to Turkey's economy and security,[29] but Turkey's ideological attachment to Western Europe has been important in intensifying its efforts to achieve European standards in consolidating

---

[27] Briefing, 13 June 1988, p. 11.

[28] On 16 November 1987, Haydar Kutlu, secretary-general of the illegal United Communist Party of Turkey, and Nihat Sargın, secretary-general of the disbanded the Worker's Party of Turkey, came back to Turkey from Europe, where they were in exile. They were placed under custody immediately after landing at Ankara Airport. Both men were accused of violating Articles 141 and 142 of the Penal Code, which at the time prohibited Communist parties and propaganda. See Briefing, 16 November 1987, pp. 8-11.

[29] See Ali L. Karaosmanoğlu, "Turkey and the Southern Flank: Domestic and External Contexts," in NATO's Southern Allies: Internal and External Challenges, John Chipman, ed. (London: Routledge, 1988), p. 336.

democracy.

In Turkey, it is widely held that the Council of Europe is a very important forum that gives expression to solidarity among the democratic regimes in Europe. According to a majority of influential actors in Turkey, including the leaders of major political parties as well as the civil servants and officers, membership in the Council of Europe was a significant expression of Europe's recognition of Turkey as a modern Western democracy.[30] Adopting European Community (EC) membership as a major policy objective, on 14 April 1987 the Turkish government formally applied to join the EC as a full member. This move led to a considerable increase in European influence on the process of democratization in Turkey.

However, the 1980 military coup and the imposition of martial law seriously affected Turkey's relations with its European allies. Turkey's membership in the Council of Europe's Parliamentary Assembly was suspended, and relations with the EC were frozen. The EC decided to block its aid program to Turkey, at a time when the country was in a precarious economic situation. Temporary suspension of civil and political rights also led to protests from some European governments, Socialist groups in various European organizations, and Amnesty International. Some organizations, such as the North Atlantic Assembly, sent fact-finding missions to investigate the human rights violations in Turkey.

Although such efforts by European and international organizations met with resistance and were interpreted as unjustified cases of external interference, pressures exerted by Europeans nevertheless did accelerate the process of democratization in Turkey. In addition to the restoration of the parliamentary system and competitive politics, which took place according to the timetable announced by the military rulers right after the 1980 coup, Turkey took a number of significant steps–discussed in Chapter 4–to adapt its political and social system to those of Western Europe.

By the end of the 1980s, European criticism had largely subsided. Turkish parliamentarians resumed their seats in the Parliamentary Assembly of the Council of Europe as early as April 1984. In May 1986, the Parliamentary Assembly of the Council of Europe removed from its agenda the item "Situation in Turkey." Turkey assumed the chairmanship of the Council of Europe in November 1986. The five states that had filed a complaint against Turkey with the European Commission on Human Rights (Denmark, France, the Netherlands, Norway, and Sweden) withdrew their complaints, and the case ended with the adoption of a positive final report in January 1987. However, as late as 1989, some issues still remained about which Europeans had reservations. Reports were filed on sporadic, if not systematic, cases of torture, although officials who were suspected of having committed such crimes were tried before the criminal courts.

---

[30]See Kenneth Mackenzie, *Turkey in Transition: The West's Neglected Ally* (London: Institute for European Defence and Strategic Studies, 1984), p. 22.

The U.S. attitude toward democratization in Turkey has been quite different from that of Western Europe. U.S. administrations have usually adopted a pragmatic approach during periods of regime breakdowns and transitions to democracy. Although in principle the United States encouraged the restoration of democracy, it carefully refrained from openly criticizing authoritarian practices on the part of the military governments.[31] The U.S. policy has at times even caused indignation in some political circles by eulogizing the military rulers.[32] We should note, however, that the U.S. administrations' unequivocal support of Turkey's struggles against the PKK has been widely appreciated in Turkey.

Yet Kurdish Patriotic League leader Jalal Talabani's visit to Washington on 9 June 1988, only a few of months after signing a "pact" with the leader of the PKK that was responsible for mass murders in Turkey, created disappointment within Turkish public opinion. With Talabani's visit, State Department officials–underlining U.S. interest in human rights in the region–declared that the Kurds should seek to satisfy their aspirations through peaceful means within the framework of the existing states in the area. This incident came as no surprise to the Ministry of Foreign Affairs and foreign policy experts in Ankara, who had concluded long before Talabani's visit that the United States had decided to place the Kurdish issue on the agenda in a systematic way. The Talabani visit only confirmed Ankara's conclusion that Washington would take up the Kurdish question within the framework of its overall strategic approach to the situation in the Gulf area, even if such a policy were to have potentially destabilizing effects vis-à-vis the consolidation of democracy in Turkey.[33]

In the aftermath of the Gulf War, Turkey achieved a bold policy reversal. Turkish diplomats, intelligence agents, and political party leaders met on several occasions with Talabani and other Iraqi Kurdish leaders. Moreover, the restrictions imposed by the military government on the use of the Kurdish language were lifted in February 1991. In line with this new policy, the new coalition government, led by Süleyman Demirel, confirmed in its program that linguistic differences within the country enriched Turkey's cultural domain. These developments paved the way for more extensive use of the Kurdish language in politics, the arts, and the media.

From an international perspective, two motives can be seen behind this policy change. First, it coincides with other measures of democratization taken previously by the Motherland Party (ANAP) governments to improve Turkey's image in Western Europe. Second, it is regarded as a step that would yield diplomatic and strategic returns by increasing Turkey's freedom of action in the region and strengthening its position to take on regional roles.

---

[31] See Theodore A. Couloumbis, *The United States, Greece, and Turkey: The Troubled Triangle* (New York: Praeger, 1983), pp. 37, 161.

[32] See, for example, the interview with Demirel, *Turkish Daily News*, 24 March 1985, p. 5.

[33] See *Briefing*, 20 June 1988, p. 11.

Conclusion

Although Turkey is situated in a highly unfavorable geopolitical area, its regime choices have not been predicated by that setting. Its geopolitical and international environments have acquired significance only in relation to Turkey's domestic sociopolitical milieu and to the profound belief of Turks in the virtues of Western democracies. Turks have been able to transform a cosmopolitan empire into a secular nation-state, with a parliamentary democracy, in one of the most strategically perilous environments of the world. It is very likely, however, that Turkey will remain a target for destabilization efforts because of its geopolitical environment.

Turkey's Western connections, however, constitute a favorable factor for the consolidation of democracy. Its full membership in the EC would undoubtedly provide a further guarantee against authoritarianism. Developments since 1980 indicate that Western European states and organizations are willing to wield considerable influence on Turkey to push for the consolidation of its democracy. So far, this potential has been used only to a limited degree. Differences between Turkish and West European political parties have prevented the efficient use of transnational linkages to promote democracy. Misinterpretations, Turkish suspicions of foreign interference, and the European lack of understanding of the Turkish situation have also stood in the way of constructive dialogue and reduced the credibility of European interventions.

Paradoxically, the political organizations that do not believe in democracy and that spread anti-Western propaganda in Turkey have maintained better linkages with Western Europe. They have actively and effectively utilized their connections, not to further democracy but to alienate Turkey from the West in general and from Western Europe in particular.

In spite of these limitations, Western Europe has been able to play a significant role in the improvement of Turkey's human rights record. Some other important developments have been critical for the consolidation of democracy in Turkey, in which the West had no recent, direct influence. The post-1980 behavior of the military leaders is a case in point. Their tolerance of Islam as a social force, and their support of liberal economic policies as opposed to the Republican principle of étatism, concomitant with the reduced degree of elitism among the civil bureaucracy, served to considerably weaken the hold of statist attitudes. The rapid liberalization of the economy and increased emphasis on local government under ANAP governments resulted in a focus on civil society and pluralism. In the long run, these developments can be expected to strengthen transnational linkages among various groups. External influences are also likely to augment the present trends even further as democracy is further consolidated.

PART FIVE

Some Critical Issues

11

Economic Growth and Political Stability

Bilsay Kuruç

From the mid-1960s until the mid-1970s, Turkey enjoyed an annual average growth rate of 6 percent in a golden age for the world economy. In the second half of the 1970s however, Turkey joined those countries that were challenged by serious economic problems. Consequently, issues relating to economic adjustment and growth have been prominent among the problems Turkey faced during the last two decades.

Economic growth became the main concern of Turkey's policymakers following World War II, especially after 1950. Full employment and the related issues of social welfare and income distribution, however, received less attention. This approach continued during the past four decades.[1]

Concern with economic growth had other policy implications as well. Beginning in 1950, and more systematically after 1960, policymakers occupied themselves primarily with the issues of high and sustainable growth rates, inflation, and external deficits and the resulting indebtedness.

Growth Performance

In the four decades since 1950, the rise in domestic demand, the high rate of public spending, and the presence of a conservative party in power to secure the policy line have accounted for the high growth performance of the economy. The entire process seemed irreversible in many respects, even during and after the short intervals of military takeovers, non-conservative coalitions, or left-of-center governments. The mid-1980s, for example, again witnessed the revival of those particular components that have been primarily responsible for sustained high growth rates.

Part of the work on the present chapter was carried out during the author's stay at the University of Oslo with a support from the Royal Norvegian Ministry of Culture and Science. The author is grateful to İlhan Uğurel and Oktar Türel for their insightful comments on an earlier version of this essay.

[1] Exceptions can be found in the second half of the 1940s and the early 1960s.

Subsidiary components of growth also had an impact on the primary set: first, the introduction of a particular growth strategy, which at times was based on import substitution and at other times on a pronounced withdrawal from it, according to the circumstances, which were determined mostly by external factors; second, the increasing influence of business interests on economic policies and management; and third, the particular impact of external funds on the policy line and political fortunes of those in power.

The Rise in Domestic Demand

After a decade of slowdown, the economy attained high growth rates in the mid-1980s, reaching rates well above 7 percent in both 1986 and 1987. The growth that actually took place, however, was not the result of the stragety adopted in 1980, as discussed in Chapter 6. It was, once again the relative rise in domestic demand, and not external markets, that motivated growth.

We can suggest that a long period of sustained growth spurred the rise of populism.[2] A more detailed analysis would reveal particular relationships, for instance, among consumption, real wages, and welfare spending. In this regard, the early and mid-1970s reflected a different pattern of economic growth combined with populism than that of the mid-1980s. In the former period, increases in real wages, consumption, and welfare expenditures were notably high, whereas in the mid-1980s, slightly decreased consumption coincided with a more radical decline in both real wages and welfare spending.[3]

In the field of investment, a mixed performance was observed. The radical turn in growth strategy introduced under the 1980-1983 military regime was further developed by the Motherland Party (ANAP) government. The traditional import-substitution line was dropped in favor of giving priority to public sector investment in infrastructure and services, among others. This change in strategy was accompanied by a shrinking investment effort in productive sectors, mainly for two reasons. First, the public sector stopped investment in, and later gradually withdrew altogether from, the manufacturing sector. Second, the high interest rate structure adopted after the three-year Standby Agreement (1980) with the International Monetary Fund (IMF) had a negative impact on the private-sector investments. In the mid-1980s, the private sector found many incentives to invest in housing, small-scale industries, and services. This profile of investments revealed a striking contrast with those of the early and mid-1970s, when both the public and private sectors were mainly oriented towards investing in a broad range of manufacturing industries.

---

[2]Korkut Boratav, "Türkiye'de Popülizm: 1962-76 Dönemi Üzerine Bazı Notlar," *Yapıt* 46 (1983): 7-18.

[3]In public investment programs, the shares of education and health dropped to 1 and 0.03 percent, respectively, in the mid-1980s.

In sum, growth during the mid-1980s was based largely on domestic demand spurred by consumer spending and on investments in infrastructure, housing, local government, and service-sector projects. The new politics became dependent upon the success of growth performance, which in turn reinforced the platform for political recruitment of an expanding group of new investors and of a tiny but important category of middle-class earners of rent and interest. The growth policies not only prepared a novel political climate but also established a new background for more active business involvement in political life.

Public Spending

There was a coincidence of growth performance, particularly in the mid-1980s and late 1980s, with growing budgetary deficits. During this period, public spending played a crucial role in the management of the economy.

In the four decades after 1950, public spending always had an appeal for the conservative governments. Following 1980, both the military regime (1980-1983) and later the ANAP governments attempted to roll back the boundaries of the public sector. However, after 1983, together with a significant rise in public spending, the proportion of public investments relative to that of private-sector investments still remained high. In the mid-1980s, the public sector's share of total investments reached 60 percent. The ANAP allocated funds to infrastructure and local government to prepare a new political base for itself. The party adopted a policy of establishing close relationships with the business circles—especially with the new generation of entrepreneurs and professionals in the rapidly growing service and finance sectors, which it expected would provide new cadres for political parties and public bureaucracy. In contrast to the earlier periods, a smaller proportion of national income was allocated to social wage, or consumption: energy, transportation, and communication sectors were awarded larger shares, whereas the share of such social sectors as education, health, and social security declined. Consequently, the contribution of public spending to economic growth decreased, contributing to a corresponding decline in the quality of education, extent of health services, adequacy of social welfare schemes, and provision of entitlements.

The policies of the ANAP government shaped the new economic weaponry. Its most frequently used tool was the pricing of the goods produced by the state economic enterprises (SEEs). In a similar vein, the government adopted the policy of allocating a growing portion of public resources through non-budgetary channels. Both practices helped the government to intervene effectively in economic and social life. However, in 1987, the limits of intervention became apparent.[4]

---

[4]Higher public prices were influential in raising the operating surplus of the SEEs from 1.6 percent of GNP in 1980 to 6.4 percent in 1988, whereas no significant productivity changes took place. However, the gross revenue of the public sector channeled to extra-budgetary funds as a proportion of consolidated budget rose to around 21 percent in 1987 and 32 percent

138   *Bilsay Kuruç*

Although public spending played a considerable role in the government's ability to obtain political support for itself, the economy, meanwhile, operated with high costs and prices. Two factors responsible for this state of affairs were the absence of efforts to reform the public sector, which in turn led to growing bottlenecks and inefficiencies, and the emphases on the formation of a mass base and recruiting new cadres, which gave rise to high costs and prices. One consequence was widening budget deficits.

A Conservative Government

Over the past four decades, conservative interests have become an ingredient of the growth performance and have shaped its specific pattern. The gradual weakening of the conservatives' popular base throughout the 1970s was reversed, first by the policies of the military regime of the early 1980s and later–perhaps more significantly–by the use of economic means available to the new conservatives.[5]

In the ANAP government, Turkey's business community found echoes of its aspirations and goals. It had been effectively organized in the 1970s, and its organizational base was not dissolved by the military regime. As a result, business interests played an influential role in the restructured politics of the post-1980 period, despite the fact that the ANAP government came into conflict at times with some of the chambers and business associations.

Following the overhaul of the growth strategy in 1980, one factor that facilitated the business community's involvement in conservative politics was the establishment of new priority sectors, or zones of influence. The representatives of the new sectorial interests developed an ongoing dialogue with the government, contributing to a greater business involvement in economic policymaking.[6]

Compared with the former conservative governments, the ANAP paid more attention to establishing ties with the business community, which it saw as its partner as well as supporter in the management of the economy.[7] In other words, it was not only that a growing number of businesspeople from sectors of financial intermediation, foreign trade, construction, ser-

---

in 1988, starting from a negligible fraction in 1983 (State Planning Organization, *1989 Annual Program*, Ankara, 1989, pp. 80-81).

[5]I use the term *new conservatism* to stand for the major political movement of the 1980s led by Turgut Özal and supported largely by various spheres of interests within the private sector. The growth policy was carried out by a right-wing political party, which also allocated the resources.

[6]Selim İlkin, "Exporters: Favoured Dependency," in *Strong State and Economic Interest Groups: The Post-1980 Turkish Experience*, Metin Heper, ed. (Berlin: Walter de Gruyter, 1991), pp. 89-98.

[7]By *business community* I mean a large band of sectors in which economic interests are led by the most active groups of businesspeople. The latter may or may not correspond to big business, but it is reasonable to assume that the big business interests will be protected and even developed further.

vices, and the like, wanted to be involved in economic decisions; it was also that the ANAP actively encouraged them to participate at least indirectly in decisionmaking. Although the government did dominate the mechanism for resource allocation, its liberal policy made it possible for the business interests to play an influential role. Ever larger percentages of public resources went to the ANAP government's own business community, thanks to the shrinking share of social consumption in government budgets and the declining role of industrial interests.[8]

The two novelties of the period were the enlarged share of rent and the growing linkages of the private sector with external finance. Higher prices of financial instruments, real assets, and commodities all helped to increase the returns on investment by the wealthy. The increased linkages of the private sector with the external world flourished mainly due to external credit facilities; it quickly developed into the establishment of partnerships and joint ventures (both were based on special contracts), deregulation practices, and privatization initiatives.

Inflation and Its Nature

We must make a distinction between the institutional framework of the industrial democracies of Western Europe, where after the mid-1940s demand-management policies had been established with the purpose of maintaining a high and stable level of employment in the economy, and that of Turkey, where, with an emphasis on growth-oriented policies, a comparable institutional setup had not been developed and may even have been totally neglected. Although in the sphere of production the Turkish public sector also played a central role, in the field of distribution it hardly resembled its Western European counterparts.

In Western Europe, strong and stable control over the government made it possible for the working class to use public policy to intervene in the distributional process in society. Therefore, the wage earners were "no longer limited to fight for their share of production on the labor market."[9] This institutional framework had been completed by circulating a sufficiently sizable portion of national income through the public sector to determine the level of economic activity and the *share* of wages, when the latter was mainly allocated to "social consumption." Economic activity was conducted within the framework of a responsible fiscal policy; one has come across a gradual evolution of income policies within an environment of

---

[8] "It is not the responsibility of the state to provide employment to everyone to steer the system in a balanced manner and at the macro level. People with skills will definitely and more easily open up new employment opportunities." Turgut Özal, speaking at the opening ceremony of the 1986-1987 academic year at Ankara University, reported in *Cumhuriyet* (Istanbul daily), 2 October 1986.

[9] Walter Korpi, "Social Policy and Distributional Conflict in the Capitalist Democracies," *West European Politics* 3 (1980): 309.

negotiable wage rates between labor and employers.

Although Turkey made some progress in social reform during the 1960s and 1970s, the links between organized labor and economic management remained negligible. In the 1980s, the public sector's diminishing role in production coincided with worsening income distribution.

By the mid-1980s, two key features of the ANAP government's economic policy had become apparent. First, the government was ignoring distributional issues. Second, its immediate priority was to maximize the resources at its disposal so that high growth performance could be achieved. The new conservatives' approach to the issue of distribution led to the labor market's being kept from potential conflicts by a combination of centralization of decisionmaking and limited wage negotiation practices,[10] parallelled by a rather pronounced antiwelfarism and maintenance of a climate of depolitization. This climate prevented the establishment of close ties between wage earners and prolabor parties.

The government's concern with keeping control over resources was not matched by counterinflationary objectives. Since the underlying aim was to increase spending to a level sufficient to support economic growth but not to take effective measures against inflation, neither a consistent fiscal discipline nor a deliberate incomes policy ever appeared on the government's agenda. These developments reveal why this period did not witness a serious effort to implement a socially acceptable model of price restraint. In practical terms, most of the price increases were absorbed by a broad category of wage earners and small producers.

The economic stabilization measures of 1980 were aimed at a sharp adjustment of domestic prices and exchange rates, as well as at curtailing of welfare spending and achieving lower real wages, which could be maintained in the absence of conflict in the labor market. Official data show that these measures resulted in an overadjustment to the crisis of the 1979-1980 period, and the inflation rate dropped to 25 percent in 1983. The impact of overadjustment, however, was mixed. The inflationary impact that could be attributed to the wageearners' behavior had already been contained by 1983-1984, but the ANAP governments continued to subscribe to the existing guidelines. In the labor market, real wages remained low, and a reversal to the negotiable rates of the 1970s seemed unlikely. Although restrictions on the conventional trade union activities continued, price movements sparked strikes after 1986. Their precipitation, however, did not lead to a modification of the norms of inflation control. Higher prices for public-sector goods and services, a remnant of the early 1980s, became another feature of the period. However, labor's political participation remained very limited and did not contribute to the persistent inflation. The overadjustment of wages and the shrinking wage share in national income

---

[10]Metin Heper, "Interest Group Politics in Post-1980 Turkey: Lingering Monism," in *Strong State and Economic Interest Groups*, Heper, ed., pp. 163-176; Ümit Cizre Sakallıoğlu, "Labour: The Battered Community," in ibid., pp. 57-69.

continued unabated.[11]

On the other side of overadjustment, with a clear shift of power to business interests, the combined share of national income of profits, rents, and interest increased significantly.[12] This new pattern of income distribution was the consequence of some supply-side measures such as higher tax rebates, exemptions, and various subsidies offered to entrepreneurs, as well as a number of financial instruments of intermediation favoring old and new upper-income groups. These measures in general led to an underadjustment of profits to the price movements.

The monetary side could be handled more easily. Persistent monetary expansion helped to serve the government's immediate aim of supplementing the resources at its disposal. As long as the public's prediction of monetary expansion was lower than the actual "invisible" target, this expansion was comfortably matched with the lack of fiscal restraints and kept interest rates within a margin sufficiently safe for both the government and the interest-seeking groups, as well as for the financial intermediation sector. To a certain extent, overadjustment of wages was the linchpin of financial and monetary balancing, which was achieved while keeping prices high.

All in all, Turkey in the mid-1980s resumed a high growth rate with a rate of inflation higher than that of the early 1970s and a gradually worsening distribution of income. The real growth component of the economic performance probably played a politically stabilizing role vis-à-vis democracy, whose crises sometimes corresponded to the fortunes of the economy. However, high inflation rates and the deteriorated income distribution may lead to political instability in the future. The Turkey of the post-1980 period has displayed not a single prospect but rather a blend of factors contributing to both stability and instability.

External Accounts

Turkey had maintained a deficit position in its external accounts for decades and sometimes met with increasing difficulties in its external payments. This was the result of fast-growing deficits and accumulated in-

[11] In the 1980s, the fall in real wages and the low level of wage rates resulted in a low-cost climate for business. Its potential impact on inflation was positive and was helped greatly by organized labor's failure in negotiating wages, because of the coercive atmosphere of the 1980s. The "stickness of wages," which is a factor in the industrial economies that explains inflationary phenomena, is not an explanatory factor concerning Turkey's high inflation in the mid-1980s and late 1980s. The wage earners of the 1980s have paid a large part of the inflationary increases. Overadjustment of wages refers to this phenomenon.

[12] See inter alia Merih Celasun, "A General Equilibrium Model of the Turkish Economy, SIMLOG-1," *METU Studies in Development* 13 (1986): 50-53; and Korkut Boratav, "Inter-Class and Intra-Class Relations of Distribution Under 'Structural Adjustment': Turkey During the 1980s," Paper presented at the Seminar on Turkish Economy, April 1988, Harvard University, Cambridge, Massachusetts.

debtedness in the second half of the 1970s. For a few years after 1980, an air of optimism prevailed among the policymakers, who planned an outward-oriented economic strategy that was to be based on the buoyancy of exports. In the mid-1980s, however, Turkey once again could not escape from external imbalances, although for different reasons.

Balance of Payments: A Serious Problem?

In the post-1980 period, the opinion that Turkey's troubles stemmed from its balance-of-payment deficits was common among policymakers. This view was carried to its extreme when payments difficulties, or, rather, foreign exchange shortages, were singled out as the primary cause of the military interventions.[13]

Like most other countries after World War II, for decades Turkey had to diversify its production. However, the country's export performance remained insignificant, whereas development imports steadily increased. The resulting trade deficit left the policymakers in a precarious situation in dealing with external balances. They therefore kept an eye on both development financing and deficit financing. Because both are inevitable for a developing country that tries to maximize its growth rate, a combination of development and deficit financing gradually became a part of medium-term policies, thereby setting the economy on a kind of debt-oriented growth strategy. The exception came in the early 1970s, when Turkey achieved a near balance in its current account, a considerable amount of foreign-currency reserves, and a negligible stock of debt with a low debt-service ratio. However, this was short-lived. In the second half of that decade, in the international climate of stagflation, the country quickly returned to debt-oriented growth, which in the past had led to an insolvency crisis.

In the earlier decades, at lower levels of development, the country was subject to relatively small fluctuations in the flow of foreign credits. Predictably, the shortage of foreign exchange caused hardships for productive sectors and consumers alike and produced an air of instability through its impact on domestic demand and the growth rate. Destabilizing factors of this kind are common in both developed and underdeveloped countries. Perhaps a feature of the Turkish case was the way in which a foreign exchange squeeze precipitated a series of crises in the political system. The outcome of the foreign exchange crisis was not a wave of popular protests, as observed elsewhere, or of particular warning signals to the politicians; the consequences of the crisis were rather a sense of mistrust, skepticism, and uncertainty, which gradually led to military intervention.

However, the international economic climate of the 1950s and 1960s

---

[13] This view was prevalent among a part of the business community in the late 1970s. It was repeated from time to time in the early 1980s by the military regimes' economists, mostly by their chief, Özal. Later, in the mid-1980s, this view gradually became one of the basic ideas on which the ANAP's conception of democracy was founded.

helped the country to achieve a relatively quick recovery from the adverse effects of foreign exchange shortages. In the wake of the political crises that occurred at the end of each of those two decades, the economy resumed its historical growth rate without long delays, and inflation was cured because of external assistance. In either cases, the external indebtedness caused considerable deterioration on the income distribution profile. Therefore, the destabilizing effects of these foreign exchange crises were rather short-lived and did not block the country's return to democracy.

Beginning in 1980, and more so in the mid-1980s, economic restructuring was again met with foreign exchange shortages. The economic performance of the mid-1980s did not significantly improve the structure of balance of payments, although in 1988 the deficit was smaller and some reserves were built. If the restructuring of sectorial priorities, relative prices, terms of trade, market institutions, and consumption habits were to produce further demands for foreign exchange, at least two conditions were vital for stability. First, a reasonably small deficit would have helped the policymakers to achieve necessary growth targets, which seemed to be the idea adopted by some–if not all–of the technocrats in the government. The alternative was to quickly achieve a surplus position, which would have enabled the government to make its repayments and to have a high profile for further borrowing, which could have refueled and sustained a high growth performance. The latter alternative, which might have been inspired by some Latin American experiences in recent years, seemed tempting to some key government figures, despite the fact that the impact on stability of net transfer of resources abroad was underestimated.

The second condition that could have contributed to stability proved far more difficult to attain elsewhere. This was the rule of "borrow less, repay less," which repuired a strong engine of growth to accommodate both domestic and external demands. The ANAP government of the period, faced with a strong domestic and a weak external demand, adopted the opposite rule of "borrow more, repay more."

Indebtedness in the Mid-1980s

The ANAP governments adopted a new policy concerning the adjustment of currency. From 1980 until 1988, the Turkish lira underwent a real depreciation of approximately 40 percent vis-à-vis the U.S. dollar. On this issue, policymakers have underlined two points: The necessity of maintaining a competitive edge for the country's exports and the inescapable adjustments that needed to be made on the currency rate due to a constantly high level of inflation. This policy of continuously depreciating currency suffered from a lack of reality, because in the mid-1980s, it was open to question whether the policy of real depreciation alone produced a significant improvement in the country's export performance and productivity or became a cure for rising prices. Export buoyancy, for example, has been largely achieved thanks to subsidies, mostly in various forms of tax rebates. Attempted corrections of internal prices by higher currency rates, however, were always followed by new rounds of domestic price hikes, which in turn were triggered primarily by higher public-sector prices. Thus, the corrections in question introduced a kind of circularity into the price dynamics.

Another feature of the period was high interest rates to match a steadily depreciating currency. But, its dampening effects aside, a constantly depreciated currency created pressures on prices, which in turn led to the adjustment of interest rates in line with the inflation rate. In addition, the government's policy of high levels of public spending relied increasingly on domestic borrowing, not on tax revenues, a policy that again was in harmony with the policy of maintaining high interest rates.[14]

The exchange and interest rates duly reinforced each other, and their interplay had repercussions on the overadjustment and underadjustment of different income groups to high level of prices. As long as the adjustment process was coupled with high prices, its impact on wage earners might have played a role in keeping them less inclined to participate, if not totally discouraged from participating in politics. In a similar vein, the increased percentage of interest repayments of government accounts might have justified the constant shrinkage of social wage items as part of prudent fiscal management.

External indebtedness rose steadily in the mid-1980s. At the end of 1987, total foreign debts were more than half of the gross national product (GNP), up from a quarter in 1980–a ratio comparable to those of the world's most highly indebted borrowers. However, two aspects of the Turkish case need to be underlined: Debt-servicing requirements reached a "hump," as the debt-service ratio increased to over 30 percent, which was much higher than that of the former growth phase in the early 1970; also, the growth performance of the early and mid-1980s was achieved with a substantial transfer of resources from abroad.[15]

As mentioned above, during this period, external credits played an unprecedented role in fueling higher rates of growth. Consistent prudence in debt repayments enabled the government to secure financial support for the priority sectors and to receive continual assistance for balance of payments. Developments in the post-1983 period showed that the government began to pursue a "growth-oriented debt strategy".[16] Compared with earlier decades, this was an important change concerning the role and

---

[14]The high rates, were predictably a function of the persistent depreciation and monetary expansion within an environment of relative shortages of domestic capital funds. A tight monetary policy, to explain the high rates was not the case in Turkey in the mid-1980s.

[15]Between 1984 and 1987, the rate of increase in total foreign debt was three times higher than that of economic growth, excluding military indebtedness. See Ömer Altay, "Türkiye'de Dış Borçların Analizi," 28 March 1988, typescript.

[16]The term *growth-oriented debt strategy* was adopted and suggested by a recent World Bank report on Turkey's prospective blueprint for external debt, fiscal policy, and growth. The report had not been cleared for publication when this Chapter was completed.

size of external funds in the Turkish economy.

The greater role played by external funds was a mixed blessing. Their uninterrupted inflow evidently contributed to the revival of domestic demand via public spending. This could not have been achieved with the low levels of domestic saving observed in the early 1980s. The comfortable room for maneuver thus obtained by the ANAP government made it clear that not only Turkey's resumption of economic growth but also the maintenance of its political stability was considered to be important by Turkey's creditors. The stability of political life was thus connected to economic growth, in which external finance played a more determining role than had been the case in earlier decades.

However, a drawback of the role of external funds was seen in debt repayments. Turkey's debt-service ratio rose in the mid-1980s. High foreign debts, with their maturity and interest structures comparable to those of the most indebted nations, obliged Turkey to transfer its own resources in considerable amounts to service external debts. This was a new and somewhat disturbing phenomenon in the country's economic and political life; an increasing percentage of net transfers could not only hamper economic growth but could also cause deterioration in income distribution by shrinking the wage earners' share.

In sum, a novelty of the mid-1980s was the economic growth effect of external funds and the net benefits of its spillover to the conservative government. However, another tendency, which has gradually built up and which could offset the economic and political gains, has been the increasing pressure on the country's capability to service its debts through production.

Conclusion

Turkey made a transition from a "low inflation, high growth" model in the early and mid-1970s to the "growth with high inflation" model of the mid-1980s, with conservative governments in power in both cases. In the latter period, although the economy attained a high growth rate, current account deficits, increased indebtedness, and a higher ratio of debt servicing accompanied the growth performance. Thus, there was a relative increase in the economic costs paid by society compared with the situation in the 1970s.

During the 1980s, the new conservatives neglected the political economy of distribution to an unprecedented degree. They supported a new and rising business class and maintained a policy of depoliticization for the rest of society. This approach was reflected in their policy of the overadjustment of wages and underadjustment of profits.

For the new conservatives, a political system based on consensus remained alien. This could have been their political model if their primary objective had been growth without inflation. Their concept of democracy bordered on exclusionary. The Turkish case resembled others in which efforts have been made to significantly restructure the economy in the direction of market forces, yet it differed from others in that Turkey has not drifted into a single-party authoritarian regime; among other things, the ANAP was removed from office in October 1991 through democratic means.

12

Education and Political Development

Joseph S. Szyliowicz

The educational system has played an important role in the dramatic changes that have transformed Turkey in recent years, both as an object and agent of change. In this chapter I examine the degree to which the educational system contributed to the military intervention in 1980 and the changes that have taken place since then in order to assess the extent to which those changes permit democracy to flourish.

Education and Political Change

In Turkey, following the installation of competitive politics in 1945, the social demand for education accelerated rapidly, and by 1980, modern educational opportunities had expanded enormously at all levels: Primary enrollments rose from 1.6 million to 5.7 million in that period, secondary low enrollments (grades 6 to 8) from 68,000 to over 1 million, secondary high enrollments (grades 9 to 11) from 22,000 to 535,000, and higher education enrollments from 25,000 to 330,000.[1] Unfortunately these gains were not accompanied by the kinds of investments that were required to maintain quality. The student-teacher ratio at all levels declined, as did the quality of teachers. Libraries and laboratories were inadequate. Textbooks and curricula needed upgrading.

The drop in quality was paralleled by the perpetuation of existing inequalities. Children who live in the underdeveloped regions of the country have less opportunity to enter and continue in the system than do those in the metropolitan centers. Some villages (primarily small hamlets) in the underdeveloped eastern and southeastern regions still lack a school, and throughout the countryside many schools have only one teacher and

---

[1] Unless otherwise indicated, the account here draws upon Joseph S. Szyliowicz, "Continuity and Change in Turkey's Educational Policies," *Journal of Turkish Studies* 8 (1984): 245.

operate several shifts a day–sometimes as many as four.[2] Overall, only 18 percent of the rural schools, compared with 61 percent of the urban schools, operate on a normal schedule. The situation at the secondary level is similar: In the 1980s, about 1,000 middle schools (25 percent of the total) were operating on either double or triple shifts, and only 157 of the 871 public *lycées* (grades 9 to 11) were operating on a full schedule. As a result, many students spend only two to three hours a day in school, usually in very crowded classrooms.

Given these conditions, we can expect that dropout rates will be high. At the primary level, for example, only 27 of every 100 entering students graduate five years later. About half of these enroll in a middle school, but only 60 to 65 percent of this group graduate in three years. Most of these (75-80 percent) go on to a *lycée*; at this level, about 33 percent fail to complete their courses. And only a small percentage of the *lycée* graduates enter a university. Only two out of every 100 students who entered a primary school enrolled in a university eleven years later.[3]

These two students are likely to be from urban centers, because the variations in the quality of education that is available in various parts of Turkey greatly affect who gains admission to the universities. The success rate on the national examination system, which screens out about 75 percent of all applicants, varies greatly by region, ranging from a high of 30 percent for the advanced Marmara region to a low of 7 percent in the underdeveloped eastern areas. Male-female disparities are also evident, although the number of women enrolled at all levels has increased greatly in recent decades. Still, only 21 percent of the male and 25 percent of the female cohorts are enrolled in middle schools and *lycées* respectively, and, most of the female students come from the more developed provinces.

In short, by the late 1970s, Turkey had created an extensive system of schooling, albeit one with serious deficiencies. Nevertheless, it had succeeded in significantly increasing literacy and enrollments at all levels–developments that in conjunction with other forces, such as urbanization and the mass media, contributed to narrowing the traditional center-periphery gap and developing a political culture, shared by elites and the masses alike, that at least on an abstract plane supported democracy.[4]

---

[2]The percentage of the population age six and over that did not complete primary school is 18.5 for the entire country, 14.0 for the Marmara region, 19.0 for the Aegean region, 35.0 for eastern Anatolia, and 44.0 for southeastern Anatolia.

[3]These inequalities are discussed by Selçuk Özgediz, "Education and Income in Turkey," in *The Political Economy of Income Distribution in Turkey*, Ergun Özbudun and Aydın Ulusan, eds. (New York: Holmes and Meier, 1980), pp. 505-508. He calculated that out of 1,000 preschoolers, 104 will graduate from a high school in the normal amount of time, another 267 will eventually complete high school, and 142 will enroll in an institution of higher learning.

[4]İlter Turan, "The Evolution of Political Culture in Turkey," in *Modern Turkey: Continuity and Change*, Ahmet Evin, ed. (Opladen: Leske Verlag, 1984), pp. 84-112; E. N. Muller, M. A. Seligson, and İ. Turan, "Education, Participation and Support for Democratic Norms," *Comparative Politics* 20 (1987): 19-33.

The specific role of the schools, however, cannot be identified with any degree of precision. Little empirical evidence is available about political socialization in Turkey, and that which is available does not permit clear conclusions to be drawn. A 1974 survey suggests that in Turkey, education and democratic values are positively related, but the relationship is not strong, because even those with little or no formal education strongly support democratic norms.[5] The fact that at best a weak relationship exists is also indicated by the results of a study of Turkish interest groups, which found little or no relationship between education and either family or personal authoritarianism.[6] Furthermore, experts do not agree on the degree to which the Turkish political culture incorporates the necessary norms to make democracy function effectively. Some scholars have concluded that it contains powerful antidemocratic values, including a limited tolerance for opposition, tendency toward violence, and a reluctance to compromise.[7]

It is plausible to assume, given the deficiencies cited above, that the culture in most schools remained highly traditional, and that they functioned in an authoritarian manner that emphazised passive learning, over conformity to rules and regulations, and the mastering of assignments through rote memorization rather than active participation in the learning process. Hence, students would be socialized into values that reinforced powerful traditional values, such as obedience and conformity rather than into those that are required for the successful functioning of a pluralist democratic system. [8]

The schools also indirectly influenced political developments by the way in which they fulfilled, or, rather not fulfill, their economic functions. They failed to provide the ecomomy with needed manpower, and shortages of skills of various kinds limited productivity and quality in many sectors. Efforts to remedy this situation by directing students into vocational and technical schools met with limited success. Altogether, the number of students enrolled in technical schools in 1978 stood at 2.4 per 1,000 population, an extremely low figure when viewed comparatively. A 1964 study, for example, indicated that this figure was 33.7 in Germany, 16.3 in France, 9.1 in Hungary, and 4.7 in Egypt. Only Syria, Greece, Thailand, Jordan, and Iraq–with enrollments between 1.2 and 1.9 per 1,000–ranked lower than Turkey.[9] Moreover, the quality and relevance of the training the technical and vocational schools provided left much to be desired. Accordingly, the economic crisis that gripped the country in the late 1970s, although due primarily to an ongoing commitment to a strategy that had outlived

---

[5] Cited in Muller et al., ibid., pp. 26ff.

[6] Robert Bianchi, *Interest Groups and Political Development in Turkey* (Princeton: Princeton University Press, 1984), pp. 293-294.

[7] Compare the work of Turan cited in note 4, for example, with the analysis presented by Ergun Özbudun in "Turkey", in *Comparative Elections in Developing Countries*, Myron Weiner and Ergun Özbudun, eds. (Durham, N.C.: Duke University Press, 1987), pp. 353-354.

[8] On this tradition, see ibid., p. 354.

[9] Cited in Yahya K. Kaya, *İnsan Yetiştirme Düzenimiz* (Ankara: Erk Basımevi, 1981), p. 175.

its usefulness (industrialization based on import substitution), was aggravated by the failure of the educational policy to keep up with changes in economic policy.

Economic factors appear to have special significance in the Turkish case because of the central role the state plays in the Turkish economy and the benefits that accrue to those who control the state. Moreover, political parties tended to be loose coalitions of persons whose power depended on satisfying their clients. Under these circumstances, it should not be surprising that during times of economic difficulty, tolerance of opposition diminished, as government leaders–seeking to maintain the allegiance of their followers at a time in which their popularity was dropping– often pursued policies that would enable them to retain power at any cost, thus provoking further internal dissension.[10]

The university played the most obvious role in influencing the country's political processes. As did schools at the lower levels, they grew greatly in numbers and size. But investments in human and physical resources did not keep pace. Between 1927 and 1981, the number of students receiving a higher education increased by 8,500 percent (the largest percentage increase of any level), but the number of faculty rose by only 4,500 percent.[11]

The quantitative growth and the resulting qualitative problems greatly precipitated violent student activism, which had been an important feature of university life in the late 1960s and, following the 1971-1973 military intervention, became widespread once again.[12] Students as well as faculty became polarized along ideological lines, and student militants fought for physical control of campuses. Nevertheless, it would be wrong to equate the political role of the universities in the 1970s with that of the 1960s, because the terrorist groups of the 1970s were no longer composed primarily of students, and the violence–which was now of higher intensity– was not confined to the campuses but took place throughout the country.[13]

The politicization of the faculty made normal academic life virtually impossible, because appointments, promotions, and the selection of deans, chairpersons, and rectors all were influenced by ideological factors. The legal position of the universities further limited the possibility of maintaining an intellectual atmosphere. In Turkey, the universities had been granted almost total academic and administrative (although not financial) independence by the 1961 Constitution and, although a 1973 law restricted their rights somewhat, the functioning of the highly decentralized system depended largely on cooperation among deans and rectors and faculties. The high level of politicization made this cooperation virtually impossible

---

[10]Turan, "The Evolution of Political Culture in Turkey," pp. 109ff.

[11]Kaya, İnsan Yetiştirme Düzenimiz, p. 174.

[12]Joseph S. Szyliowicz, A Political Analysis of Student Activism: The Turkish Case (Beverly Hills, Calif.: Sage, 1972).

[13]Sabri Sayarı, "Patterns of Political Terrorism in Turkey," Terrorism, Violence, and Insurgency 6 (1985): 40-1; Sabri Sayarı, "Generational Changes in Terrorist Movements: The Turkish Case." Santa Monica, Calif.: The Rand Corporation, July 1985.

to achieve.

Educational Change in the 1980s

Upon seizing power in September 1980, the military leaders moved decisively to depoliticize the universities. Believing that the faculties had contributed significantly to the polarization and violence of the 1970s by socializing students into extreme right-wing and left-wing ideologies rather than with the ideals of the Atatürk revolution, they enacted a sweeping new Universities Act, which separated "academic" from "administrative" autonomy and established a three-level hierarchy capped by the High Board of Education (YÖK) with extensive powers over the universities. Its membership consisted of eight persons chosen by the president, eight persons elected by the Council of Ministers, and eight professors selected by the Inter-University Board–a second-level body that was composed of rectors and professors and that was expected to deal with academic matters. Each university handled its own affairs, but faculty could no longer elect deans and rectors. Clearly, the universities had lost their autonomy; control now resided in the YÖK, which was dominated by members appointed by the state and headed by the former rector of Hacettepe University, Professor İhsan Doğramacı. The YÖK promptly embarked upon a series of reforms, most of which have been extremely controversial. It greatly expanded the system of higher education and passed numerous decrees concerning curricula (including the expansion of teaching on the Atatürk ideology) as well as student and faculty behavior.

Convinced of the need to purge the system, the military dismissed or fired many faculty members and encouraged others to retire. In some cases, the military acted directly; in others, the new rectors and deans who had been appointed took the initiative. The purge, which began in the summer of 1982, took place in waves and evinced different forms: outright dismissal (the most severe, since the individual lost numerous rights), termination of contract by the university, and resignations by individuals for various reasons, including a reluctance to be assigned to vacancies in the provincial universities. It is difficult to assess precisely how many people were involved, because people quit the universities for different reasons–some of which, such as low salaries and the numerous other constraints, had little to do with YÖK–and also because the available data are not fully compatible. Official statements indicate that a few hundred were involved; some critics put the number at over 4,000. Both of these figures are suspect; more realistic is the finding of one careful study, which listed 1,188 persons. Subsequently, this list was expanded to 1,323 plus another 75 firings by the martial law authorities, giving a total of about 1,400 persons.[14] The validity

---

[14] "Ek Liste: 400 Öğretim Üyesi Daha," *Bilim ve Sanat* (Istanbul monthly), April 1984, pp. 4-5.

of this figure is strengthened by data from the State Institute of Statistics, which listed a decrease of 1,890 faculty members (8.5 percent) between 1981 and 1984.[15] This suggests that about 500 persons abandoned an academic career for reasons of their own.

Whatever the exact figure, it is obvious that a significant number of persons left academia, with important consequences for the remaining faculty and for institutions–some of which were affected more than others. The primary targets were those that were considered centers of radical activity, such as Ankara University's Faculty Political Sciences and the Middle East Technical University.

The military also decided to expand the educational system but it did so without serious planning. In fact, the decisions ran counter to the recommendations of at least one State Planning Organization (SPO) study. No attention was paid to manpower requirements; the increases reflected possibilities and interests rather than a rational response to national needs. Whatever the policy process, in addition to three private universities, Turkey now contains fifty public universities, ten of which were created by turning various academies and institutes into new universities. These institutions faced severe problems with facilities and faculty and have struggled for many years. In addition, the overall number of students enrolled in higher educational institutions nearly tripled between the 1980-1981 academic year, when the number stood at 237,000, and the 1989-1990 academic year when 644,000 students were attending a facility of some sort. In addition, an "Open University" based on television courses enrolls another 150,000 students. Excluding Open University enrollments, 6.2 percent of the eligible cohort (19-22 years) was enrolled in a higher education institution in 1980-1981, 10.8 percent in 1985-1986, and 11.2 percent in 1987-1988.

The YÖK and its supporters consider that their policies have led to significant achievements. In addition to the increase in enrollments and the establishment of an open university, they point to higher standards in the provincial universities, the treatment of higher education as a system, the establishment of postgraduate institutions in every university, an increase in the number of scholarly publications, and improvement in student performance because of constant monitoring.[16]

These claims, however, must be placed in context, because the new system is beset by a variety of problems. The first of these will probably be resolved in time, but for now significant administrative shortcomings are commonplace since the universities had to suddenly accommodate large numbers of new units–each with its own standards, culture, and structure. Thus, although one of the goals was to achieve centralization and unifor-

---

[15] *Statistical Yearbook of Turkey* (Ankara: State Statistical Institute, 1987), p. 118.

[16] For a useful elaboration of these points, see Galip Karagözoğlu, "1981 Higher Education Act of Turkey After Five Years of Practice," November 1986, typescript. See also *Yüksek Öğretimdeki Gelişmeler* (Ankara: YÖK, 1988).

mity, the system remains marked by many disparities.[17] Second, it remains regionally unbalanced. Although educational opportunities have been distributed more widely, the geographical distribution is still poor. There are eight universities in Istanbul and five in Ankara, whereas the Aydın plain has only one university which is yet to admit students. Third, the distribution of students by fields is more skewed than it ever was. In 1974-1975, 53 percent of all university students were studying social sciences and the humanities; by 1982-1983, this figure had climbed to 66 percent.[18] Thus, the system is graduating large numbers of poorly prepared students in areas that do not relate closely to national needs. The demand for some specializations–such as medicine, mechanical engineering and agricultural engineering–is not being met, whereas simultaneously the already serious problem of unemployement is being aggravated.[19]

Most important, there is little evidence to demonstrate that academic quality, the most important element of any educational system, has improved. It has not been easy to fill the vacancies, let alone to find qualified persons to accommodate the expansion. Efforts were made to recruit foreign academics, former diplomats, civil servants, and others with varying qualifications, but larger classes and fewer electives are now commonplace. The student-faculty ratio which stood at 11.3:1 in 1980, climbed to 19.6:1 by 1985.[20] YÖK officials argue that the provincial universities have faculties that are more adequate than before, but their data also indicate that the student-faculty ratio has dropped again in both urban and provincial institutions in recent years: In 1981, it stood at 34:1 for the universities located in Istanbul, Ankara, and Izmir and 30:1 in the provincal universities, in 1983, the figures were 18.6:1 and 15.8:1, respectively, and in 1985, the ratios were 28:1 and 22:1.[21]

YÖK has tried to improve the situation of students by reorganizing such services as health, food, housing, and extracurricular activities, and it has also attempted to raise standards in various ways, such as by tightening examination requirements, the number of times students can take examinations, and the like. However, most faculty members believe that the quality of education has deteriorated everywhere, although some institutions have suffered less than others. The problem of quality is a serious one. Professor Doğramacı noted that some medical students do not even know "where the liver is." And, he once asked, "Who makes our cities

[17]Saim Kaptan, *Türkiye'de Yüksek Öğretim ve İnsangücü Hedefleri* (Ankara: Devlet Planlama Teşkilatı, 1982), pp. 2ff.

[18]Ibid., Table 13, p. 31.

[19]At the end of 1980, 37,000 university and high school graduates were seeking employment; in 1982, 2,300 architects registered for 364 positions, 573 chemists for 36 jobs, 910 administrators for 60 positions, and 84,000 persons applied for 7,000 openings in the Ministry of Education (ibid., p. 26).

[20]*Statistical Yearbook of Turkey*, 1987, p. 117.

[21]The figures are from İhsan Doğramacı, "The Turkish Universities," *Higher Education in Europe* 9 (1984): 81-82; and Karagözoğlu, "1981 Higher Education Act of Turkey," pp. 28-29.

ugly with terrible projects? Our engineers and architects."[22]

The fundamental problem is that the policies of the past few years have not created an environment most faculty view as conducive to quality teaching and research. The YÖK was widely regarded as a bureaucratic center that has long functioned as a controlling body. Faculty members pointed to the fact that all universities were treated alike, even though there were major differences in the resources, capabilities, and needs of different regions. Centralization had obvious political implications as well, for it raised important questions about the kind of university system that is most compatible with a modern, democratic society and whether one that is administered from the center in this manner can best meet the needs of an increasingly diverse and pluralistic society.[23]

Moreover, the system has maintained existing inequalities: The children of elite parents go to select high schools where the language of instruction is English, German, or French; are tutored to do well on the university entrance examinations; and enroll in the best universities or, increasingly, choose to go abroad. Many are also troubled by the decision to allow the opening of three private universities, Bilkent in Ankara, and Koç and Galatasaray in Istanbul. Bilkent, Koç, and Galatasaray possess better physical resources and a fine faculty attracted by salaries considerably higher than those at the public institutions. Further plans are being made to open additional private universities in Istanbul.

These initiatives have been interpreted by some academics to mean that the government wants to see the universities linked more closely to the private sector through creating new institutions on the U.S. model and by forcing the state schools to turn to the private sector for support. They fear that higher education is being divided into two systems (a few select institutions meeting the needs of the modern sector and the elites, with the remainder geared to the masses and the traditional economic sectors), and that the universities will acquire a particular ideological orientation and become functionally subservient to the needs of industry.

The YÖK's efforts to reform the internal functioning of the universities have also aroused controversy. Change was not necessarily bad; many aspects of academic life needed reform, and some of the YÖK's policies might have improved matters, but far too often these were implemented in a way that alienated faculty. For example, the YÖK's attempts to standardize curricula were carried out in an arbitrary manner that did not allow for meaningful faculty participation. Its design for a centralized foreign journals documentation center and its attempt to regulate dress and work habits were also not favorably received. Nor has the implementation of a new personnel act, which reorganized the traditional chair hierarchy into a new pyramid based on departments, received unanimous approval.

---

[22] *Hürriyet* (Istanbul daily), 28 January 1983.

[23] By the early 1990s, however, the YÖK became more of a coordinating and less of a controlling body.

New regulations, the loss of many of the best people, a perceived loss of control in many areas, and severely limited support services have all affected faculty morale negatively. In addition, the chronically low salaries have lagged far behind inflation. As a result, many faculty members are no longer committed and do the minimum that is required. Furthermore, even the dedicated instructors confront major obstacles in attemping to get the students to become active participants in the learning process and thus to prepare them for citizenship in a democratic society. And since the appeal of a career has diminished and there are fewer entrants, important questions about the size and quality of academia in the future are being raised.

We also cannot overlook the possible return of student activism. Many students are unhappy about various aspects of university life, including its quality. A good student specializing in physics, for example, complained in a letter to a newspaper about the problems he encountered in trying to become a solid professional.[24] At present, the students are quiescent even though many of the factors that lead to activism are present. Two explanations can be advanced to explain this phenomenon. First, many may have low expectations; they may be satisfied with the quality of the education they are receiving and with the opportunities that await them, because mobility is relative and many of the students are "second-generation mobiles." They are doing better than their parents and may eventually find employment in the informal sector or work in a family enterprise. Similar considerations may apply to the thousands of students enrolled in the Open University. Second, we should not overlook the nature of the political environment; key political elites are unlikely to tolerate any renewed student politicization. Since this is widely recognized, students may be unwilling to run any risks by engaging in activities that might threaten their future. Still, we cannot rule out the possibility that the present pattern of depoliticization will change in the future, especially if the unemployment situation deteriorates and the legitimacy of the political system is eroded.

The fate of employment opportunities for university and other graduates will be determined by the rate of economic growth, and in this regard as well, the new university system is not functioning in a way that meets the country's needs for manpower. The universities are failing the country in the area of research. They are producing only a limited amount of research and have weak linkages to the productive sectors. Furthermore, higher education is not integrated with the primary and secondary levels, so flows of graduates are not directed toward those areas of greatest need for industrial growth.

Although no coherent system that encompasses all levels and types of education has been created and little long-range manpower planning has

---

[24]*Cumhuriyet* (Istanbul daily), 3 August 1983.

taken place, the lower levels of the system have seen significant change because the government took various steps to raise the quality of the poorly trained labor force. It sponsored an important literacy campaign, targeted at women, shantytown inhabitants, and rural labor. Beginning in 1981, 826,559 persons enrolled in 33,336 courses.[25] A new curriculum that incorporates modern pedagogical practices was also introduced. In terms of content, one important change has taken place–an emphasis is now placed on language and history in a manner that is consonant with Atatürk's principles.

These developments, however, have not been accompanied by the kinds of investments that are required to transform the system. In fact, investments in education as a percentage of total investments fell to a low of 4.3 percent in 1982, half the percentage that prevailed in the early 1970s.[26] And the decline has continued. Between 1980 and 1987, education's share of the budget fell from 12.5 percent to 8.5 percent; educational expenditures as a percentage of the GNP dropped from 3.5 percent to 1.9 percent. This decline represents a 40 percent drop in spending per pupil during this period.[27] Without a change in this pattern, it is difficult to see how education's serious shortcomings can be remedied or how the system can contribute in a positive way to the achievement of development goals.

One of these shortcomings involves the teachers, whose numbers and quality are lower than is desirable due to the poor conditions under which many of them work. In late 1982, for example, it was estimated that three hundred thousand teachers lived in inadequate housing.[28] Not surprisingly, the profession was chosen by few students who took the university entrance examinations. Essentially, only students with poor qualifications and humble family backgrounds become teachers.[29] It is obvious that no significant change in the quality of the educational system can occur until the status of teachers is upgraded, and teaching becomes, as it once was, a respected and honored profession.

The one area that has received significant new resources is vocational and technical training, historically a bottleneck to economic growth. There are simply too few well-trained engineers, technicians, foremen, and supervisors to permit Turkey to compete effectively in the international economy. A recent World Bank study, for example, found that the staff of the Electric Authority, rather than consisting of at most 50-65 percent unskilled or semiskilled workers, had 80 percent of its members in that category.[30]

---

[25]The General Secretariat of the National Security Council, *12 September in Turkey: Before and After* (Ankara: Ongun Kardeşler, 1982), pp. 286-287.

[26]*Eğitim Sektör Raporu* (Ankara: State Planning Organization, 1985), Table 146, p. 406.

[27]"A Survey of Turkey," *The Economist*, 18 June 1988, p. 23.

[28]*Tercüman* (Istanbul daily), 8 November 1982.

[29]Galip Karagözoğlu and K. B. Murray, "Profile of New Teachers in the Turkish Educational System," n.d., typescript.

[30]"Staff Appraisal Report, Republic of Turkey, Non-Formal Vocational Training Project," World Bank Report no. 6360-TU, 12 November 1986, p. 3.

Similar problems have handicapped many other sectors that must play a leading role if the new export-oriented strategy is to succeed. In 1980, Turkey had 7 engineers, 9 technicians and 0.5 foreman per 1,000 workers in the manufacturing sector, compared with 5, 2, and 4 for Greece (1971), 14, 37, and 19 for Israel (1970), 22, 35, and 10 for West Germany (1970) and 33, 24, and 47 for the United States (1970).[31]

To deal with these problems, the government sought and obtained the support of the World Bank for four important projects. The first established a nonformal vocational training program to provide those who leave school and others with skills that will enable them to find employment.[32] The World Bank has also supported the Ministry of Education's efforts to upgrade the secondary-level industrial schools. Although their number expanded from 176 in 1978-1979 to 301 in 1982-1983 (by 71 percent), in that same period the number of students only increased from 100,457 to 126,710 (26 percent) and the number of graduates from 28,545 to 39,250 (38 percent).[33]

Turkey lacked an integrated national industrial training system, and there were no arrangements for preservice training programs for industrial technicians. Accordingly, the YÖK established about sixty higher vocational schools, two-year postgraduate institutions attached to universities. Many are located on campuses so that they can share facilities and benefit from the university's resources. Unfortunately, these expectations have not been realized; the links to the universities create certain problems, notably regarding to the instruction that is provided by faculty. The training tends to be abstract and engineering-oriented rather than geared to the specific needs of technicians.[34] In addition, the schools are characterized by various weaknesses, including limited physical facilities, inadequate and obsolete curricula, poorly trained teaching staffs, and weak linkages to the industries they are expected to serve.[35]

A final area that is relevant to a consideration of the relationship between the educational system and future political developments is religious education. The number of students in religious schools grew astronomically since the 1950s, rising from 876 in 1951 to 5,507 in 1961, 46,400 in 1971, 201,000 in 1980, and 238,000 in 1985.[36] The implications of this trend for

---

[31] A. Vural Türker, "The Development of Two-Year Postsecondary Technical Training Programs," Paper presented at the American Vocational Association Convention, New Orleans, 30 November-4 December 1984, Table 1, p. 3.

[32] "Report and Recommendation of the President of the IBRD to the Executive Directors on a Proposed Loan to the Republic of Turkey in an Amount Equivalent to US$58.5 Million for a Non-Formal Vocational Training Project," World Bank Report no. P-4385-TU 18, November 1986, p. 12.

[33] *Technical and Vocational Education, Turkey* (Bangkok: n.p., 1984), p. 29.

[34] "Staff Appraisal Report, Republic of Turkey, Second Industrial Training Project," World Bank Report no. 7038-TU, 7 March 1988, p. 3.

[35] Türker, "The Development of Two-Year Postsecondary Technical Training Programs," pp. 21ff.

[36] *Statistical Yearbook of Turkey, 1987*, p. 123.

the country's future continue to be debated, but this issue appears to have been somewhat depoliticized. There seems to be recognition that from the viewpoint of the state, as well as of the parents and students, such schooling is justified. Many Turks strongly favor religious instruction and have contributed to the construction of religious schools. Since the students are mainly from lower-class backgrounds, these schools provide an important channel of mobility and their graduates can find employment in a variety of areas. From a societal perspective, religious education, the expansion of religious instruction in the public schools, and the introduction of Arabic need not be regarded as a retrogression from Atatürk's principles. The military moved sternly against religious extremists but recognized that Islam, when viewed as a progressive faith and a moral teaching, could play a critical role in combating ideological extremists of the left and right and in promoting social unity.[37] Whether religious instruction will play such a role remains to be seen; many intellectuals have serious reservations.

Conclusion

The promotion of exports is a fundamental element in the new strategy upon which Turkey's economic future depends. Economic growth is positively related to the movement toward a more open, pluralist political system that is marked by greater cohesion and elite responsibility than existed before. There is, of course, a reverse relationship. Before the 1980 intervention, the educational system had a retarding influence upon the economy because of the general level of education the populace had acquired, the limited provision of specific skills, and the amount and quality of scientific research that was being carried out. It also contributed to the political paralysis of the 1970s.

The governments that have ruled Turkey since 1980 have attempted to change this situation. But although many changes have been made and some important advances have been registered, much remains to be done before the educational system functions in such a way that it promotes economic growth and is fully supportive of democratic processes.

Perhaps the most fundamental need is a recognition of the importance of education and the willingness to commit the necessary resources. For many decades education has received inadequate budgetary allocations. Only with adequate financing can the necessary reforms be implemented. These involve two general areas, the first of which is higher education. The policies that have been implemented in the past decade have not created a system that can educate people appropriately or that can generate and diffuse knowledge in the amount and quality that are required. Similar considerations apply, albeit for different reasons, to general secondary and primary education. Its deficiencies (high rates of waste, low quality, and

---

[37] David Kushner, " Turkish Secularists and Islam," *Jerusalem Quarterly*, no. 38 (1986): 96.

significant inequalities) combine to provide most Turks with a rudimentary education that does not prepare them to function effectively in a modern, democratic society.

Thus, Turkey faces a difficult challenge in the years ahead. It must improve the quality of its educational system while it simultaneously seeks to meet other needs, which also require significant investments. In a sense, the developments since 1980 have provided a time zone in which a democratic process free of past weaknesses can be built. This process, which seems to be underway, can flourish only if economic conditions continue to improve. But Turkish industry must now compete in terms of quality and price in the international marketplace, and it can do so only if the educational system provides it with the manpower and research inputs a country at Turkey's level of development requires–particularly one that aspires to become a member of the EC. If Turkey is to achieve this goal, it must bring its educational system up to European standards, and it must do so within the next few years. Yet these standards are improving so Turkey must move faster and further if it is to create the kind of educational system that will permit it to meet the challenges of the 1990s and beyond.

13

Islam in Mass Society: Harmony Versus Polarization

Şerif Mardin

Anyone who takes up the study of modern Islam in Turkey faces a methodological problem: how to gauge the role of ancient institutions that are operating under modern conditions. Islam has undergone many changes throughout its history, but it has never faced changes as stark as those that have confronted it in the nineteenth and twentieth centuries. This is more true of Turkish Islam than it is in other countries of the Middle East.

In part, the role of Islam as an ancient institution with deep roots in Turkish society has been a function of rememoration–that is, the reenacting of what the believers rightly or wrongly considered to be the unchanging core of Islam. At present, this version of Islam is drawn from scholarly translations of basic Islamic sources into Turkish and from popularized "catechisms" with wide circulations but also from submerged popular make believe (that is, *l'imaginaire sociale*), where Islam's mythical expression is paramount.

There have been signs, moreover, that the popular make believe has become increasingly active throughout the world in modern times as an element of rememoration. One example suffices: *The Washington Post* of 6 January 1990 reported a mass murder performed by followers of a religious cult whose members believed they had to perform a sacrifice before traveling to the West, where they could be cleansed and could reach for a "golden sword."

The very fact that the study of Turkish Islam demands an estimation at three different levels–the scholarly, the popularized, and the mythical–shows how difficult it is to form a picture of Turkish Islam simply in terms of the received sources of Islam. But a student of modern Turkish Islam encounters even more difficulties. Part of the role religion assumes in modern Turkey is a function of the reaction to new social conditions: economies of scale, the mobilization of the periphery, mass society, politicization, mass media, the disenchantment of the modern world. A complete picture of Islam would therefore take into account interaction of what I have termed *received sources* with new social conditions.

Elites, Masses, and Islam

It is obvious in this perspective that a capsule study of Islam in Turkey is doomed to be somewhat superficial. What we can bring out in such a study are cues to trends and directions, one of the most important of which is related to the changing social structure of Turkey in the past fifty years. Most important in this respect is the transformation of a rural society led by a bureaucratic elite to a largely urban society led by politicians with roots in the periphery. In the Turkey of the 1930s and 1940s, policy was made at the center of Turkish society and transmitted to an overwhelmingly rural population through what may be described as the midway station of men of substance in the provinces. In the following decades, the center began to lose its dominant position.

By *center* I do not mean a locus or a geographical area but rather the group of leaders who saw themselves as responsible for elaborating policies for the country and who had the power and the authority to carry those policies through. The advent of competitive politics in the mid-1940s changed this picture. The attempt of the new parties to garner votes, the need to build a clientele–in short, the participatory nature of the new political system–brought the rural masses into the limelight and enhanced the role of provincial notables who earlier had operated as midway stations in the "nerves" of government. Of necessity, the role of the bureaucrat was diminished, and the bureacratic elite was downgraded. Roles were reversed: The provincial notables were now propelled into Parliament by their rural constituencies, but they had to harken to demands that came out of the rural areas in unprecedented numbers.

The utopian element that appeared in the first decades of the Turkish Republic–the attempt to build a country anew–slowly disappeared and was replaced by the down-to-earth demands of the rural population. The modernization of Turkey was still on the agenda of the new politicians, but it was supposed to be promoted by support for the needs of villages and provinciality and by encouragement of their economic pursuits rather than by blueprints for the establishment of a new society. New ideas described as *conservative* were now expressed in Parliament. These were often ideas that promoted the retrieval of Turkey's Islamic inheritance, which had been jettisoned during the years when secularism had become official state policy. But, in fact, there was more continuity between the secular policies promoted by Atatürk and the new emphasis on religious values than meets the eye.

This link emerges clearly if we see both of these policies as attempts to establish a moral code for society. The bureaucrats, the politicians, and–most interesting–the intellectuals, who figured as the ideological apparatus of the secular republic, had never stopped propounding the theme of the "degenerative" aspects of modern Western civilization. 'Kozmopolit' continued to be an insult in secular, Republican Turkey. The example to be followed was a sanitized version of Western culture, cleansed from what was perceived to be its libertinism. The antidote officials offered to counter the effects of exposure to Western civilization–which was the main plank in their program–was that a strong cultural anchor (fervent nationalism) would enable Turkey both to profit from Westernization and to keep the social integrity that was also one of their primary aims. Such a view of the strategy to be adopted vis-à-vis the West without succumbing to its blandishments had been a leitmotif of virtually all Turkish thinkers–both progressive and conservative–since the mid-nineteenth century.

In Sultan Abdülhamit II's (1876-1909) views, religion took the place of nationalism, but his main theme was the same as that of his liberal enemies: Adopt the technology, reject the mores. This attitude does not seem to have been necessarily Turkish or Ottoman. Pan-Slavism was built around the same values, and in the far Pacific islands, nativistic movements showed a similar cast. This worldwide reaction to the explosive invasion of Western civilization into established culture areas of the globe should be evaluated as a response to the unprecedented acceleration of social changes in the nineteenth century. The form this took in Turkey– following a number of avatars and after the introduction of competitive politics–was the attempt to reintroduce Islamic values in Turkish society as a countervailing force to balance what Turkey was felt to have lost during the modernization of its educational and cultural institutions.

Part of this reaction is understandable, as an example shows. In the 1930s, *à la Turca* music, the classical music of Ottoman culture, was proscribed by the Turkish Republic as inducing sloth and pessimism. Western polyphonic music was to replace the sounds of the *kanun*, the Ottoman cither. For the population, which was exposed to the blaring of the loudspeakers of ferries plying the Bosporus, incessantly repeating Ravel's *Bolero*, this was an unpleasant way of being introduced to the West. More was involved here than aesthetic shock: The republic had not been able to propagate a social ethic that was sufficiently meaningful to the rural masses to enable them to react positively to its modernization drive. This was its main failing, and it was especially galling to the Muslim population of Turkey. All students of Islam know that a widely used characterization of Islam involves its penetration into every interstice of social life. From this, commentators on Islam have depicted a society extremely dependent on religion for its very functioning. But this description, which is no doubt veridical, is still incomplete: What we need to know is *how* religion penetrates into social institutions. Up to the present, the regulatory aspects of Islam have been underlined in establishing the influence of religion in

society. This takes in a description of the way Islamic law operates in
Muslim society and also the ways in which religion regulates individual
values.

Different Faces of Islam

But the paramount influence of Islam in society can only be understood if
we add three dimensions of social analysis that have only recently become
available for the study of Islam, although they have been used by modern
sociologists for the study of other societies. One of these is the idea of
culture as language, the second is the conception of *habitus* promoted by
the French sociologist Pierre Bourdieu,[1] and the third is the elaboration in
the use of the "everyday" (*alltäglich*) in Michel de Certeau's conception of
the "quotidian."[2]
To start with the first of these ideas, we can more thoroughly conceive
of the pervasiveness of the social influence of Islam if we see it as an *idiom*,
by which I mean a set of conceptual facilities that enable one to classify
the stimuli that come from the ambient world according to a grid. This
grid is also a key that will allow us to elaborate social projects. It might
provide a key at the personal level, on how to win friends, for example,
or at an institutional level on how to build up coalitions, for instance. In
other words, religion in this case appears not only as a cosmology but also
as a set of social strategies and tactics: *Adab*–that is the store of knowledge
a Muslim gentleman should have at his command–is a good illustration
of the workings of Islam in this mode. What Bourdieu tells us is that the
space-time configuration of Islam is also an aspect of Islamic culture that
we have to reconstruct to understand how Muslims behave in a Muslim
society. Finally, what de Certeau tells us is that every culture has devised
ways of deflecting the abstract pattern of high culture on which it is built
at the level of "everyday usage."
Islam provided patterns for Turkish Muslims to follow in these spheres,
which is why it was important for them. Kemalist secular culture left
these pockets of Turkish culture empty in the sense that it consisted only
of general injunctions to take the West as an example. It provided no
equivalent for the widely used Islamic idiom, it did not understand the
degree to which existing space-time configurations were rooted and it had
no strategies of the quotidian to offer the masses.
A law such as the one passed in Turkey in 1986, which gave stronger
control to the police in controling public morals, may be seen as having
originated from a diffuse popular demand for the reestablishment of social

---

[1] Pierre Bourdieu, *Outline of a Theory of Practice* (Cambridge: Cambridge University Press,
1977).
[2] Michel de Certeau, *The Practice of Everyday Life* (Berkeley: University of California Press,
1984).

control–an aspect of the revival of religion that secularists will always underline. However, the large attendance at prayers at the mosque could be understood rather as a consequence of patterns of communal geography and space-time configurations. Turks' enthusiastic response to democracy may be linked to a continuation, in a different mode, of de Certeau's popular strategies of the debunkment of higher culture, of which the shadow play character Karagöz provides a good illustration.[3] In the most general sense, the loss of Islamic culture may be seen as the loss of an idiom governing social relations.

I claim that understanding the gaps left in the idiom of everyday relations in secular-Republican Turkey constitutes a first step in understanding the religious situation in this country in our time. But this only provides a start in analyzing the complexity of the revival of Islam in Turkey.

A second important dimension of modern Turkish Islam is related to unanticipated consequences in the religious sphere of the secular reforms of Atatürk. In bringing these paradoxical outcomes of reform to the surface we should pinpoint that the Islamic revival began in Turkey in a setting in which there were no ulama–doctors of Islamic law–left to expound their ideas. These religious functionaries had been relieved of their responsibilities in 1924 by the abolition of the ministry to which they were attached, from which followed the cessation of their salaries–a neat, single stroke that took the ulama out of circulation. This absence of legitimate religious personnel–except at the lowest level of mosque ministers and employees of the Directorate General of Religious Affairs– is one of the important differences between Turkey and Iran. In Iran, even under the monarchy, the ulama retained their own institutional support, whether in the public–if not official–recognition of their social status, their educational institutions, the pious foundations they controlled, or the contributions of their "parishioners." In Turkey, the absence of ulama with a recognized status enabled many more laypersons to be vocal in religious affairs; it also propelled into the religious arena men who claimed they had religious knowledge but who were often not well versed in religious sciences. Also, a class of lower-level religious personnel, which had not been eliminated by the abolition of the Ottoman Ministry of Religious Affairs, surfaced as religious leaders. In Ottoman history, these men, who occupied the lower range of the religious hierarchy, had often been leaders of the masses in expressing grievances against the bureaucracy. They now took on this role again, but this time actively opposing to secularization.

The reforms of Atatürk and his founding of a republic provided the provincial politicians of the 1950s with a platform through which to express their opinions, which had no equivalent in the Middle East in the sense that the democratic process was legitimatized in principle during

---

[3] The puppet shadow character Karagöz represents the simple, but cunning, man in the street, and confronts Hacivat–the educated fellow who gives himself airs. See Raphaela Lewis, *Everyday Life in Ottoman Turkey* (New York: Dorset Press, 1971), pp. 124-125.

Atatürk's years in power and the years that followed his death. The provincial politicians who acceded to power in the 1950s–unbeknownst to themselves–carried in their cultural store this Kemalist inheritance, as well as their Muslim values.

The interaction of the new preachers with the new political class enabled the politicians of the 1950s to use the preachers' religious network and that of the clientele they controlled to promote their own careers. Politicians, in return, had to pay the piper, which in their case meant supporting demands for an increase in the numbers of religious personnel and better emoluments and for support for the organization of Koranic teaching. One should note that this use of social networks has not profited the "clerical" Muslim parties that surfaced in Turkey from the 1970s on. The average voter support for the most successful of these parties has hovered between 10 and 12 percent; political parties as corporate entities have been much slower to promote religion in Parliament than have individual politicians. But the reverse is also true–namely, that many Turks with strong religious beliefs have supported parties other than those that are clerical. There is a sense, then, in which we can state that religious currents have been incorporated into midstream Turkish politics. What this midstream produces, however, is an increasing number of "seminars"–that is, high schools with elaborate programs of religious studies running in parallel with the normal high school curriculum. This is the specific form in which the support of a religiously conservative electorate is rewarded by the politicians. A further, more detailed explanation of the Turkish Kulturkampf is necessary at this point.

The same 1924 statute that disestablished the ulama in Turkey also granted the state a monopoly in education and abolished the higher religious schools known as *medrese*. The main influence of contemporary Turkish Islam, originated in Parliament, was the extent to which the early republican educational regime was modified. Religion was reintroduced at various primary and secondary levels. Today, an extraordinarily large number of high school-level seminaries have become part of Turkish secondary education. The promotion of this type of school, however, is not simply the result of a clerical conspiracy; these establishments are very popular with parents. The reason for this popularity seems to be the same one that, according to T. Zeldin, promoted the growth of Catholic schools in France in the nineteenth century: The schools have provided a frame of discipline and a sense of direction for their students, something parents find comforting.[4]

---

[4]Theodore Zeldin, *France, 1848-1945. Vol. II. Intellect, Taste and Anxiety* (Oxford: Clarendon Press, 1977), pp. 147-154.

Toward Islam as a Civil Religion

The idea that religion was being used as a tool by politicians in the 1980s needs, therefore, to be modified. For one, the first few years of the 1980s, before the general elections of 1983, were years during which the military established strict controls over religious currents. But more important, the politicians of post-1980 Turkey have only gone halfway to meet the real demands of a vocal electorate. Again, the phenomenal growth of *lycées*, with a parallel program of religious and secular studies, should be evaluated in the light of a seldom-quoted statistic: Between 1978-1979 and 1984-1985, the percentage of women students in *lycées* grew from 0.1 to 15 percent. Whether segregated or not, what counts here is the secular education offered in these schools.

But a scrupulously fair survey of the influence of Turkish education in the 1980s would not stop with underlining the contemporary flight from the secular values of the early Turkish Republic; it would also show a reverse movement, which can be termed the *capture of the secular discourse,* by younger Turkish Muslim intellectuals. A Turkish fundamentalist, such as the poet İsmet Özel, for instance, feels no compunction in titling his autobiography *Waldo Why Aren't You Here?* [5] The "Waldo" of the title is Ralph Waldo Emerson, and the phrase refers to an item in American intellectual history. The fact that Özel has a two-page quotation from Marcel Proust in the same book seems to indicate that the attempt by the Republic to familiarize Turks with French literature has not been ignored.

At the other end of the spectrum are the demagogic speeches of popular leaders propagated through cassette recordings, but neither this leadership nor its clientele should be attributed to Islam. What seems to be happening is that countries with Muslim population are undergoing a process of social transformation, which took place much earlier in Western Europe. There, too, the wrenching of the rural social fabric, the social problems created in the wake of industrialization, the mobilization of the masses, and changes in links within the family established the basis of social disorganization. The demagoguery that is one aspect of the revival of Islam in Turkey and its association with the popular mythical make believe are the corresponding Turkish products.

Where this mythical make believe has crossed with a stratum on the move, it has promoted an autonomous identity. By *identity* I do not mean only an anchor for an individual but also a boundary-constructing force that shapes a collectivity. What we have seen in post-1980 Turkey are steps toward the construction of such a collectivity rather than a conspiracy by politicians to "use" religion. If this is true, then the secularists–instead of bewailing the rise in the friction between secular and religious groups (which no doubt increased in the 1980s)–should try to devise a strategy for understanding this force and, possibly, for coming to terms with it. An

---

[5] İsmet Özel, *Waldo Sen Neden Burada Değilsin?* (Istanbul: Risale Yayınları, n.d.).

optimist would point out that in all cases in which political and economic spheres have become increasingly differentiated, the influence of religion has also been transformed.

The fact that many young laypersons in the post-1980 period have been engaged in what can be termed a hermeneutic exercise for enriching their Muslim culture, and the fact that they take the Western philosophic discourse seriously, shows the other aspect of the issue. The inheritance of many republican institutions, which have acquired legitimation, and the continuity of its social fabric in present-day Turkey necessarily move religion in the direction of a general secularization. In the long run, it may be possible to think of the transformation of Turkish Islam into a "civil religion."

PART SIX

Leading Elites

14

Kenan Evren as President: From Conflict to Compromise

C.H. Dodd

The central question I examine in this chapter is extent to which the presidency of the Turkish Republic, as it was fashioned in the 1980s, contributed to the viable democracy that was the aim of the new Constitution. This is not easy to determine because of the difficulty of defining democracy. Members of the European Parliament have been among the foremost critics of the Turkish democratic system of government set up in 1982, but they do not refer to any official definition of liberal democracy. There is no definition in the Treaty of Rome. In fact, discussion has usually focused on two features of democracy: human rights and competitive political parties.

One difficulty with this emphasis is that it ignores pressures on political decisionmaking emanating from a variety of groups in society operating outside political parties. But more important in Turkey's case is the fact that criticism has often overlooked the fact that liberal democracy is not only a form of politics but is also a form of state. Like other types of state, liberal democracy has to be able to maintain order, to provide coherent government, to establish the rule of law, to dispense justice, and to have some thought for the longer-term public interest. As happened in Turkey in the 1970s, political inputs can become too strong for the basic institutions of the state–hence the development in the late 1970s of serious debate on the need to create a strong presidency after the current French fashion.

The Development of the Turkish State and the Role of the President

Turkey has a firm, if not a liberal-democratic, state background–a by no means an unfortunate heritage. The Ottoman Empire was an authoritarian, bureaucratic, patrimonial state. Atatürk's Turkey was ruled largely by an enlightened elite, which aspired in its best endeavors to develop and protect the public or general interest within the framework of Atatürkist values. The word state (*devlet*) can therefore easily conjure up values somewhat akin to those found in continental Europe. The modern Turkish state is in some administrative respects heir to the authoritarian Ottoman state, which was mainly represented by the civil and military elites who recognized the authority of the sultan. With the new Fundamental Law, or Constitution, of 1921, the elites' situation was greatly changed. Allegiance was thenceforth owed to the Grand National Assembly, which took on all legislative and executive authority; there was no mention of the state.[1] This was an important break with the past that was not immediately apparent. The bureaucratic elite, in particular, played a large role in Atatürk's one-party state. But with the development of multiparty politics after World War II, the exposure of the bureaucratic and military elites became obvious, and their position was less secure.

Under the 1921 Constitution, there was, then, no separate legitimate executive authority from whom these elites could draw legitimacy. There was no president of the republic. The only executive authority was the president of the Grand National Assembly, who was ex officio chair of the Council of Ministers. The council, which was elected by the assembly, chose one of its own members as chair. The assembly, immensely proud of its revolutionary role and jealous of its authority, closely controlled the ministers in charge of the executive department, whom it also elected to office. In practice, it became very difficult for the government to act at all in these conditions. Deputies tended to lose sight of the fact that democracy is, after all, also a form of *government*. It was not without cause, therefore, that on 29 October 1923, Atatürk declared in his advice to the assembly that what was needed was a republic; this would solve the problem of coherent government.

In fact, a republic had already come into existence with the earlier declaration that sovereignty belonged to the nation and the abolition of the sultanate in 1922. Mustafa Kemal's proposal was for a head of state, a president of the republic–a move preempted any designs to have the caliph fill such an office. The proposal was accepted by the assembly, and Atatürk was duly elected president of the republic. He was allowed to choose the prime minister, who then appointed a government, which was to be approved in turn by the assembly. The government was now more independent of the assembly, but the presidency had gained little except that as head of state, Atatürk attracted the allegiance of the people. The president could not ultimately act independently of the government and the assembly, however. What had occurred was some separation of powers; the convention, or assembly, type of regime had changed into one that was more parliamentary in character.

---

[1] For an illuminating account of early constitutional history, including constitution making, see Suna Kili, *Turkish Constitutional Developments and Assembly Debates on the Constitutions of 1924 and 1961* (Istanbul: Robert College Research Center, 1971).

The Presidency in the 1924 Constitution

Turkey now had a president, but the office was confirmed in the Constitution of 1924 only after vigorous and heated discussion in the assembly. This occurred because the Constitutional Commission's proposals were for a strong president; these included the power of the president to dissolve the assembly, to head the armed forces, and to promulgate (or not promulgate) legislation made by the assembly. The proposal that the president could have the power of dissolution (a power also given to the assembly itself) ran into particularly deep trouble. In the face of repeated assertions that the assembly was the sole representative of national sovereignty, the proposal had to be withdrawn. So, too, did the recommendation that the president should be commander in chief of the armed forces.

In the end, it had to be accepted that supreme command was vested in the Grand National Assembly; only in wartime was command to be given to a person appointed by the president, although that appoinment had to be proposed by the Council of Ministers. On the matter of the president's power to return legislation to the assembly, the proposal was also weakened in favor of the assembly: The president's "veto" could not be used in cases of financial and constitutional legislation, and in all other matters, it could be overridden by a simple majority in the assembly, not by the two-thirds proposed. The assembly also insisted that the president must be chosen from among the members of the assembly, and it restricted the presidental term to four years (instead of the seven proposed) to coincide with the parliamentary term. The attempt to create a stronger presidency was roundly defeated. The president was head of state but lacked any substantial independent power.

If Atatürk could not dominate the Grand National Assembly as president, which was necessary if the revolution were to be pushed through, the troubles beginning in 1925 allowed him, and later İsmet İnönü, to dominate it through the Republican People's Party (CHP)–soon the sole party in existence. The major role of the presidency was to lead the Atatürkian revolution, but this leadership rested on Atatürk heading the party, which has not been an unimportant precedent.

This situation changed with the transition to a multiparty system after World War II. As presidents, both Atatürk and İnönü had been identified with the aims of the CHP (which led the revolution); during the decade from 1950 to 1960, Celal Bayar was mostly aligned with the new Democratic Party (DP) government. In fact, the insistence on a very large measure of assembly supremacy in the making of the 1924 Constitution did not take into account the powerful results of tight party discipline, which led to both the assembly and the president coming under the influence of the party in power. The focus of this power lay in the prime minister from 1950 to 1960. His position was further enhanced over that of the president mainly for two reasons. First, Bayar did not have the status of İnönü, and second, the prime minister, Adnan Menderes, had the legitimacy of popular election in a system that was now quite open and competitive. The 1924 Constitution received some of the blame for the emergence of this new "democratic tyranny" although Menderes's opponents sometimes blamed governmental authoritarianism and the manipulation of the Constitution by the government. The virtual absence of checks and balances in the Constitution was often pointed out.

Although theoretically this Constitution provided for the supremacy of the legislature over the executive, in practice, this situation was reversed. It was the government which dominated the Assembly. The President, the prime minister, and other members of the Council of Ministers, and the president of the Assembly, were all members of the majority party. This situation led some people to believe that in the 1950s the Council of Ministers functioned as the executive organ of the majority party.[2]

This belief was encouraged by partisan amendments to the electoral law to give the majority party an increased number of assembly seats. This and other moves of questionable political morality helped to create a high level of interparty adversarialism and fostered a deep suspicion not only that a democratic tyranny was in the making but also that the Atatürk revolution was in danger of erosion at the hands of the DP government. These were the most important factors behind the military intervention in 1960.

The Presidency in the 1961 Constitution

In the making of the 1961 Constitution, the remedy for recent difficulties was mainly seen to lie in creating more checks and balances, principally by creating a constitutional court and a second chamber. There was also provision for greater independence of the judiciary, but there was no further separation of the executive and legislative powers. For the promotion of pluralism, the universities and the media were given more freedom, interest group activity was encouraged, labor unions were allowed the right to strike, and legislation was introduced to provide for a system of proportional representation.[3] The clash of interests emanating from society was expected to keep Turkish democracy truly democratic. It was a plausible and persuasive theme, but reality did not meet expectations. The antagonisms among political parties and political personages spread to some important institutions in society and to some social groups, to such an extent that they were a major factor in the violence that developed and became intolerable on two occasions during the following two decades.

---

[2]Ibid., p. 22.

[3]For the making of the 1961 Constitution, see Siyasal Bilgiler Fakültesi İdari İlimler Enstitüsü, *Anayasa Tasarısı ve Seçim Sistemi Hakkında Görüşü* (Ankara: Ankara Üniversitesi Siyasal Bilgiler Fakültesi, 1960). See also Walter F. Weiker, *The Turkish Revolution, 1960-1961: Aspects of Military Politics* (Washington, D.C.: Brookings Institution, 1963) and C. H. Dodd, *Politics and Government in Turkey* (Manchester: Manchester University Press, 1969), pp. 108ff.

It was claimed by subsequent governments that the liberal measures introduced prevented a firm and dynamic government from emerging, but at the time the Constitution was made this was not foreseen. In fact, the chair of the Constitutional Committee, Professor Enver Ziya Karal, maintained that "the primary characteristic of this Constitution is that it is a revolutionary [*inkılapçı*] constitution . . . and is revolutionary because it includes and gives legal value to the reforms of Atatürk . . . and has brought the principles that will clear the way for our nation's tendency and aptitude to move forward."[4] The potential problem was whether social unity and secularism, two major Atatürkist principles, were going to prove compatible with "revolutionary" liberal principles.

In reviewing the position of the president, the framers of the 1961 Constitution chiefly had in mind the need to ensure that the president was politically impartial. After the election, the president was to sever all political party connections. The new constitution tried in this way to prevent a repetition of dominant-party government. The president was still to be elected by the Grand National Assembly–now by a joint session of the National Assembly and the new Senate. In order to ensure the election of a politically impartial president, a two-thirds majority was specified for the first two ballots, after which a majority vote sufficed. The term of office was extended to seven years, thus overlapping the terms of offices of both houses, but the president could not be reelected.

Although the president was supposed to be more impartial, the measures taken did little to make him more powerful, which would have been one way of checking on a government that was too partisan. He was given important appointing powers–fifteen members of Senate and two judges on the twenty-member Constitutional Court–although on the nomination of other bodies. Some wanted to empower the president to dissolve the Grand National Assembly, but this was granted only under closely defined and exceptional circumstances. It was actually proposed during the debate on the role of the president that he should be elected by universal suffrage in order to enhance his authority, but this was rejected on the grounds that it would introduce a political element to the office–the very thing the framers of the Constitution were trying to avoid. Nor were the president's delaying powers over legislation increased, although he could refer proposed legislation to the Constitutional Court. In sum, the president was expected to be impartial, but the tradition of supremacy of the assembly was too strong to allow him to be made powerful. This also coincided with the dominant philosophy that the mandate for government and the power to check government were both increasingly to come from outside–from the new civil society in the process of formation–and that these forces would be shaped by the assembly. Technically, dominant-party government would be avoided through the operation of proportional representation–which

[4]Quoted in Kili, *Turkish Constitutional Developments*, pp. 71-72.

largely turned out to be the case. At this juncture, the president was not regarded, at least by the civil intelligentsia, as the guardian of the state.

One element in the new Constitution that could be seen to negate this view, however, was the position now occupied by the military that was closer to political decisionmaking. Although the president continued to fill the position of commander in chief (representing the Grand National Assembly, as mandated in the 1924 Constitution), the chief of the general staff–the de facto commander of the armed forces–was made responsible to the prime minister, a point left unclear in the 1924 Constitution. In addition, a National Security Council–a mixed military-ministerial body–was established in the 1961 Constitution, with the president as chair, although the prime minister assumed this role in the absence of the president.

The "impartiality" of the presidency now began to take on a new meaning. It often came to be seen as guaranteed only by the election of presidents of military provenance. The first president was General Cemal Gürsel, the leader of the junta, who was followed in 1965 by Cevdet Sunay, chief of the General Staff–who resigned in order to be elected president by agreement of the political parties. However, allegations soon were made that Sunay favored the Justice Party (AP), although these claims were refuted by Sunay, who declared that the armed forces and their commanders were not the instruments of one policy or another. This did not stop Osman Bölükbaşı, leader of the Nation Party, from declaring, "In no country run really democratically and where the national will is respected has a person leading the army become president of the Republic in the way Cevdet Sunay has done . . . . No citizen can but feel anxious about the future of our country and democracy if electing the chief of the general staff for president becomes a custom, and a kind of 'heir to the throne' tradition is created."[5]

It is interesting that this statement contains two criticisms of presidents from the military–that they do not guarantee impartiality and that the appointment of persons of such backgrounds denies the very idea of democracy. In 1973, the retired admiral Fahri Korutürk was elected president by agreement among the parties. He was acceptable to the military, but the military candidate, Faruk Gürler, chief of the General Staff, had been rejected by the political parties, who also would not allow the extension of Sunay's term of office. These events underlined the point that even if the military were convinced that it was acting impartially in advancing military candidates for presidential office, it was going to find few who believed this. Clearly, during the 1970s, after the experience of a military intervention in 1971, the political parties were united in not wanting to see a military influence perpetuated in politics through the election of former military officers to the presidency. In fact, the new left-of-center CHP, under Bülent Ecevit, was actively trying to disassociate itself from the military connection, which had been reinforced in 1960-1961. And the military was unpopular with the AP after that party's virtual ejection from office by the military in the "coup by memorandum" of 1971, despite the seemingly better relations that had developed starting in the mid-1950s.

When the office of the presidency again fell vacant in 1980, there was an impasse. Both major parties advanced the names of candidates least likely to find favor with the other party. With such hostility between the major political parties, there was little chance of finding an impartial president. The military was not pressing a candidate, perhaps having learned a lesson from the events of 1973. Yet the impasse was one of the factors in the situation that reinforced the military's belief that it had to intervene in order to save the state.

In the late 1970s, both major parties were seeking the appointment of a sympathetic president; despite growing political and social violence, neither really relished the prospect of a president with a military background. In these trying circumstances, a number of proposals began to circulate in intellectual circles, including proposals for a more powerful and more independent presidency. Inspired in part by the French examples, these proposals included rights to dismiss Parliament, to veto legislation, and to be popularly elected. A president with a military background was not specified, but the military was thought to be close to these circles.[6] In this submission, what was now being sought was not an impartial and a judicious arbitrator but a weighty arbiter.

The Presidency in the 1982 Constitution

In the end, the 1982 Constitution did not produce such an arbiter, but it did fashion a somewhat stronger presidency.[7] Impartiality requires that the president should not belong to a political party or remain a member of Parliament. It seems he is expected to be elected from among the deputies, but the nomination of persons from outside the assembly is possible if it is proposed by at least one-fifth of all deputies. The president serves for seven years, thus overlapping the parliamentary five-year term, but may not be reelected.

The president is now equipped with powers of appointment: He appoints all members of the Constitutional Court,[8] one-quarter of the mem-

---

[6]See C. Dodd, *The Crisis of Turkish Democracy* (Walkington, England: Eothen Press, 1983), pp. 65ff. and Mehmet Ali Birand, *The General's Coup in Turkey*, trans. M. A. Dikerdem (London: Brassey's, 1987).

[7]See the very useful chapter by Ergun Özbudun, "The Status of the President of the Republic Under the Turkish Constitution of 1982: Presidentialism or Parliamentarism?" in *State, Democracy, and the Military: Turkey in the 1980s*, Metin Heper and Ahmet Evin, eds. (Berlin: Walter de Gruyter, 1988), pp. 37-45.

[8]He selects one member from the three names submitted by each of a number of bodies: the Council of State, the High Court of Appeals, the Military Court of Appeals, the Supreme Military Administrative Court, the Court of Accounts, and the High Board of Education. He also appoints three other members.

bers of the Council of State, the chief prosecutor and his deputy, the members of the Court of Appeal, the members of the Military Court of Appeal, the members of the Supreme Military Administrative Court, and all members of the Supreme Council of Judges and Prosecutors. He also appoints the chair and members of the State Supervisory Board, and he can instruct this body to carry out investigations into and inspect all public bodies, including public professional organizations, employers' associations, and labor unions. He also appoints the chief of the General Staff (who is responsible to the prime minister, however) on the nomination of the Council of Ministers. Although in making appointments to posts the president generally has to choose from among persons nominated by other institutions of state, this is nevertheless an important area of influence. In such circumstances, nominations are not normally made if a person is likely to be unacceptable to the appointing authority.

The president's powers to participate in the political process in other areas were also augmented. He calls the National Security Council into session, prepares its agenda, and presides over it. Moreover, the Council of Ministers now has "to consider with priority" (Article 118) recommendations made by the National Security Council designed to safeguard the existence and independence of the state, the unity and indivisibility of the country, and the peace and security of society. This is a more important role for the military than that mandated in the 1961 Constitution.

The president also now has power to dismiss the Grand National Assembly and to call new elections. This power can only be used, however, in certain stringent conditions of impasse. Also he has not been given the right to act alone in the interests of law and order in conditions of emergency, as was sometimes proposed prior 1980. A state of emergency can only be declared by the Council of Ministers, although on such occasions the council must meet under the chairmanship of the president. Even then, the decision must be submitted immediately to the Grand National Assembly for approval, as do any decrees made as a result of the declaration of an emergency.

The president's delaying powers over legislation have not been developed, but he continues to have the right to submit legislation to the Constitutional Court. The right to submit suits of annulment to the court is now given to fewer bodies than was true in 1961, so the president's influence can be said to have increased in this respect. He can also submit laws relating to the Constitution to a referendum, even though they were passed by the required two-thirds majority in the assembly. This gives the president a degree of access to the expression of the popular will. Under an amendment (May 1987), if the president does not reject a proposal for constitutional amendment supported by more than a three-fifths, but less than a two-thirds, vote, he must refer it to a referendum. This provides a check on his impartiality but does not add to his power.

The decrees embodying presidential decisions are countersigned by the prime minister in all cases except those specifically mentioned in the Constitution as being within the power of the president (and not subject to appeal, it may be noted). He does not, therefore, have any general residual power. Overall, the president has only a few more strictly executive powers than did the president under the previous Constitution. Where his position is stronger is in his general controlling and investigatory powers and his powers of appointment. These do not constitute his being an arbiter, but he is the guardian of the state.

A comparison of the oaths sworn by the president under the 1961 and 1982 Constitutions is instructive. In the 1961 Constitution (Article 96), the president is required to swear "I will not deviate from the principles of a democratic state based on the rule of law and human rights, that I will be free from bias." In the comparable article of the 1982 Constitution (Article 104), there are some interesting additions. The president is now required to swear "I will always strive to preserve the Constitution . . . and the secular republic guided by the tenets and reforms of Atatürk." In addition, in the 1982 Constitution (Article 104) the president is obliged to "ensure the implementation of the Constitution and the steady and harmonious functioning of the state organs." Clearly, as head of state the president is not expected only to be impartial; he has the active role of supervising the working of the Constitution in the light not only of the requirements of democracy but in accord with Atatürkist principles–among which secularism is given particular mention. If not an arbiter, he is certainly intended to be a protector, which is more than being an impartial figurehead. At this point, we might ask what sort of role President Evren has filled during his tenure (1982-1989) and to what extent he has been able to fulfill the duties imposed upon him in the absence of substantial independent powers.

Kenan Evren's Presidency

President Evren was an active and outspoken president who paid particular attention to visiting all parts of the country and to addressing a wide range of his fellow Turks. As the size of his majority (92 percent) in his 1982 election showed, he was very popular. Although he could not avoid being a father figure he did not promote the cult of his own personality. Nor did he even seem to relish being regarded as head of state, despite his being described as such in the Constitution.[9] For him, this was perhaps too authoritarian, or it may have implied too much power within the context of Turkish history. What the president stressed in his speeches was not the state but rather a variety of attitudes that were consonant with the role he clearly accepted–that of defender of the Constitution and of the

---

[9]The point is illustrated by Metin Heper, "The Executive in the Third Turkish Republic, 1982-1989," *Governance* 3 (1990): 299-319.

Atatürkism that, rightly or wrongly, was seen to underlie it.

To take the constitutional aspect first, there was much emphasis in his speeches on the need for security, especially for a firm stand to be taken against terrorism. The best way to prevent terrorism from arising again, in the president's view, was for the political parties and others participating in the political system to combine to prevent it–which had been the attitude of the military before intervention. There was little or no philosophizing over other possible causes of the terrorism that emerged. He had a strong tendency to emphasize the personal responsibility, or irresponsibility, of the political leaders. The people were not blamed or cajoled; it was not suggested that they were responsible for getting the government they deserved.

In line with his defense of the constitutional settlement of 1982, the president was opposed to any amnesty for those who had been convicted of crimes since the military intervention. In the case of the former politicians who were banned from playing political roles in the new regime, he did not, however, prove inflexible. He modified an earlier pronounced disinclination to permit the return of former political leaders to politics, to the extent of allowing a referendum on this issue to take place in 1987.

This flexibility did not seem to make the president popular with many members of the new, revived parties, however. In an address to the assembly in 1985, Evren criticized the former politicians. He noted that in the past the country had paid a price for a "speaking" Turkey and that those who should be silent were talking everyday. Former prime minister Süleyman Demirel responded with a four-page tract on the requirement in the Constitution for an unbiased president. This was hardly as serious, from the point of view of bias, as the president's clear intention prior to the 1983 elections to persuade the electorate to vote for the now-defunct National Democracy Party in preference to the Motherland Party (ANAP) under Özal.

This "bias" could, with leniency, be interpreted as stemming from a desire to protect the achievements of the 1982 Constitution in the best way possible–and certainly, Evren quickly accepted the ANAP once it was victorious. What seems to be stressed was not the detail of the Constitution, but rather its essential character, which was seen to incorporate the principles necessary for an orderly, liberal, and democratic state. In 1986, in a speech in Kahramanmaraş, Evren strongly defended the Constitution. The events of 1980 were not a coup, he said, but were a defense of the republic against anarchy. If the Constitution were "punctured," he went on, the conditions that had existed prior to 12 September would return. But, he continued, the military had not interfered in politics since the 1983 elections, knowing it would lose its prestige if it did so.

This sort of consideration with regard to the military nevertheless did not prevent the president from suggesting that political crises could again lead to military intervention. In May 1988, at a time of incidents of leftist violence, Evren warned that if the political authorities did not do their duty, the armed forces could not stay silent. More than just this outbreak of violence was involved, however. This was a period during which open attacks on the 1980 military intervention were being made by the former political leaders who had been admitted to politics after the September 1987 referendum. Evren was vigorously criticized for his remarks, notably by Demirel, and for neglecting the fact that only the Grand National Assembly could call upon the armed forces to do their duty. In the upshot, Özal came to Evren's defense, asserting that the president was a believer in democracy, although he denied any danger of military intervention.

In his speeches, the president also tried to inculcate the moral values and social behavior he considered appropriate for Turkish public life. There was a good measure of idealistic Atatürkism in the way he recommended showing consideration for the political opposition and its points of view and in the way he hoped for, and believed in, the reasonable and sensible participation of the common person in politics. He was suspicious of political activists, having pointed to the danger of politicizing certain key ministries, such as the Ministry of Education. This was not a fear of a return to the widespread politicization of governmental and other public institutions, which was rife before 1980; it was rather a concern with the specific problem of the revival of Islam, which had taken on new dimensions since 1980 and is discussed below.

Prominent in the president's speeches was discussion of Turkey's national independence and integrity. He did not refrain from commenting on foreign affairs. In this respect, he criticized the European Parliament's views and verdicts on Turkish affairs, blamed the United States Congress for being duped by Turkey's enemies, and deplored Europe's unreasonable hostility to Turkey because it is a Muslim country. In June 1987, he also expressed himself forcibly on alleged foreign aiding and abetting of Kurdish dissidents, even threatening that Turkey might withdraw from NATO. More serious was his statement in June 1988 that there could be no Turkish withdrawal from northern Cyprus except as part of an overall settlement of the Cyprus problem–a warning, it seems, to the governmnet in its negotiations with the Greek government at the time.

In these last instances, the president was moving from the general to the more specific–from the domain of the state to the world of politics–and the two are not easy to disentangle, since a general statement may well be prompted by a particular problem. Also, these matters were in the field of foreign affairs. But the president certainly did not think it necessary to refrain from commenting on particular topics of current internal political import, sometimes suggesting a line of action before the issue had been considered by the relevant political, administrative, or judicial authorities. His forthright views concerning those who might be under judicial investigation, such as members of the Confederation of Revolutionary Labor Unions (known by its Turkish acronym DISK), were criticized. So, too, were his strictures on two United Communist Party members who returned to Turkey and were arrested in 1987–namely, Haydar Kutlu and Nihat Sargın.[10] He also commented on matters such as the lifting of solitary confinement, the alleged intention of hunger strikers to draw adverse attention to Turkey from outside, and proposals to transfer cases being tried in military courts to civil courts. He also objected to, and prevented, the appointment of persons associated with former extreme right-wing parties as higher public servants; he is also said to have asked for alternative names to consider when ratifying the appointment of ministers in certain cases.[11] This intervention in political affairs was not partisan, however. These matters of political dispute were essentially concerned with matters of government and administration and with the defense of the principles guiding the 1980 military intervention.

The president was perhaps most irritating to the government in his penchant for remarking on governmental shortcomings. He did not refrain from commenting adversely on inflation, unemployement, the amount of foreign debt, and the like. One intrusion into matters of government that was resented involved his strictures on the lack of progress being made in the huge Southeast Anatolian Project (for the damming and distribution of the Euphrates waters). His call for a seperate ministry to handle the project was rejected. Criticized for his outspokenness, Evren reminded the public, among whom he was undoubtedly popular, that he was not the sort of president to sit inside his residence in Ankara and sign laws and decrees but that he would speak up on matters of national significance.

The president had a marked tendency to comment on matters important to the military, whether materially or ideologically, which suggests that to some degree, he was still a spokesperson for that interest. One matter of particular interest to the still staunchly Atatürkist officer stratum of the military was secularism, which the Constitution, it will be recalled, also requires the president to defend. Evren did not emerge as antireligious in outlook, and he was conscious of the contribution of religion to general moral standards.[12] But he expressed a good deal of disquiet about religion, in both its social and political aspects. He gave his views on girls wearing headscarves in a visit to a girls' school in January 1985, remarking that religion was a matter between God and the individual and implying that headscarves did not further that relationship. He returned powerfully to this theme in his 1987 new-year message, and it could be implied from his remarks that the military would, if necessary, move against religious fundamentalism.[13] Evren also expressed fears about the infiltra-

---

[10] *Yeni Gündem* (Istanbul weekly), 22-28 November 1987.

[11] Heper, "Executive in the Third Turkish Republic," p. 312.

[12] In 1982, Evren allowed the Muslim World League to finance Turkish "clergy" working among Turkish workers outside Turkey. He also visited Saudi Arabia (February 1984), where he spoke out against Israel.

[13] *Briefing* (Ankara weekly), 5 January 1991.

tion of religious extremists into the armed forces, which many saw as the principal bulwark against religious fundamentalism. Reports in the press in January 1987 alleged that there had been meetings of army officers to warn the president against fundamentalism, but such reports are not easily corroborated.

On the subject of military recruitment, in an altercation with Demirel, Evren expressed his view that those who graduated from the religiously oriented high schools (the *İmam Hatip* schools) could not become army officers. Demirel pointed out that the curricula of such schools were state approved and that their pupils could go on to become, say, engineers or doctors, implying that they could also become military officers.[14] Later in the same year, the president requested an explanation of the proposal to offer courses in Arabic script in secondary schools.[15] On these matters, the prime minister strove to adopt a middle course, aware of the extent of religious (which is not the same as fundamentalist) support for the ANAP. There is a well entrenched secular elite in Turkey, and those who are religious are not necessarily fundamentalists. Influenced perhaps by the military and by his own military–and very Atatürkist–background, the president seemed more concerned about the threat to the secular state than did most of the political and civilian elites. Although he was outspoken on a number of sensitive matters, the president did not seek to enchance his role. Even in matters affecting religion he accepted compromises initiated by the prime minister, who, although respecting the president's position, became increasingly more confident and took over tasks he would previously have left to the president.[16]

Relations between the president and the prime minister were sometimes strained, especialy when the President was seen as invading the sphere of government, which his broad supervisory role over the administration inclined him to do. But a good deal of harmony prevailed. In cases in which the president returned draft legislation to the Grand National Assembly for consideration, compromises were reached, with the President's views often being firmly, although tactfully, rejected by the government. As early as 1984, the president was unable to amend legislation providing for early local elections.

More positively, the president was helpful to the government on a number of issues. For instance, he did not allow an investigation into alleged corruption by a government minister to be handled by the State Supervisory Board (over which he has authority), on the grounds that this would imply a lack of confidence in the prime minister. Nor in 1984 did the president invoke the Constitution (Article 84) to prevent deputies who transferred to other parties by simply by crossing the floor of the chamber from participating in subsequent elections. This, he said, was a matter

---

[14]Ibid., 19 January 1987.
[15]Heper, "Executive in the Third Turkish Republic," p. 310.
[16]Heper makes this point in ibid., pp. 313ff.

for the assembly.[17] The president tried to take a firm line in restricting the appointment of public servants because their political allegiances, on the grounds that the bureaucracy should be impartial. But he had to give ground here, because he was obliged to recognize that governments can legitimately argue a need for leading bureaucrats who are enthusiastically committed to the execution of the government's policies and personally acceptable to the ministers. Nor did president object to administrative control of the machinery of the state being undertaken in practice by an Inspectoral Board set up in the prime minister's office, despite the existence of the State Supervisory Board under the president's authority.[18]

It might be said, in conclusion, that the president was criticized much more for expressing his views on matters of current political or judicial dispute than for his attempts to gain greater control over government, which were rare. He was regarded as stepping outside the requirements of his office when he warned of possible military intervention if the conditions that existed before 1980 should reappear.[19] It could be argued, however, that insofar as he was transmitting military views, he was performing a service in the interests of realism and, in the longer term, in the interests of democracy.

The president's condemnation of major parties that were involved in politics before 1980 did not endear him to the members of those parties who were now in the assembly. The deputies belonging to Demirel's True Path Party, together with some from the Social Democratic Populist Party, refused to stand when the president delivered his opening address to the 1987 Grand National Assembly. Yet the president had not ultimately stood in the way of their return to politics, despite the constitutional prohibition; nor did he prove to be inflexible in other matters. He listened to government advice in making appointments, and even in religious matters, he accepted a good deal of compromise, although his influence here–reflecting the strong views of the military–was allegedly important in restraining the religious wing of the ANAP.

In sum, President Evren was not an arbiter, in Gaullist fashion, nor did he seek to create an executive that rivaled the government. In fact, beyond a general surveillance of the administration, he did not have a powerful executive role. The executive in the Turkish unitary system of government lies within the government. More important, he did not seek to assume political leadership. With the return of competitive politics, which he did not try to prevent, he could not have done.

President Evren attempted to maintain the prime Atatürkian values of secularism, national independence and integrity, and a unified society in

[17]Reported in ibid., p. 312.

[18]See Lütfi Duran, "Cumhuriyetin 'Yürütmesi': Kuvvetli İcra mı, Kişisel İktidar mı?" in Bahri Savcı'ya Armağan (Ankara: Ankara Üniversitesi Siyasal Bilgiler Fakültesi, 1988.)

[19]See "Demokrasinin Sürekliliği ve Cumhurbaşkanının Konuşması," Yeni Forum (Ankara monthly), 15 May 1988.

two broad ways.[20] First, he proclaimed these and associated norms to the public at large on numerous occasions. Second, he tried to ensure that these norms permeated the spirit of the administration over which he had broad surveillance. Interpreting these functions broadly, he did not hold back from making outspoken comments on the administrative performance of the government and sometimes on judicial matters, which caused friction. He also represented the common person to some extent; he was folksy in the Turkish way and provided a popular personalization of the state.

Yet the presidency came to have less real power, or authority, than had been expected to be the case in 1983. Metin Heper has shown how Özal gradually asserted his power over the government after 1983, continually gaining confidence and becoming "less hesitant in asserting the prerogatives of the political executive."[21] President Evren was elected by popular vote, which gave his presidency a degree of popular legitimacy, but under the Constitution this cannot recur. He had a certain amount of executive power in his powers of appointment and surveillance, but in later years his influence over processes of constitutional change was somewhat reduced. And he was powerful as head of the state only insofar as large sections of society accepted the norms he preached and acted upon them. President Evren undoubtedly realized the limitations of his office and adjusted his role to that required in a unitary state such as that of Turkey, in which the political initiative came increasingly from society through the operation of the party system. Evren took seriously the role of guardian of the state and the Constitution, but having no political base, he could not develop independent powers sufficient to allow him to achieve this objective with any ease. He had a strong personality but lacked political dynamism. Özal would later show how the powers of the presidency could be expanded.

Conclusion

It seems impossible for Turkey have an impartial president to guard the Constitution, except save in one or two circumstances. The first is the relatively easy and short-term case of a military-backed president, assuming that the military remains Atatürkian in spirit and is not infiltrated or politicized. The political parties would almost certainly reject this, as they did in 1973; it seems to be an affront to democracy. The only other albeit long-term, circumstance would seem to be to encourage the development of a truly pluralist society, which means not just the expression of diversity but development of the awareness that diversity must be reconciled in the public interest and that the modes of reconciliation–as embodied in the

---

[20]When Evren was presented with an Intellectuals' Petition in May 1984, he sharply reminded the intellectuals concerned that it was absolutely necessary to abandon all division in society (including that of the intellectuals). Reported in *Yeni Gündem*, 22-28 November 1987.

[21] Heper, "Executive in the Third Turkish Republic," p. 314.

stable institutions of a liberal and democratic state–have to be generally accepted and respected by all political actors.

Long inured to the tradition of the state, the politically rather moderate Turkish public would no doubt be glad for some reassurance that democracy is not simply government and its opposition, which results in disruption that the military corrects at times on behalf of the state. They would perhaps welcome the idea that democracy is a state itself and that not only the president but all political actors would realize this.

Too much credence may unfortunately ultimately be placed on the notion that a "civil society" composed of free and interacting individuals and groups will of itself create a viable democracy. This development, coupled with a free market, may curb party domination (and intraelite conflict) by taking the pressure off government as the source of all bounty. The danger is that it can lead to an irresponsible *enrichissez-vous* type of society, where material gain is the dominant value. That would not please the military or the now stronger, puritanical Islamic right. By virtue of his powers of surveillance over the state, the president has some opportunities to alert public opinion to the need for a "civil" society, but the qualities of impartiality and vision are little promoted by the presidental system set up under the 1982 Constitution. President Evren's presidency nevertheless came close to success in these respects during difficult times.

15

Turgut Özal's Presidency: Crisis and the Glimmerings of Consensus

Metin Heper

In October 1989, for only the second time since the transformation of the Turkish political system in 1945 (from a single-party to a multiparty regime), Turkey elected a president with a civilian rather than a military background. The first such president was Celal Bayar, who was elected during the 1950s. Thereafter, from 1960 to 1989, all Turkish presidents were either actively involved in the military interventions that took place during this period, staying on at the helm of the state after the military returned to the barracks, or they were retired military men who were elected as president by political parties anxious not to alienate the military.

Given this particular background, the election by Parliament of Turgut Özal as president in 1989 constituted a watershed in the development of Turkish democracy. Özal had been prime minister in the Motherland Party (ANAP) governments since 1983, and his bid for presidency caused a great deal of controversy both before and after his election, virtually amounting to a new crisis of political legitimacy. Although it seemed that the democratization process in Turkey would not to interrupted by further military intervention, the political tension created by this controversy pushed Turkish democracy into a similar political crisis.

Toward the 1989 Presidential Election

Because of past political dynamics concerning the presidency, toward the end of the 1980s the question of who should become the next president of Turkey once again became extremely critical.[1] For a while, even the

---

[1] This chapter draws largely upon a complete survey I made of three dailies (*Hürriyet and Milliyet*, both published Istanbul, and the *Turkish Daily News*, published in Ankara) and of some issues of two additional dailies (*Cumhuriyet* and *Tercüman*, both published in Istanbul),

possibility of President Kenan Evren continuing for a second term was considered. However, once it became clear that Evren had no intention of serving for another seven years, attention focused on Prime Minister Özal as the most likely candidate, because ANAP had the necessary majority in the Parliament to elect him as president.[2] A controversy started immediately, concerning the potential candidacy of Özal, in the press and among leading past and present politicians, as well as in intellectual circles.

Some opposed Özal's becoming president by arguing that he would not represent what the state stood for in Turkey. A minority in this group argued that the president should represent all of the political parties, the implication being that Özal would continue to have sympathy only for his former party. The majority considered the presidency as being above party–a representative of the Republic's fundamental norms and institutions, the general interest, or of commonsense. It was implied that the presidency under Özal would not promote these norms and institutions. The arguments advanced in this context were that Özal would continue to act in a partisan manner, and in any case, his personal characteristics– "lack of seriousness", "inability to elicit respect", "a tendency to ignore established rules and regulations", and the like–would prevent him from displaying the behavior expected of a head of state.

On 26 March 1989, local elections were held in Turkey. Early in the campaign, the governing party, the ANAP, tried to restrict its propaganda to local issues and the success of ANAP mayors during the 1980s in dealing with those issues. The opposition parties, however, quickly nationalized the debate, and what were supposed to be *local* elections soon took on the characteristics of *general* elections. At the elections, when the ANAP lost the bulk of the mayoralties, a very important dimension was added to the controversies about the impending presidential election–the questions of whether the Parliament now represented the people, and, if it did not, was it constitutionally and politically appropriate for that Parliament to elect the next president.

As far as some of the former politicians–of different political persuasions– were concerned, the result of the local elections did not justify the representativeness of the Parliament being questioned. The majority in this group believed that although the way people voted in the local elections could not altogether be overlooked, no one was entitled to conclude that the present Parliament could not, constitutionally speaking, elect a president. But they did feel the results of the local elections obliged ANAP deputies to elected a president who would be acceptable to a large crosssection of the people in the country.

Most of what I think could be considered as independently minded members of the press and the intelligentsia subscribed to this second view. They argued that the issue of legality should be clearly separated from

---

from 1 January 1989 to 15 January 1992.

[2] The ANAP was founded by Turgut Özal in 1983.

that of what is politically appropriate. They thought the Parliament, with an ANAP majority, was entitled to elect a president but that ANAP leaders should first confer with the leaders of the two opposition parties in the Parliament–the Social Democratic Populist Party (SHP) and the True Path Party (DYP)–and that even if an ANAP deputy is eventually elected president, he or she should be someone who would act in a nonpartisan manner. The bulk of the journalists and intelligentsia disagreed with this view. In their thinking, legality and political ethics could not be separated. The situation dictated that politicians should pay attention to the people's wishes; the electorate were not behind the present Parliament, and, thus, this body had lost its right to elect a president who was supposed to represent the people as a whole. The journalists and intelligentsia in question concluded that under the circumstances, the people rather than the Parliament should elect the next president. Some even rejected the idea of an election, whether by the Parliament or the people, as a means of determining the person who would be head of state. They reasoned that the presidency was too important an institution in Turkey and that party politics should not play a role in selecting the incumbent. What they proposed as an alternative was not quite clear. They seemed to opt for the selection of the president by acclamation, but how this would take place was not apparent. One thing was clear: They were strongly against the election of Özal by a Parliament dominated by the ANAP.

An even more extreme view held that the ANAP government itself was not legitimate. One student-of-law-turned-columnist claimed that a political party that loses its political support would also be deprived of political legitimacy. Another student of law, who had headed the commission that prepared the draft of the 1982 Constitution, asserted that the ANAP government was not legitimate, because the last general elections (in 1987) were carried out according to an election law based on a proportional system of representation–which significantly favored the political party with the plurality of votes–and consequently that this election law was incongruous with the principle of equality before law, stipulated by Article 10 of the Constitution.

Turning to the political parties in the assembly, before the 26 March 1989 local elections, SHP Chair Erdal İnönü had been sympathetic to the idea of the ANAP's parliamentary majority electing the president, provided that the ANAP deputies nominated their candidate after consulting with the opposition parties in the Parliament. Following the elections, however, İnönü argued that the election of the president by the ANAP majority in the Parliament would amount to disregarding the national will, because in effect, a minority would capture the state. Consequently, İnönü repeatedly pressed for early elections. The ANAP government did not go along with this demand, and İnönü even indicated that as a last resort, the opposition parties might "return to the fold of the people"–that is, the opposition deputies would resign from Parliament–and force an early election. In the end, he did not pursue this strategy and, in fact, resisted pressures from some within his own party–including, for a while then secretary-general of the party, Deniz Baykal–because, İnönü felt such a move would not be in the best interests of the country. İnönü did not question the authority of the Parliament to elect a president or the legitimacy of the president so elected, yet he made it clear that his party could not work with such a president. He argued that if the ANAP deputies elected the president all by themselves then there would be two separate state structures–one favored by the ANAP and the other supported by the opposition parties, and for that matter by the majority in the country. He pointed out that Özal's election would drive the country into turmoil; sharp, spontaneous reactions would come from different quarters; and it would be difficult to predict the direction in which the regime would evolve in the future.

İnönü himself had chosen to remain within the normal parliamentary rules. His party, however, over which he did not always have firm control, tended to display a more militant attitude. As early as May 1989, Baykal had implied that if the ANAP deputies chose to elect the president without consulting the opposition, the SHP would boycott the election. Soon İnönü, too, adopted this view. The party's position was that the presidency was a symbol of unity among the political forces in the country, and, as such, it had to have behind it either adequate electoral support or the support of the major opposition parties in the parliament. A faction within the party, led by the secretary-general, argued that one could have consensus between the ANAP and the opposition parties only on the subject of an early election and not on a candidate for president. The secretary-general categorically stated that a president elected by an "artificial parliament" would be an "artificial president." He added that Özal's evaluation of the issue (taken up below) did not reflect a healthy psychological state of mind. The other opposition party in the Parliament–the DYP, led by Süleyman Demirel– adopted an even more intransigent stance. Not only following but before the local elections, Demirel had a rather uncompromising attitude. He said that less than a 50 percent majority in the Parliament would be inadequate to elect a president and rejected as inappropriate the suggestion of nominating a candidate through a dialogue among the political parties. His proposal was that the people, not the Parliament, should elect the president.

Following the local elections, Demirel questioned not only the representativeness of the assembly but also the legitimacy of the government. He claimed that the results of the local elections had created a situation such that the national will was no longer represented, because the parliamentary majority now enjoyed the support of only a minority of the electorate. According to him, the government was now no more than an "unjust occupier," because it was a government without the people. This radical approach on Demirel's part may be explained by the fact that since

1983, he had accused the ANAP government of being a product of the 1980 military intervention. According to him, it had come to power in 1983 through unequal competition, because the SHP and the DYP were not allowed by the military to participate in the general elections of that year. Furthermore, he argued, the ANAP had maintained its parliamentary majority in the 1987 elections because of an election law that, due to an amendment made by the ANAP majority in the assembly, unduly favored the political party thad had the most votes.

Thus, it was difficult for Demirel to come to terms with the ANAP, and Özal in particular, on any issue. He took revamping altogether "the regime distorted earlier by the military and later by the ANAP" as his sole mission. He called on everybody to assemble under a flag and wage a struggle against the present regime through democratic means. To him, no solution other than the election of the president by the people was acceptable. When asked if he had in mind a particular person within the ANAP or without as a suitable candidate for the presidency, his response was that he had never thought about it because that was not the issue. Not unexpectedly, he was very critical of, and had a condescending attitude toward Özal, and at times, when engaged in a public debate with him, he did not mince his words.

Özal did not help to ameliorate this rather tense political atmosphere, and the constant barrage of harsh criticisms made him more stubborn than he might have been in different circumstances. First, he categorically rejected the claim that the local elections showed that the ANAP had lost its political support and was therefore obliged to hold early general elections. He gave the example of the Conservative government in Britain staying in office after having faced defeat in the local elections. Second, he pointed out that according to the Constitution, the political parties in the Parliament could not nominate candidates, because the president is elected by secret ballot. Consequently, it was inappropriate for the political party leaders to agree on a joint candidate and impose that candidate on the Parliament. Özal asserted that arriving at a consensus on this issue would not be a democratic act. He argued that Parliament should not be subjected to any kind of pressure; it should elect the president by its own free will.

Third, continuing on the same theme but with a significant variation, Özal noted that the claim that a person elected president by the Parliament could not take over that duty was undemocratic. He asked, "How those people who take unto themselves the responsibility of determining who should or should not be elected president, consider themselves as democrats?" By stepping up the severity of his offensive, Özal claimed that in the past (in 1973), Demirel's previous Justice Party (AP) had the majority in the Parliament, but it was afraid of the military, so it could not elect a president of its own choice; the Republican People's Party (CHP) (the predecessor to İnönü's SHP) also had a share in this "crime."[3] And in response to the question, What would be your attitude if you become a candidate and the opposition parties do not participate in the presidential election, Özal said, "That I do not know. But, if, by engaging in such an act, they make it known that they do not attribute legitimacy to the Parliament then their own legitimacy would be open to question."

On 18 October 1989, Özal formally declared his candidacy for presidency. He did so only after conferring with some leading members of the ANAP. He ignored the views of more than thirty ANAP deputies who asked Özal not to become a candidate but to determine the candidate together with the other parties in the Parliament. These parliamentarians warned Özal that if he did not go along with their proposal, after his election disputes concerning his presidency would not come to an end, and such a conflictual situation would not bode well for the future of the democratic regime in Turkey.

The Özal Presidency

Özal was elected president on 30 October 1989. The next day, an editorial in an Ankara daily argued that the era of controversial presidency had begun. Indeed, from the very beginning, both İnönü and Demirel were resolved to have nothing to do with the president. As a first indication of this approach, the SHP and the DYP deputies did not participate in the presidential oath-taking ceremony in the Parliament. However, at least initially, İnönü was not inclined to keep the issue alive indefinitely. He said that neither the people nor they should constantly preoccupy themselves with the controversial nature of the presidential elections. In contrast, Demirel was not willing to let Özal off the hook so easily. He decided to hold a number of public rallies, and tell the people what had really happened.

From the inception of his presidency, Özal added fuel to the flames by acting as though he were working closely with the ANAP. He urged the party members to elect the new prime minister (Yıldırım Akbulut) as chair of the party at the party's next congress. The ANAP deputies readily complied with Özal's wish. Özal's partisanship–meddling in ANAP's internal affairs–began to harden İnönü's attitude toward him, too. İnönü came up with the following argument: While he was prime minister, Özal adopted an anti-secularist stance. Now it is not possible to assume that he, as president, represents the national will and unity. Furthermore, he now acts as the de facto leader of the governing party. Under the circumstances they could not have anything to do with him.

---

[3]Here, Özal's account of the presidential election is partly true: At the time, the AP and the CHP refused to elect the military's candidate (the then chief of the general staff, who had resigned from his post for this purpose) but then did elect a retired admiral.

Undeterred by such criticisms, Özal continued to maintain close relations with his former party. He frequently received groups of ANAP deputies and conferred with them on party affairs. The chair of the party organization paid regular visits to the presidential palace. And occasionally, Özal would not refrain from openly criticizing one of the other opposition parties.

This approach on Özal's part was coupled with his predilection for taking into his own hands matters in which he had special interest, even when, according to the Constitution, those matters had to be dealt with by the government. Initially, he paid particular attention to the economy.[4] Özal quickly established autonomous links with the relevant key ministers and bureaucrats, he received regular briefings on the economy at the presidential palace, and he announced the economic measures that were to be adopted. The next issue in which he played a relatively active role, although not on a continual basis, was law and order. When, for instance, the activities carried out by the separatist groups in southeast Turkey reached a critical level, Özal took the initiative: He convened the National Security Council and invited the opposition leaders to the presidential palace with the stated purpose of obtaining consensus on how to deal with the problem.[5] Then with the eruption of the Gulf crisis in August 1990, he began to play an active role in foreign affairs. In fact, he completely sidestepped the government; among other things, he conducted a telephone diplomacy with both President George Bush and Middle Eastern leaders. In the process, Özal forced the government and the ANAP deputies to adopt an active policy in the Gulf conflict, in spite of the apparent opposition of the Foreign Ministry and the military establishment.

Özal's dominance of the executive—on those matters in which he chose to be actively involved—created havoc in the government. There was much confusion and debate over the lines of responsibility. Consequently, within one year of Özal's assuming the presidency, the minister of finance and customs, two foreign ministers and the chief of the general staff resigned.[6]

Özal felt there was nothing improper in the way he conducted his presidency. He did not think he was overstepping his sphere of jurisdiction, because he thought the Constitution gave him wide powers; in this respect, Özal argued, the Turkish Constitution was very much like the [1958] French Constitution save on one or two matters. Because Özal also felt that he was fully qualified for the job and that he should not deprive the

---

[4]During his prime ministership, the economy was also his primary preoccupation. See Metin Heper, "The State, Political Party and Society in post-1983 Turkey," *Government and Opposition* 25 (1990): 321-333.

[5]I say *stated* because the opposition leaders later claimed that the real purpose behind the meeting was an effort on the part of the president to legitimate his presidency.

[6]During this period, the minister of defense also resigned; it was not, however, entirely clear whether he, too, had resigned for the reason noted here. The minister said that an intolerable lack of trust had developed on the part of Prime Minister Akbulut toward him, as had become obvious in a conflict between them concerning a local party issue.

nation of the opportunity to benefit from his long-accumulated knowledge and experience; he thought he should use all of the powers bestowed upon him by the Constitution. Nor did Özal think he was acting in a partisan manner. He elaborated: Just because he was the president, he could not bring his "views to an average"; he would go on expressing his long-held opinions; if what he said seemed to some as favoring the ANAP that was not because he discriminated between the political parties but because his views and those of ANAP would coincide, which was only to be expected since he had founded that political party and had been its chair for a long time; if another political party came to office he would still voice his opinions, and it would be up to those in government to pay or not to pay attention to his views. He also rejected the claim that he was usurping the powers of the prime minister by arguing that as head of state, he could not be expected to stay idle in the face of problems that threatened the vital interests of the country. He also claimed that when carrying out his duties, he always conferred with others, and although he expressed his views on matters that were the government's responsibility, the final decisions were always taken by that body.

However, the opposition leaders were not convinced, and in fact they ignored him. Following Özal's election as president, İnönü was prepared to let bygones be bygones, provided that Özal acted in a nonpartisan manner. Özal showed no intention of doing so, and İnönü joined Demirel and began accusing Özal of violating the Constitution (by his "partisan" approach and "doubling as prime minister") and again started to press for an early election, which both opposition leaders perceived as the only means to defuse "the fast developing political crisis in the country."[7] İnönü's criticism of Özal at first had a moderate tone; later, it reached a very high pitch. During the Gulf War, in response to Özal's adoption of an active policy (for instance, letting the United States use the jointly run bases in Turkey), and to his apparent readiness to participate in the war if Turkey's vital interests came under threat, İnönü went so far as to state that Özal should not be allowed to be engaged in a gamble for his personal political ambitions and that the Turkish soliders' blood cannot be spilled for furthering political ends.

In contrast to İnönü, from the very beginning, Demirel was not prepared to give Özal even the benefit of the doubt. When he was asked what his attitude toward Özal would be if as president he acted in a nonpartisan manner, Demirel responded by saying that if he now changed his attitude toward Özal's presidency, all the criticisms he had previously made regarding this issue would be invalid. He thus constantly argued that the impasse Turkish politics faced could be overcome only by removing Özal

---

[7]The opposition leaders were so incensed by Özal's partisan conduct of his office that they avoided all public ceremonies he attended. On one occasion when, by coincidence, they happened to attend the same ceremony, Özal and İnönü sat next to each other, but they did not even look at each other, let alone shake hands or talk.

from his post; this could be done by changing the Constitution. The Constitution would be amended by his own party, alone or in conjunction with the other opposition parties, following an early election. Thus, Demirel, too, insisted on an early election; he thought that in an early election, the ANAP would face a crushing defeat.

As the ANAP again refused to hold early elections, at a number of public rallies Demirel urged the people to raise their voices against the government. This strategy failed to bring the desired result, but the rallies further heightened political tension in the country. This tension became still more acute when the two opposition parties started talking of mobilizing "the organized sectors of civil society" against the government. These parties also contemplated the wholesale resignation of their deputies from the assembly as another tactic for forcing the government to hold early elections, but they put that idea aside temporarily when the Gulf War erupted. İnönü, however, continued to have sharp exchanges with Özal, whereas Demirel chose to have a period of neutrality.

As the sharp confrontation delineated above unfolded, Turkish politics plunged into another round of a legitimacy crisis. This crisis led to a situation in which every issue was evaluated by the opposition leaders, not in terms of its own merit but of whether the manner in which that issue was handled would legitimize Özal's presidency. If they concluded that such a possibility existed, they adopted an intransigent attitude. Among other things, it was for this reason that they refused to see Özal, even when he invited them for consultations during the Gulf War. In turn, Özal at times hesitated to take timely action (for instance, when the insurgency in southeast Turkey had escalated) lest he would again face severe criticisms. On other occasions, he acted without attempting to consult the opposition leaders, as he might have done in normal circumstances. Even when Turkey faced a war situation, the polity was badly divided; some supported Özal to the bitter end, whereas others were completely against him. Particularly toward the end of the period under consideration, neither side was prepared even to attempt a reconciliation. The only hopeful sign was the scaling down of the confrontation between Demirel and Özal.

What seems to be a more fundamental mending of fences between Özal and the opposition leaders started to take place at a later date, but not before a further deterioration of their relations. In June 1991, Mesut Yılmaz was elected chair of the ANAP, and soon after replaced Yıldırım Akbulut as prime minister. As premier, Yılmaz did not act in a subservient manner to Özal, as his predecessor Akbulut had done. He conceded that Özal had been "the spiritual leader of the ANAP" and that he would continue to benefit from Özal's experience and foresight; yet, he pointed out, it was time that the ANAP governments began to operate without Özal's day-to-day guidance. In fact, Yılmaz asked civil servants not to brief the president or to receive instructions from him without his knowledge. He wanted to see the president acting within his own sphere of jurisdiction and not transgressing on the government's prerogatives. When Özal again was not careful on this score, Yılmaz displayed a calculated patience; he handled his relations with Özal skillfully and almost always had his own way. However, even when at times their relations were strained, Yılmaz never questioned Özal's legitimacy as president; on the contrary, on that issue, he always defended the president.

In August 1991, the Yılmaz government decided to hold early elections (on 20 October 1991). Because both Demirel and İnönü were resolved to remove him from office, the outcome of the elections was critical for Özal. Basically for this reason, but also because he continued to feel he was morally responsible to the party he had founded, Özal began campaigning for the ANAP, although without referring to the party by name. He told the people that Turkey had made tremendous progress during the 1983-1991 period (the years the ANAP had been in office) and that voters should vote in such a way that progress would not be arrested.

Not unexpectedly, Özal's active propaganda on behalf of the ANAP drew sharp reactions from the opposition leaders, particularly Demirel. Demirel argued that in the elections, the opposition parties had to fight against the "Çankaya [the Presidential Palace] Party," too! He concluded that the upcoming elections were a "war of independence" from Özal.

Özal was again undeterred. He pointed out that nobody could stop him doing things he thought were in the best interests of his country. He challenged the opposition leaders' declarations that when they came to power, they would ask him to account for his deeds by claiming that he was accountable to God only. Özal said that he was even ready for an end like that of Adnan Menderes, who was prime minister in the 1950-1960 period, and was hanged by a court decision following the 1960 military intervention. Demirel retorted: "The President is talking in delirium; does he mean he will escape the country when we come to power?"

At the 20 October 1991 elections, Demirel's DYP and İnönü's SHP singly or together were unable to capture the two-thirds majority in Parliament necessary to amend the Constitution and remove Özal from the presidency. Still, as the leader of the party with the plurality of seats in the Parliament, and as one who had challenged Özal all along, Demirel felt compelled to immediately consult party leaders in the Parliament in order to find out what can be done concerning the presidency issue. After having talked with them he announced that there was an agreement in principle on the need to remove Özal from the presidency; all that was necessary was working out the details of removal. The issue, however, was not so simple; the religiously oriented Prosperity Party's leader, Necmettin Erbakan, seemed ready to give his support only in exchange for being included in the coalition government, but Demirel had no intention of including him. Demirel had rather disappointing working relations with him during the late 1970s when Erbakan, as the leader of the now defunct National Salvation Party, was Demirel's coalition partner.

At this juncture, Özal invited Demirel to the presidental palace to discuss matters pertaining to the forming of the government, well before he was supposed to do according to the constitutional traditions. Before inviting Demirel, Özal had made a rather conciliatory statement: "My era came to an end. During the 1987 election campaign as the then prime minister, I made certain promises to the people. So I had a moral responsibility to make good on those promises. We have just had new elections; now those who obtained a mandate from the people will rule. I will go on expressing my views; but it is up to the future governments to take them into account or not."

When he received the invitation from Özal, Demirel hesitated, then decided to go. His long years in the government and his memories of the harm bitter conflicts among the political elites had done to Turkish democracy in the past must have forced him to end his personal feud with Özal. He said that going to the presidential palace was difficult for him; but he must not let personal feelings direct state affairs. Rather defensively he added that he will go and see Özal because he did not wish to see a fight at the top echelons of the state apparatus. But that did not mean that he would stop trying to remove Özal from office. However, he did stop trying to topple Özal from power after their tete-à-tete at the presidential palace. It was reported that at the meeting, Demirel pointed out that the country faces critical times; the problem at hand can be solved only if everybody serves within his sphere of authority; Özal replied indicating that as the President he shall do whatever he is supposed to do according to the Constitution. At long last, Demirel had given up challenging the legitimacy of the presidency and Özal had promised not to meddle in governmental affairs.

Conclusion

The political tensions that troubled Turkey in the late 1980s, although they could ultimately be traced to the perennial cleavages that divide the state elites from the political elites, this time did not take the form of direct confrontations between those two groups. Instead, the conflicts of recent years essentially sprang from the efforts of the 1980-1983 military regime to effect a gradual transition back to democracy. With this goal in mind, the generals kept many pre-1980 political figures (including Demirel) from participating in the general elections that were held at the end of the interregnum in 1983. Özal escaped these restrictions, and his ANAP came to power. This led both İnönü and Demirel to think that Özal was no more than a pawn of the military, even though Özal's ANAP had distanced itself from the military more than had the other parties that competed in the 1983 general elections. When İnönü and Demirel's ire toward Özal is taken into account, along with the latters's occasionally inflammatory counterblasts and his high-handed style as president, it is easy to see why Turkish democracy suffered another round of a legitimacy crisis in the 1980s.

There is, however, reason for optimism, because Turkey's political leaders–although fond of invective and intransigence–have nevertheless shown flashes of prudence and the ability to learn from past mistakes. Cases in point include İnönü's initial patience with Özal, Demirel's restraint during the Gulf War, Özal's intermittently displayed concern for shielding the presidency from unnecessary controversy, and, most recently and significantly, glimmerings of harmonious politics following the 20 October 1991 elections.

Indeed, at the end of 1991, many people in Turkey thought that the Demirel of the post-20 October 1991 election era was a "reformed" Demirel– a wise and prudent statesman. For his part, İnönü, on the whole, has been a moderate leader. He becomes angry only when he is overly frustrated; however, he never carries a conflict to the bitter end. Özal had always strong opinions. Yet, perhaps grudgingly, he increasingly accepted the fact that in an essentially parliamentary system of government, such as the one in Turkey his prerogatives as president were necessarily limited. Turkey entered 1992 with at least a working relationship between its three top political leaders–a feat never achieved before.

16

Journalists as Champions of Participatory Democracy

Gérard Groc

Ideally, civil society is an entity free from the encroachments of the state. Mass media should reflect and, if necessary, defend the autonomy of civil society; it should provide a check on a political government–particularly an opportunistic one. However, mass media should not unnecessarily exploit and exacerbate popular resentments. In this chapter I address the question of whether the Turkish press could take on such a role.

An Overview

In Turkey, the evolution of the press, as with democracy, has been fraught with contradictions. Its history begins in 1831 with the publication of the first official newspaper, *Takvim-i Vekayi*. The press is, therefore, one of the oldest and most venerable institutions in the country. Throughout the vagaries of its evolution, its right to exist has never been questioned. It has acquired experience as well as some degree of credibility. It has also developed a keen sensitivity to the aspirations of the people. Westernization, which was the hallmark of the Kemalist period, largely facilitated the contact of the Turkish press with the presses of other countries and with developments worldwide. Moreover, throughout its history, talented journalists recognized and shared the value of independent thinking and helped to build a true journalistic tradition on their largely shared ideals.

The first Republican Constitution of 1924 included a clause on the freedom of expression (Article 77), of which the press seems to have been the most obvious–or at least the most regular–beneficiary. During the single-party years (1923-1945), however, the press was perceived as an instrument of government and was brought largely under governmental control. Newspapers were founded, following decisions from above, to serve the government or its loyal opposition; hence, newspapers functioned mostly as organs of a party, thereby projecting a particular ideology.

Having been created as partisan structures rather than as a natural extension of civil societal institutions, newspapers were geared to reflect political alignments. They would instinctively take a partisan line, a stance that proved fatal in the 1970s. Being deeply engaged in political debates, but sitting on the margin of social life, the Turkish press pushed itself into a corner because of its overriding desire to represent the intellectual and urban elites of Istanbul. From the start, but even more so under Atatürk, the press devoted all of its energy to supporting the "progressive" cause and ideals of Westernization, and it increasingly took on the role of a didactic intermediary between an idealized West and a society "in need of reform." Consequently, it kept its distance from the general public, whose "ignorance and obscurantism" it openly resented, and opted for expounding the positivism subscribed by the culture.

In fact, in the absence of anything worthy of the name *public opinion*, the press gradually acquired not only the role of conveyor of opinion but also of "source of opinion." It often acted as if it were the only interlocutor of government and, ipso facto, the sole and self-appointed, representative of civil society.[1]

Those ruling the country took advantage of this confusion on the part of the press. During the 1980-1983 period, the press was confronted by the military authorities and forced to accept rules it could neither read-ily conform to nor outright resist. The civilian government, formed in 1983, adopted a similar strategy in imposing its own will on the press. The ingredients of governmental control included continuing the policy of depoliticization (which posed particular difficulties for a press so deeply engaged in polemical confrontation), breaking up traditional solidarity groups in the journalistic world, and creating a competitive milieu with the other branches of the media–particularly television. The government's aim was to reduce the critical influence of a mainstream lobbying group, which had formed around Kemalist traditions and was sure of its legiti-macy as well as of international support. In the absence of any other form of public expression, this influential lobby group could become too consis-tent and too well-informed an adversary for a new political order that to some extent was still considered to lack in legitimacy.

In contrast to the situation that existed during the military rule, after 1983 the press reemerged not only as the champion to claim lost liberties but also as a potentially effective troublemaker for the government. It con-stantly attempted to reveal the government's weaknesses by revealing the disagreements within the Motherland Party (ANAP), criticisms directed

---

[1] Even recently, one could find examples of this confusion: A well-known journalist with the Istanbul daily *Hürriyet* also worked as a special correspondent for a leading British daily, thereby becoming a source of British public opinion on the Turks and of Turkish public opinion on the British. *Hürriyet* must have taken great pride in referring to the opinions of the English press.

at and the "mistakes" made by the government. To the government, the press represented the archetypical, and in a sense untouchable, survivor of the old order and the chief proponent of those very values and claims the government was anxious to circumvent by any means.

In response, the press put up a stiff resistance to the government and chose as its weapon an argument with which it could trap the ANAP government in its own game. Through concrete examples, it attempted to show that the democratic evolution of which the ANAP boasted, both within the party and in society, was superficial. The press's most effective tool in this conflict was that of enhancing the notion of participatory democracy, and in the process, it began to voice the particularistic aspirations and demands of some disparate civil societal groups.

Oddly, this particular pattern of resistance to the government in turn led to some fundamental changes within the press itself. Some segments of the press discovered a hard-hitting, and thus a rather effective, style, which it had not adopted previously. But since not all journalists and papers joined in the attack, this new aggresiveness also exposed the hitherto unrevealed heterogeneity of the press and, therefore, one of its weaknesses.

Is it valid to say that the crisis in the Turkish press in the 1980s was part of a general trend observed in all Western countries–one of a new sensationalism in some newspapers and increased competitiveness of television? To be sure, there was a similarity, but this alone does not explain the salient attitudes of Turkish journalists–their reactions to, hesitations over, and struggles against sudden and destabilizing developments. These developments, moreover, appeared to have been strongly supported by the ANAP governments, with the aim of inducing the press to abandon its previous modus operandi discussed further below.

The Changing Press

The 1980-1983 Period

For three years after the 1980 coup, the press represented practically the only expression of "public opinion," in part because the military-backed government took stern measures against various groups, a new constitution was prepared, and various reforms were implemented. During this period, the press faced great difficulties. The military, with its "state of siege" argument, blocked the democratic process by censoring virtually all freedom of expression.[2] Consequently, most of the newspapers directly connected with political groups disappeared. The government attempted to discredit the major newspapers in the public eye by holding them re-

---

[2]The 1982 Constitution is noteworthy for the clauses limiting dissemination of news: Article 26 (Liberty of Expression and Propagation of Ideas) bans the use of languages other than Turkish; Article 27 (Scientific and Artistic Liberty) proscribes the intent to modify Articles 1, 2, and 3 of the Constitution. (From the early 1990s on, the use of Kurdish was allowed.)

sponsible for the pre-1980 events.[3]

A second policy, less precise but more far-reaching in its implications, was the virtual depoliticization of public debate. The military undertook to enforce this policy by means of a series of constraints on the journalistic profession.[4] The depoliticization policy itself adversely affected the small local (or localized) press, which constituted a diverse group of papers that appealed to varied interests and streams of thought.[5] The local papers were later left alone after many had already disappeared. At the national level, a new sensationalist press appeared, of which the best-known examples were the Istanbul daily, *Tan*, and the Istanbul weekly, *Hafta Sonu*–both regarded as mediocre by most professionals, but each a real commercial success. The success of the Turkish boulevard press may have reflected a general trend experienced in the West, but its launching at this time also revealed the extent to which the military government had succeeded in turning public attention from politics to trivia by restricting freedom of public debate in the media.

A third and later change was the new phenomenon of a gradual takeover of the press by rich businessmen.[6] Not having any professional interest in journalism, businessmen-turned-publishers viewed the press primarily as a money-making business venture and used any means necessary for that purpose: cover girls on the front pages, belly dancers sent to readers' homes as prizes, offers of free books and encyclopedias, cars, and even apartments as prizes to be won in lotteries. This new approach to journalism marked

---

[3] In its 15 May 1988 issue, *Nokta* published a list of twenty-nine editors who were currently in jail or detained; some of these were sentenced to such terms as 661 or 748 years in prison. Also see *Cumhuriyet*, 15 January 1989.

[4] Here are a few examples of intimidation: (1) September 1982: An article on wheat producers led to the trial of *Cumhuriyet* on the claim that the paper was sowing disorder with its pessimism (acquitted); (2) May 1983: Nadir Nadi, owner of *Cumhuriyet*, was sentenced to two months and twenty days for "inciting youth to armed rebellion" (decision rescinded in September 1983); (3) November 1983: Metin Toker, another well-known name in journalism, was sentenced to three months in prison with no possibility of remission or appeal, for violating Decision 76 of the National Security Council (sentence deferred for four months); (4) December 1983: Four journalists from the ultraright-wing *Hergün* (which, furthermore, had been banned since 12 September 1980) were sentenced to twelve months in prison for insulting a former director of religious affairs; (5) 1 to 7 December 1983: *Hürriyet* was suspended for publishing the death announcement of a former Communist leader.

[5] *Milliyet* of 28 May 1986: "According to L. Akçan, President of the Anatolian Press Union, there is at present a total of 745 publications (391 dailies and 354 periodicals) published in 64 Provinces; over the last two years, 244 publications have disappeared."

[6] This style of journalism was initiated in February 1982 by two young businessmen. A new addition to the Turkish press was the daily *Güneş*, which brought the number of national dailies up to six. *Güneş* caused a splash on its first appearance. Its owners, Istanbul businessmen, put a great deal of money into building up an impressive editorial staff and acquiring advanced printing equipment. By offering the highest salaries on the market and paying "transfer" fees, *Güneş* gathered the best names in the Turkish press under its banner. The result was a combination of in-depth reporting, serious political commentary, scandals, and tabloid-type articles, in colour if possible, like most of the Turkish dailies. The Sublime Porte [the press district of Istanbul] will never be the same again, commented one professional. (*International Herald Tribune*, 10 March 1983).

the beginning of a process that led, for the first time in its history, to the domination of the Turkish press by business interests, as a result of which journalism was gradually transformed into a solely commercial venture.

These changes naturally led to tensions within Istanbul's Fleet Street and to a cutthroat competition in which the traditional press, or what remained of it, became vulnerable; faced with new and often untrustworthy competitors, it could not continue its old habits. Certain previously respectable newspapers were unable to stand on their own. *Günaydın*, for example, succumbed to the temptation of commercial rewards by turning to sensationalist journalism and was taken over by the owner of *Tan*. Others, on the verge of bankruptcy (e.g., *Milliyet*, allowed themselves to be bought by financial groups, and some diversified their activities–for instance, by publishing popular supplements and the like. Few among the "committed" newspapers managed to survive. These included *Tercüman* (supported since the 1960s by the financial backing of its businessman proprietor Kemal Ilıcak, and later kept afloat by the Bulvar group that have always come up with sensationalist news) and *Milli Gazete* (whose sales dropped from 20,000 in 1987 to 12,000 in 1988), both of which represented the right, and on the left *Cumhuriyet*, which for a long time made it a point of honor to continue its political line and had a circulation of about 100,000–in contrast to the first copies of *Tan* whose circulation was 700,000. But later, *Cumhuriyet* too, could not escape from diversifying its coverage and activities.[7] The only daily paper that survived this period relatively unscathed was *Hürriyet*, which did not regain its 1960s sales record of one million but which, by diversifying its news coverage and remaining on the whole a reliable and nonpartisan paper, held its status as a successful independent daily.

Still, by the end of this period, the press was effectively destroyed. The aims of the military government campaign had been to skim off undesirable opinions, to break up the internal solidarity in the journalistic world, and to introduce a new concept of the press. It is hardly surprising that the bulk of the press, therefore, aligned itself with the opposition. We must add, however, that having been viewed as victims of authoritarianism, these spokespersons for public liberty enjoyed broad, if tacit, recognition as the sole surviving standard-bearers of democracy under trying circumstances.

Confrontation with the ANAP Government (1983-1991)

After the formation of a civilian government in 1983, the relations between the press and government became even more complex following the emergence and progressive crystallization of the antagonism between them. Three developments must be mentioned that when viewed simultaneously, seem to work at cross-purposes to each other but that in fact

---

[7]See Orhan Koloğlu, "La Presse turque, evolutions et orientations depuis 1945," in *La Turquie en transition*, Altan Gökalp, ed. (Paris: Maisonneuve, 1986), pp. 184-185.

combine to produce the desired result of weakening the independence of the press. First, return of the civilian regime lessened the pressure from the military and somewhat improved the margin within which the press could maneuver. Censorship was still exercised by means of military tribunals; however, the military gradually softened its intransigence and its desire to closely control the press.[8] Second, the press found itself pitted against other media and was particularly threatened by impressive advances in television.[9] The third development was the growing conflict between the press and the new government.

A broad segment of society, including the plurality of the voters, viewed Prime Minister Özal as one who had disassociated himself from the previous regime and who had even imposed himself on the military hierarchy. However, the mainstream press joined the bulk of the intellectuals and opposition politicians in claiming that Özal was the direct descendant of the authoritarian period from whose shadows he emerged.

From the start, the success of his election and his personal views permitted Özal to appear as the reformer of the old order, who aimed to liberate social, political, and economic life from the weight of the state, from which society had long suffered. Özal's ANAP, at least until 1987, had the widespread backing of the public and consequently had an absolute majority in the Parliament. As such, it could easily translate its reform projects into reality. And from the start, Özal was able to take initiatives against the will of the military, as elaborated in Chapter 3. These initiatives were considerably more important than the critical articles in the mainstream press were prepared to recognize. For instance, the government party was able to get its candidate elected as the speaker of the Parliament, defeating the candidate preferred by the military. The Özal government, made up of factions of different persuasions, claimed it represented the "central pillar" (*Ortadirek*), the members of which were presented as the main beneficiaries of the new policies.[10]

Still, the Özal government faced a number of dilemmas. It profited from the rules and regulations enacted during the previous military rule but from which it wished to distance itself. The party was based on a combination of moderate and extremist political orientations, which it used to trample on the ruins of the old parties; at the same time, it needed an image

---

[8] According to *Milliyet* of 15 February 1986, in 1985 and 1986, there were 294 proceedings against journalists and 160 judicial seizures. A detailed look, however, reveals that most of these resulted from actions taken preceding the return of power to the civilians in 1983: Sixty-one journalists were taken into custody; the prosecutor was able to press charges against twenty-six of them, and the rest were released because of insufficient evidence. For 1985, the respective figures were sixty-three and three.

[9] The evolution of the audiovisual figures is revealing. The number of television receivers doubled between 1980 (3.3 million) and 1984 (6.3 million), reaching about 7.2 million in 1987, and the number of radio sets increased from 4.2 to 5.7 million. (*İstatistik Yıllığı*, 1985, 1988).

[10] "Central pillar" was ambiguously used by Özal to refer to the entire range of economically productive groups, including workers, the salariat, and middle-class professionals and enterpreneurs.

as a party of reform. Consequently, the government went over the heads of the press to seek a direct relationship with the people and to secure their approval of the policies it pursued. The ingredients of the Özal government's program included depoliticization, an iconoclastic (in Kemalist terms)–that is market-oriented–economic policy, a social policy viewed by the radical secularists as reactionary, and a liberal stance concerning age-old traditions at the communitarian level. In view of these factors, we can conjecture, the government could not tolerate a press acting as a censor according to worn-out criteria. The government's intolerance was to be all the more intense, since, it now felt, it could reach people directly without the intermediation of the press.

Thus, the government began to accuse the press of total indifference to the processes of social and political emancipation it was bringing about and to its parallel efforts at dismantling certain structures of the Kemalist state. It accused the press of having nostalgia for the old order. The press responded by denouncing the hypocritical reference to democracy, pointing out that certain authoritarian arrangements remained intact and that the new policies, at least as far as the economy was concerned, had no popular support. In fact, what continued to be controversial was the claim by both sides to the true expression of popular aspirations, and this struggle reflected all of the ambiguities usually found in the terms *liberalization* and *democratization*–two concepts and processes that often traverse the same paths, that bring similar arguments to the surface, but that eventually lead to different outcomes.

The struggle went through several stages, but Özal's true strategy became apparent only in the years 1984-1985. He felt the newspapers were losing ground, because they were caught up in a new competition with the other media. Consequently, they were being gradually abandoned by advertisers.[11] He was careful not to curtail the written message, as the military had done, but adopted a more subtle strategy: He exerted financial pressure on the newspapers. By increasing or decreasing different

---

[11] From 1980 to 1986, different media received the following share of the advertising funds (as percentages):

Year	The Press	Television	Radio	Others
1980	51.0	34.2	3.4	11.4
1981	50.7	38.5	3.7	7.1
1982	52.1	35.8	4.2	7.9
1983	55.7	30.5	5.1	8.7
1984	48.2	39.9	4.1	7.8
1985	37.5	52.5	3.1	6.9
1986	33.2	58.6	2.5	5.7

Source: *1986 Reklam Harcamaları*, (Istanbul: Manajans Thompson, 1987), p. 24. Just in the month of March 1987, television attracted at least 8.08 billion liras in advertising on its two channels (*Cenajans'tan*, May 1987).

forms of subsidies, he accentuated the competition among the newspapers and made them gradually realize their vulnerability. As noted above, few newspapers succeeded in resisting the policy of sales promotion.[12] I should also mention some of the consequences of the competition among the newspapers: increasing the use of color, expanding the printing and distribution networks,[13] dumping advertising tariffs and sale prices, and the like.[14]

The first real assault on the press took place in 1985, with the introduction of the value-added tax (VAT), which was initially applied to newspapers at the exceptionally high rate of 10 percent but was later reduced to 5 percent, in line with all other products. In June of the same year, the government–which held the monopoly on the sale of paper–suddenly increased the price of paper by 49 percent,[15] the immediate result being that over the years, the price of a daily newspaper rose steeply.[16] Another device typical of the prime minister's policy was to require "naughty" magazines, such as the Turkish versions of *Playboy*, to hide their covers under a plastic cover, which, of course, caused a rise in costs, and cut their circulation by 50 percent.[17] Did Özal want to virtually strangle the press? Certainly not, but he wanted to prove that he could subdue it: Stubbornness on the part of the press in not undergoing the evolution he wished could lead to the erosion of its independence.

In a previous study,[18] I concluded that, using measured doses of pressure, the ANAP government gradually proved it was able to deal with the press. Özal managed to control the papers by manipulating production costs and by forcing the papers, which were increasingly subject to

---

[12]Figures published by the daily *Posta* show that in 1986, *Hürriyet* gave away fifty-two cars, followed by *Tan* with twenty-five. In 1985, *Milliyet* offered a fortnight's holiday to three hundred readers. *Tan* gave out five cash prizes, *Günaydın* four. The same year, *Milliyet* handed out more than four sets of encyclopedias, twelve villas, and three summer houses; *Hürriyet* distributed twenty-five manuals and brochures on various subjects.

[13]In Turkey, almost all newspapers are printed in Istanbul, İzmir, Ankara, Adana, and Erzurum.

[14]Such dailies as *Tan* have always managed to keep their sale prices below those of other newspapers. In February 1992, *Tan* was selling at 1,500 liras, whereas *Cumhuriyet*, *Milliyet* and *Hürriyet* had reached 2,500 liras.

[15]On 15 January 1989, the increase reached 61.9 percent.

[16]By way of comparison, in 1986, on average, one month of a daily newspaper (including Sunday papers) cost 4,500 liras, against a minimum wage of 30,000 liras. In 1984, the average monthly income in Turkey was 24,000 liras and in 1985, 26,000 liras.

[17]On 12 March 1986, a law was enacted on "Regulation of Publications Harmful to the Young," better known as *Muzır Kanunu*. On 20 February 1987, *Cumhuriyet* surveyed the year 1986 and learned that thirty-six actions had been brought against five dailies, ten actions against weeklies, and ten actions against monthlies. The set fine for the dailies could reach 350 million liras, according to a complicated calculation (varying from five to fifteen times the value of half of the average daily circulation of the highest-circulation paper). The law was softened for the small newspapers, whose fines were calculated on their own average circulations.

[18]Gérard Groc, "Aspects de la presse turque," Paper presented at the symposium Aspects de la Turquie Actuelle, Paris, October 1986.

variations in sales figures, to adopt short-term thinking. The newspapers, which were now quite expensive, could lose readers, and they did. As early as 1985, the considerable rise in the price of newspapers resulted in readers' reducing the number of papers they read everyday. The newspapers now became easy prey for businesspeople seeking an intellectual halo or a cultural patronage with tangible benefits. A dramatic example of the changed circumstances was the rise in early 1989 of a press magnate who had no previous connection with journalism. Having the financial means to acquire Haldun Simavi's large *Günaydın* and *Tan* Group in June 1988 for 80 billion liras, in January 1989 Asil Nadir took over the Gelişim Group, which included twelve different publishing houses that owned fourteen journals, including the famous *Nokta*, and published twenty-four encyclopedias. Toward the end of 1989, as a natural outcome of Özal's liberalism, this newcomer owned nine dailies–including three of the country's largest–and eleven magazines, all with national readerships; naturally, he had significant influence on the content of these publications.[19]

Reaction to the Changes

The only direct response to this evolution by journalistic circles was the autumn 1985 publication by the *Hürriyet* Group of a daily paper, *Hürgün*, whose virulent and incisive tone–set by left-leaning journalists– attempted to show the authorities that it was still possible to offer a critical view of the government, and even to level damaging charges against the government, while remaining within the law. This experiment, however, came to a sudden end after forty-five days of publication, with no explanation either to the general public or to the paper's employees. Generally speaking, with the exception of the powerful *Hürriyet* Group, none of the newspapers felt strong enough to attempt to reverse the trend chronicled here.

However, a subtle reaction did take place that produced a fundamental reorientation on the part of the press. For the first time, the press became involved in public debate, which was no longer exclusively confined to political polemics. The daily life of society was placed in the foreground of the news; the press went out of its way to reflect as faithfully as possible the conditions of life in different spheres of society, which it tried to uncover– among other ways–by means of survey research.

A range of innovations was introduced that affected even the layout of the newspapers. New sections were added to the papers. The economics pages, for instance, rose in importance during the military period, because they were the only possible outlet for criticism. After this period, the

---

[19] In *Cumhuriyet*'s case, one of the practical consequences was the start of the publication of a sports supplement on 7 May 1985. An interesting by-result, still according to this survey, was that the popular leftist newspapers were gradually turning into newspapers for intellectuals and more cosmopolitan readers (52 percent of readers spoke a foreign language), the liberal professions (46 percent), and computer users.

foreign news pages became special sections in almost all of the newspapers, because comparison was the best way to highlight the situation in Turkey.

A thirst for information in society progressively led different publications to develop supplements on a variety themes, responding to (or sometimes anticipating) new cultural, social, or sporting interests. Some daily papers began to release with their weekend editions a weekly magazine that attempted to reproduce the reporting style of the weeklies.

All in all, the main changes consisted of a more detailed search for news and an increased use of new tools. The newspapers themselves, anxious to measure their impact, felt the need to know their public. It was no coincidence that in 1985, both *Cumhuriyet* and *Hürriyet* carried out surveys to learn their readers' profiles, with the aim of better defining their relationship to their readers. At the end of 1986, the Piar/Siar Institute (a public relations and survey research organization) devised and carried out the first major survey, which was intended not only to measure the readers' affection for their usual paper but also the general attitude of the population toward all media. It also aimed to define the roles of different media in providing news.[20] The institute attempted to establish an accurate interpretation of the total press results, basing this not on 3 million daily *readers*, but on 15 million daily *readings*, which gave a theoretical result of four readers per copy.[21]

The major newspapers became more concerned with the quality of their news, both to set themselves up as independent interpreters of public opinion and to distinguish themselves from the banal tabloids, such as *Hafta Sonu* and *Tan*.[22] We should also note that the world of the press indirectly benefited from the purge of the universities in 1982-1983, because from that time onward, the press inherited a number of former university faculty, who brought to journalism their knowledge, intellectual perspective, and a deep commitment to social issues. Late Uğur Mumcu, an influential columnist who was a former academic, became a source of inspiration for these newcomers.

Also to be noted was the rising interest in this period in information technology which attempts to bring together all of the information on a particular subject, including scattered data from various sources. Whatever the motive, religion was one of the most discussed subjects in both *Cumhuriyet* and *Nokta*. The latter weekly also published numerous reports of varying allure on issues (often to do with sexual behavior) that were of questionable relevance to Turkey but whose merit lay in the fact that they dared to take up several novel topics and expose Turkish society to a frank

[20]The survey was systematically updated from September 1986 onward.

[21] This figure was obtained by balancing multiple readers of one copy of a newspaper with those who read several papers.

[22]For example, *Tan* was initially run by a handful of editors whose primary instrument was not a pen but, rather a pair of scissors aimed at lurid articles adopted from Western magazines.

discussion of subjects that had previously been considered improper. The newspapers now sensitized to finer analyses of the news but not always able to carry out such studies themselves, also began to report on surveys and studies undertaken by others on a host of subjects, such as education, leisure, the environment, and the like.

There also appeared more polemical, but still innovative, styles of news presentation–for example, using the newspaper as a vehicle for the public airing of various individual complaints against petty local autocrats and injustices perpetrated by them, which central authorities had failed to address. *Sabah* was the first paper to run such items, followed by *Hürriyet*. There is no need to underline the success of this type of journalism. In 1987, Chernobyl and AIDS, for instance, allowed the press to take on the role of an efficient and competent detective, compared to the dilatoriness and silence of the powers that be. Here, the press seemed to have realized that by improving its news gathering and reporting in a society avid for information, it had found an extremely effective weapon against the government–particularly against a government that, although declaring democratization as its goal and contributing to the spread of the concept, nevertheless did not always provide the means to achieve it. The press, happy to catch the government in its own trap, tried to be a new pole of attraction; it wanted to satisfy the citizen's legitimate curiosity and to redirect the reader's attention–for so long fixed on the state–to the performance of the government. The press offered the citizen a true opening to information, knowledge, taste, and culture–thus beginning to prepare the ground for the emergence of a civil society that was not dominated by a monolithic state.

The traditional press suffered greatly because of the sensational papers mentioned above. If the sensational papers began to enjoy a certain amount of success, it was because, for the first time in Turkey, they became accessible to a less demanding public and thus broke with the politically committed style of an intellectual, urban press. These newspapers have undeniably increased the usual reading public, a conclusion that is supported by the fact that *Tan* and *Sabah* have been the country's most popular newspapers. And it is not a foregone conclusion that, having become used to reading newspapers, the less demanding public will always remain interested only in the sensational.

By the beginning of the 1990s, the developments took on a new twist. The press, ever more boldened, played a critical role in bringing down the ANAP government; in the campaign leading to the October 1991 general elections the bulk of the press acted virtually as another opposition party. It bitterly criticized everything the ANAP stood for and asked for the further democratization of political life. In its eyes, the ANAP was the single most important obstacle to the consolidation of democracy in Turkey.

This view was shared by the True Path Party (DYP) and the Social Democratic Populist Party (SHP), which together formed the coalition government after the October 1991 general elections. Because both of these parties had been champions of democracy when they were in the opposition, and because the 1990s in general ushered in a new era of democratization–as reflected, for instance, in the Paris Charter, to which Turkey became a signatory–further liberalization of the press laws was now in the offing. In any case, by early 1992, the coalition government had adopted a tolerant attitude toward the press.

Conclusion

The press in Turkey played a critical role in the country's political development. From the nineteenth century on, journalists took their place among Turkey's leading elite groups. Consequently, in the turbulent Turkish politics, they became the proponents of competing and often hard-to-reconcile worldviews; thus, they found themselves in the midst of fierce political struggles. In the process, they became champions of democracy at all costs–a political stance that often brought them face-to-face with repression.

The post-1980 period was a replay of this scenario. During the 1980-1983 interregnum, the bulk of the press was the only opposition to the military-backed government. The press acted so despite the great odds (including legal prosecution) it faced. Journalists' confrontation with the central authority continued following the reinstallation of competitive politics in 1983, and at that time they greatly contributed to further democratization of the political life in Turkey. However, journalists' emphasis on participatory democracy placed them on a collision course with the ANAP governments, which stressed liberalism more than democracy.

The October 1991 general elections brought to power the DYP-SHP coalition, whose views on democracy differ little from those of the bulk of journalists; both seem to emphasize participatory democracy, at least in rhetoric. This bodes well for the freedom of the press; its implications for the consolidation of democracy which requires not only democratization but also prudent government, are, however, a moot point.

PART SEVEN

The State, Civil Society, and Democracy

17

Toward an Autonomization of Politics and Civil Society in Turkey

Nilüfer Göle

In terms of the state-society relationship, the post-1980 era has been a turning point in Turkish political development. During the 1980s, the autonomization of civil societal elements from the grip of the center–a process that started in the 1950s–became even more pronounced. This autonomization has, in fact, taken on a novel pattern. Whereas the *modernizing* elites of the earlier decades took as their basic mission the secularization of Turkish politics and the transmission of Western values to that polity and to society, the *technocratic* elites of the 1980s defined their goal less in terms of educating the people than of synthesizing Islamic values and pragmatic rationality.

A New Discourse

During the 1980s, political discourse tended to shift from confrontation to tolerance. Rather than questioning the legitimacy of the regime, debates centered on specific public policies. In other words, a search by political actors for a tacit contract on parliamentary democracy underscored the new political discourse.

The political dynamics of the 1960s were based on the confrontation between leftist and rightist ideologies. This conflict resulted in armed clashes between the two camps during the 1970s. However, from the early 1980s on, the political debate centered on policy rather than political ideology. Because of this new political contest, the leftist and rightist movements of the 1970s, which rejected the existing order, left their places to moderate social democratic and center-right parties.

This softening of ideological conflict was a significant development, because previously in Turkey differentiation and pluralism– whether economic, political, or cultural–had hardly been tolerated. Every attempt

213

on the part of civil societal elements to free themselves from the domination of the state had led to repression by the state. For example, the
growth of a market economy in the 1950s–that is, of an economic sphere
independent of the state–was not considered to be in the national interest
by the Kemalist and leftist intellectuals. Similarly, the leftist movements
(an ideological differentiation) that flourished in the 1960s were seen as
threatening the national unity and territorial integrity of Turkey.[1] The Islamic movements of the 1970s were also condemned as reactionary forces
standing in the way of progress. The military interventions of 1960-1961,
1971-1973, and 1980-1983 can in fact be perceived as state reactions against
the "unhealthy" autonomization and differentiation of economic, political
and cultural groups.

In the post-1980 period, a dialogue was established among the proponents of different ideologies. For the first time, Islamicists, leftists, and
liberals debated around the same table. These debates provided, symbol-
ically and literally, a context in which pluralism could take root. And in
the process, a quest for consensus, began.

It is undoubtedly possible to attribute these developments partially to
opportunism and expediency on the part of the politicians and partially
to the fact that at least in the early 1980s, the political elites had to steer
in difficult waters and consequently were careful not to rock the boat.
Whatever the intentions of the politicians may have been, we can note on
the basis of clear evidence that since the early 1980s, the political pendulum
has shifted from ideological combativeness and confrontation to a search
for pluralism and consensus. Moderating forces were always available to
step in whenever conflicts tended to intensify and effectively to prevent
the situation from getting out of hand.

Although in one sense the 1980s' decade could be called a period of
depolitization,[2] it was also one that witnessed the emergence of new political issues closely connected with the new social cleavages that were
formed in the 1980s. As ideological confrontations over systemic preferences (mostly over socialism versus capitalism) abated, conflict over
"grand" issues in the abstract were replaced by debates on more immediate problems. Issues such as pollution, public health, and tourism began
to be considered important items on the political agenda. Earlier, political
opposition had been characterized by total rejection of the system itself,

---

[1] These modernizing elites had been heir to a tradition, extending back to Ottoman times, of
oversensitivity concerning any possible disintegrative influences. See Şerif Mardin, "Power,
Civil Society and Culture in the Ottoman Empire," *Comparative Studies in Society and History*
11 (1969): 271.

[2] During this period, restrictions were placed on political participation and the expression
of different views. These restrictions included preventing political parties from establishing
auxiliary units and keeping interest groups from expressing their views on matters not
immediately related to their concerns. See İlter Turan, "Political Parties and the Party System
in Post-1983 Turkey," in *State, Democracy and the Military: Turkey in the 1980s*, Metin Heper
and Ahmet Evin, eds. (Berlin: Walter de Gruyter, 1988).

leaving little room for debate on specific policies and thus preventing the formation of public opinion around current issues–a sine qua non for a democratic polity.

The overriding tendency to pursue utopias was inspired by Republicanism, which offered a powerful example of the way in which utopias could be achieved tabula rasa. Only in the 1980s did future-oriented revolutionary political utopias lose their appeal, a change that permitted a more diverse spectrum of political participants. Women, ecologists, veiled students, and homosexuals and transsexuals appeared on the political scene and brought to the agenda such themes as environmental protection, female identity, and individual freedom. These themes, once ignored and even scorned by committed utopianists steeped in the protest tradition, now began to constitute–even if in a restricted sense–a bridge of sympathy between the new, "marginal" groups and the public at large. Unprecedented kinds of political action followed to further the new causes: women marching to protest being battered by men, people joining ecologists in demonstrations to save turtles, Islamicist women students resorting to hunger strikes against university dress codes that banned the "Islamic outfit" in the classroom, and homosexuals and transsexuals making public demands for protection of their civil liberties. These new protest movements and their proponents were neither written off as ridiculous, reactionary, or decadent nor considered trivial by the public at large.

New issues and their expression seem to have attracted broad public attention. Women's rights, for example, received wide coverage in the media rather than remaining a cause célèbre among a small group of activists. Similarly, the unexpected popularity of the novel *Kadının Adı Yok* (Woman Has No Name), written by Duygu Asena in the mid-1980s, reflected the public's interest (also possibly its curiosity) in the new theme of feminism as conveyed in contemporary fiction. Forms of expression underscored the contemporaneity of the issues raised. Even the neotraditionalism of Islamicist university students was projected in the form of modern political expression. The protesting women students in their Islamic outfit were far from a typical representation of traditional Muslim women: They have broken loose from the private sphere to which the fundamental orthodoxy of Islam was supposed to relegate women; they violated the principle of segregation of the sexes by choosing to attend the university alongside men; and finally, they had chosen to make public demands on the system as citizens. It is not a coincidence that a diametrically opposite group, homosexuals and transsexuals, also began to voice their claims in the public sphere in the 1980s.[3] Finally, the increasing popularity of the Green Movement can be said to reflect modern human beings' consciousness of the natural environment.

---

[3] In moralistic cultures, the demand for individual liberties comes first from the suppressed groups and concerns those issues most profoundly repressed and, therefore, hidden within the private sphere.

Toward a New State-Society Relationship

The change in the nature of political discourse seems to be related to a deeper change in the relationship between the state and society: It was the replacement of radical opposition by centrist alternatives that can be said to account for this fundamental change. However, macrolevel political variables alone do not provide an adequate illustration to help us to grasp the transformation, because authoritarian tendencies exist at the level of social actors themselves–that is, at the level of their *imaginaire social*.[4] In this sense, ideological-political configurations are closely interrelated with the utopias envisioned by social actors and with the nature of social relations among them.

Single Actor Syndrome

The decade of the 1970s in Turkey witnessed political fragmentation and ideological polarization, accompanied by political violence. Unlike many other countries, in which terrorism involved basically vertical state-society relations, in Turkey violence was horizontal–among social actors themselves–and therefore greatly hindered the flourishing of a civil society.

Authoritarian tendencies embedded in social struggles in Turkey can be traced to the "single-actor syndrome" and the "hypertrophy of political expressions."[5] Both phenomena are related to the fact that social actors, who consider their role in the evolution of their society to have been insignificant, feel alienated from that society. As a consequence, social actors tend to be detached from the established social order and identify themselves either with the utopia of a future society (leftist movements) or with the utopia of a past that never existed (rightist movements).

This escapism of the social actors, manifested in their efforts to distance themselves from contemporary reality, heavily influenced the formulation of political doctrines in Turkey. The absence of the present in their consciousness led to their failure to distinguish between ideology and utopia. Whereas ideology enables social actors to situate themselves within the present social orders, utopia is undetermined in space and time. Ideology is informed by reality, utopia by imagination. If utopia remains totally isolated from ideology, it will become rigid, a situation described by Paul Ricoeur as "the pathology of utopia."[6] In that case, social movements will give way to doctrines, and may even lead to violence, as happened in Turkey.

---

[4]Cornelius Castoriadis defines the notion of *imaginaire social* as the creative capacity of society. (*L'Institution imaginaire de la société* [Paris: Seuil, 1975], p.7.)

[5]For a study of engineers and ideology in Turkey from this particular perspective, see Nilüfer Göle, *Mühendisler ve İdeoloji: Öncü Devrimcilerden Yenilikçi Seçkinlere* (Istanbul: İletişim, 1986).

[6]Paul Ricoeur, "L'Histoire comme récit et comme pratique," *Esprit* 6 (1981): 163.

When utopia is not linked to ideology, the pattern of action is not derived from the present social relations; on the contrary, action is guided by authoritarian efforts to achieve a utopia characterized by perfect social and political order and absolute harmony. In the case of the leftist utopia, this is a classless society; in the case of the rightist utopia, it is a past golden age set in the future . In neither case is there a place for a differentiated society or social conflict resembling reality. The elements of diversity and conflict are introduced by ideology.

When a social actor identifies with the absolute values of an ideal society rather than with the existing patterns of social relations, he or she develops a condescending attitude toward other actors who identify with the existing social order. Differentiated social identities and horizontal social relations which characterize civil society, are rejected by social actors who identify with utopian values. The prevalence of a utopian orientation in society leads to the single-actor syndrome, which characterized Turkey in the 1970s, as did the hypertrophy of political expressions that dominated, if not completely suppressed, the social ones.

Catharsis and Pluralism

Centrifugal forces may cause the disintegration of civil society, which, in turn, may call for direct intervention by the state. The 1980 military intervention in Turkey enabled the state to suspend the autonomy of the political system and impose itself on society in the name of national unity. Attempts were made to legitimize this repression by making reference to the major themes of the early Republican period–particularly to nationalism and secularism. Contrary to its basic motives, the military intervention served as a catharsis; it constituted a watershed in the center-periphery relations in Turkey. Thereafter, the gravity of responsibility for social engineering began to shift from the state elites to the political elites and social actors.

Thus, the relative autonomization of the political system and social sphere from the domination of the state elites has characterized the new era in Turkey. The separation of these spheres had its root in the 1950s, when the Democrats were in power. Since then, the developments toward a market economy, the establishment of professional organizations, and the birth of a working class movement have all contributed to the emergence of a distinct social sphere.

Since the interregnum of 1980-1983, political elites and social actors have striven to redefine the relations among the state, politics, and society. The first step was the relative autonomization of the political system. The success scored by the Motherland Party (ANAP) in the 1983 general elections showed how the electorate actively responded to even the smallest democratic margin permitted by the military. At that time, of the three political parties that were allowed to compete, the ANAP was considered to be the only one that was opposed to the military. And, once in power, the ANAP began dismantling the state by its policies of decentralization of government, privatization of the state economic enterprises, and reorientation toward a market economy.[7]

The development of liberal, Muslim, and leftist movements demonstrated the basic dimensions of the autonomization of civil society. The liberal discourse, which was rediscovered and became fashionable after 1983, developed simultaneously with a market economy. Whereas during the 1950s the pro-private-sector policies were introduced mainly by the political elites, during the 1980s liberalism took the form of an entrepreneurial spirit among the people themselves. We can speak about the salience of market values even in the absence of a genuine market economy when we witness enterpreneurs trying to carve out for themselves an economic space independent from the state. The transition in Turkey from a Jacobin tradition to one based on the recognition of *homo economicus* led to the emergence, on the political-cultural level, of pragmatic values.

The kind of liberalism that took rise emphasized neither liberty in a more general sense, nor the autonomy of the self in Kant's sense of the "self-determining" individual, but rather the separation between the realm of the state and that of society. More specifically, because liberalism in Turkey did not imply individualism, it basically led to the separation of economics from politics. As a result, it also led to a search for microlevel solutions, pointed to the need for decentralizing the state's power, and served as a catalyst to project pragmatic values into political culture.

Islamicist movements constituted another dimension in the development of an autonomous societal sphere. It would be oversimplification, if not reductionist, to consider them exclusively as a reaction to modernity. It is important to remember that in most Muslim countries, the resurgence of Islam was related to the modernization process. Islamicist movements did not merely involve fundamentalism; they also allowed political participation by new social groups that began to experience upward social mobility and, for the first time, attempted to acquire an urban identity. The Turkish case followed this general pattern.

If the liberal movement represented the economic dimension of the autonomization of civil society, the Islamicist movement represented the cultural dimension. Because it is mostly derived from a traditional understanding of ethics, the Islamicist movement challenged the idea of a unilinear model of progress that was cherished by the modernizing elites.

The leftist movements of the post-1980 period constituted yet another dimension of the autonomization of social groups. The leftist approach during this decade was less utopian and more ideological; protest was pragmatic and not visionary. Other social movements–such as those of the ecologists and the feminists as well as homosexuals and transsexuals–were

---

[7]See Metin Heper, "The Motherland Party Governments and Bureaucracy in Turkey, 1983-1988," *Governance* 2 (1989): 457-468.

similar in nature and further contributed to the emergence of truly diverse identities in civil society.

Political Parties in the Post-1980 Era

Turkish politics in the 1970s was marked by increasing polarization, leading to the erosion of the center. The two major parties of the period, the Republican People's Party (CHP) and the Justice Party (AP), shifted their ideological orientations further to the left and the right, respectively, in order to keep their supporters from being proselytized by their radical rivals.[8] The divergence of ideological orientations was reversed in the 1980s, and the dynamics of political competition became governed by a realignment of ideologies toward the center. The centrist right was brought to the fore as a result of new values and new cadres introduced by the ANAP.[9] As ideological restructuring took place, political discourse shifted from a combative to a more tolerant tone: Pragmatic values were introduced, and a synthesis of market economy and Islamic values was attempted.

The ANAP's mode of political action encouraged consensus rather than confrontation. The party placed emphasis on moderation and during the 1983 and 1987 general elections, staged colorful, but inoffensive, political propaganda campaigns. The ANAP candidates clasped their hands over their heads and tried to give the impression of a unified Turkey.

Research conducted in 1987 has shown that the idea of a consensual society propagated at the time by the ANAP was well received by the people.[10] The electorate seemed to have enthusiastically received the slogans of "social harmony" and "let us not return to the pre-1980 period." ANAP's success could be attributed to, among other things, its ability to promote itself as a new party that was above the ideological divisions of the previous period and that offered social peace.

Social harmony did not mean depoliticization; rather, politics was to be conducted in a different style. For example, in a village, people of opposite political convictions could now patronize the same coffeehouse, which was inconceivable during the 1970s. When engaged in a politically "hot" debate, the people now often managed to remain calm throughout.

---

[8] Turan, "Political Parties and the Party System in Post-1983 Turkey," pp. 66-67.

[9] Üstün Ergüder and Richard I. Hofferbert have underlined the similarity of the ANAP to many Western right-of-center parties and have argued that the ANAP neutralized and reintegrated antisystemic tendencies. See Üstün Ergüder and Richard I. Hofferbert, "The 1983 General Elections in Turkey: Continuity or Change in Voting Patterns," in *State, Democracy and the Military: Turkey in the 1980s*, Heper and Evin, eds., p. 99.

[10] I carried out a qualitative study in several cities–İzmir, Istanbul, Manisa, Gaziantep, and Erzurum–on the ideological conceptions of the voters belonging to the two major parties, namely, the ANAP and the SHP. This study was followed by a quantitative survey. The present account is derived from these two studies: "Anavatan Partisi Seçmen Davranışları Araştırması," July 1987, typescript; "Seçmen Davranışları Araştırması," June 1988, typescript.

All in all, the people seemed to learn quickly, a development that boded well for the consolidation of a pluralistic regime.

The liberal movement was interpreted by the ANAP in terms of microlevel solutions to economic and social problems. The ANAP adopted a policy-oriented rather than a politics-oriented approach; it did not define its identity in terms of "big" issues. In a similar fashion, the electorate explained its support for this party in terms of services rendered, not in terms of ideological convictions. Such concrete policies as the value-added tax (VAT) rebate, emphasis on municipal services, and application for full membership in the European Community seemed to be of primary importance for the electorate, whereas conservative values were relegated to the private sphere of the family.

As a result, the relations between the people and political parties underwent profound changes. The people came to consider their relationship with political parties in terms of a simple give-and-take;[11] they no longer took their party affiliation as a Catholic marriage. Floating votes increased.

Parallel to these developments, the image of a popular politician also changed. The majority of the people now preferred an "entrepreneurial politician" (işbitirici politikacı)–a politician who managed to get things done fairly quickly–to a "politician of conviction" (dava adamı). As prime minister in the 1980s, Turgut Özal provided an outstanding example of an entrepreneurial politician, whereas Süleyman Demirel (chair of the AP and prime minister before 1980, the chair of the True Path Party (DYP) from 1987 to 1993, and currently president) was considered to be a politician of conviction par excellence.

The ANAP also attempted to introduce a synthesis between a market economy and Islamic values. The party was defined as "conservative progressive," which meant it showed loyalty to Muslim cultural values along with an orientation toward a Western pattern of development. Elsewhere, I have referred to the ANAP leaders as "Islamicist engineers."[12] many of them personally held traditional Islamic values regarding the individual, family, and society; but because of their professional backgrounds, they adopted the norms of Western rationality.

Thus, the ANAP's restructuring of the Turkish center-right was realized through a combination of a moderate political discourse, a pragmatic engineering ideology, and conservative social values. Toward the end of the 1980s, whether the ANAP would remain as the party of the center-right right seemed to depend on its capacity to govern effectively, as well

---

[11] Üstün Ergüder has shown how by emphasizing tangible results, the ANAP attempted to radically change the relations between the government and citizens, especially at the municipal level. See Üstün Ergüder, "Decentralisation of Local Government and Turkish Political Culture," in Democracy and Local Government: Istanbul in the 1980s, Metin Heper, ed. (Walkington, England: Eothen Press, 1987).

[12] Nilüfer Göle, "Les Ingénieurs islamistes: une nouvelle forme de modernité turque?" Paper presented at the conference Horizons de Pensée et Pratiques Sociales chez les Intellectuels du Monde Musulman, Fondation Nationale des Sciences Politiques, Paris, 1-2 June 1987.

as on its internal unity. The party has often been seen as a "superficial" (and thus a transient) one, embodying the sharply divergent political tendencies that were formerly represented by the CHP, the AP, the National Salvation Party, and the Nationalist Action Party. Religiously conservative and ethnic-right elements had greater control at the grass-roots level; the leadership group, many members of which adhered to liberalism, had less support within the party. Toward the end of the 1980s, the liberal leadership group made strenuous efforts to have greater control over the party organization.

Following the March 1989 local elections, at which the party fared very poorly, a soul-searching began as to whether the party should place greater emphasis on a liberal-centrist identity. From June 1991 on, under Mesut Yılmaz's leadership, the party's liberal-conservative image was maintained, but the religiously conservative faction became somewhat weakened.[13] In the October 1991 general elections, the party came in second after the DYP; it fell from government but proved not to be a transient political entity. The DYP, the other center-right party, appeared to be better organized and to have a more homogeneous structure under Demirel's leadership. Until after the October 1991 general elections, the party stayed with its old conception of politics. It continued to place emphasis on regime issues and did not contribute to the emergence of new parameters in politics. Following the elections, however, Demirel suddenly adopted a rather conciliatory political stance, as elaborated in Chapter 15. The Social Democratic Populist Party (SHP), the DYP's coalition partner following the October 1991 general elections, was led by the moderate and suave Erdal İnönü, although in many ways the SHP resembled its predecessor, the CHP: elitism is dominant in the "social-democratic" SHP, which is also riven with internal conflict between İnönü and former Secretary-General Deniz Baykal. Still, in the early 1990s, both DYP and SHP leaders adopted the conciliatory styles of politics that had been started by the ANAP in the 1980s. At the 1991 general elections–alongside the ANAP–the DYP, the SHP and the Democratic Left Party, also conducted lively, but inoffensive election campaigns.

Conclusion

The post-1980 era in Turkey was a turning point, because the state-induced modernizing movement (Westernization), which had started in the mid-nineteenth century and had become institutionalized during the 1920-1980 period, virtually came to an end as the leading political paradigm. With the relative autonomization of economic activities, political groups, and cultural identities, an autonomous societal sphere began to develop,

---

[13]This was achieved by not placing some members of this faction in electable spots on the party lists in the October 1991 general elections.

and the focus has increasingly shifted from the state to society; consequently, the modernizing elites began to lose their power to transform the
society from above, and were increasingly replaced by more representative
elites. Paradoxically, the latter were mostly technocrats who belonged to
the center-right political parties. Their prevalence resulted basically from
their attempts to reconcile technological change with traditional values, an
attempt that paved the way to politics of harmony, an essential ingredient
for the consolidation of democracy.

18

Prospects for a New Center or the Temporary Rise of the Peripheral *Asabiyah?*

Faruk Birtek

I begin with the assertion that whether the Turkish elections of 1950 constituted a democratic revolution still depends on how the forces and processes it unleashed might develop in the future. The tone of the 1990s will be a significant determining factor. The crucial question is whether the republic's institutional structure and the principles of democratic politics are ultimately compatible.

My view is that Turkish political institutions are currently on the verge of a possible radical restructuring that would mark 1950 as a rupture with the past. I see an emerging trend toward political reconstruction that will radically alter the traditional center-periphery rift in the Turkish polity.[1] If this trend is not realized, the prospect of forging a new consensus, a new political grammar, and a new forum for political discourse will once more be limited by the rise of a *peripheral asabiyah*[2] and the "authoritarianization" of the center. In the latter case, the more the periphery becomes politically active, the more the center will respond by asserting its administrative, rather than its political, identity, thereby reducing the possibility for flexibility and change.[3] The state would then rapidly become isolated, its social

---

I am grateful to Binnaz Toprak for her insight and contribution to the development of this chapter and to Carol Bertram.

[1] On this center-periphery rift, see the articles by Şerif Mardin, "Ideology and Religion in the Turkish Revolution," *International Journal of Middle East Studies* 2 (1971): 197-211; and "Center-Periphery Relations: A Key to Turkish Politics?" *Deadalus* 102 (1973): 169-190.

[2] For the concept *asabiyah* (literally 'good solidarity') as a peripheral political configuration based on closeknit ties, see F. Gabrieli, *Encyclopedia of Islam*, 2d. ed. (Leiden: E.J. Brill, 1960 [1954-], p. 681.

[3] Faruk Birtek and Binnaz Toprak, "The Conflictual Agendas of Neo-Liberal Reconstruction and the Rise of Islamic Politics in Turkey: The Hazards of Rewriting Modernity," *Praxis International* 13 (1993): 192-212, discusses in detail how "administration" might overtake

structure segmented. With increased distance among social groups, there would be a reversion to a sort of Durkheimian "mechanical solidarity," which would reduce political activity to the satisfaction of short-term interests, further reducing the prospects for the development of a consensual democratic polity.

Centrism in the Early Republic

From its inception, the Turkish Republic's centrism has been at once its great virtue and its fundamental weakness. Like the French Third Republic, which was shaped and subsequently dominated by the Radical Socialists, the Turkish Republic's formation between 1923 and 1950 was dominated by the Republican People's Party (CHP). Notwithstanding the most obvious parallel between the cases– namely the dominance of Durkheimian principles[4] there is one critical difference: The CHP came into its own in 1924 only by eliminating what little representational political structure had existed before. The CHP's strategy sowed tension between the Republican institutions it helped to form and the concept of representational democracy.

One defining principle of the Republican state was its radical secularism. In the absence of social revolution, this radicalism served only to increase the center's isolation from the already estranged periphery.

The root causes of this separation can be found in the fact that the CHP's radical secularism drew part of its inspiration from the Enlightenment tradition. The pagan nationalism of post-Enlightenment Europe–especially France, which had severed the ties between church and state–was incorporated into the official ideology of the early republic. Of equal importance was the new optimism that dominated Europe, at least until World War I. This attitude advocated social and political progress through a positivist pursuit of science, which, it was hoped, would replace God-centered politics with an enlightened public mind. Thus, the concept that citizenship was acquired through membership in the nation, and not through ethnic or religious affiliation, became a central tenet of the new vision in Turkey. Republicanism assumed that the particularist notion of ties based on kin, family, religion, and ethnicity would give way to universalist norms that would integrate Turkish culture with Western civilization.

Although republicanism envisioned membership in a universal international culture, its Durkheimian vocabulary made no allowance for the Muslim communal vestiges of Turkish culture. Accordingly, the legislation enacted in the first two decades of the republic was designed to replace Islamic communalism with a new mode of social solidarity constructed along the lines of progress. The French model, especially the form it took

---

"politics."

[4]See inter alia Mardin, "Ideology and Religion in the Turkish Revolution."

under the Third Republic laicism, was adopted as the mainstay of official ideology.

It is obvious that such a radical reorientation would provoke a reaction. The rebellion of 1925 could therefore be considered the Turkish Vendée. It is impossible to judge whether the rebellion reflected popular opinion; yet, when the republic crushed the rebellion, it merely succeeded in intimidating and not eradicating Islamicist currents as the radical Republicans had hoped. Islam retreated from the public arena but remained a dynamic force in popular culture and gained the potential to influence future opposition to the republic by all peripheries.

Several factors explain the strength of Islamic ideas in Turkey. One often-mentioned contention is that secular ideologies have had only limited success in replacing religious faith as a cohesive force. This argument is frequently applied to the case of Kemalism. This new state ideology, based on pagan nationalism and emphasizing Turkey's eventual integration into Western civilization, was unable to establish itself with most of the population as a viable alternative to traditional Islamic principles.[5] I think this failure had to do with the specific sociopolitical context of Kemalism and not with its substance.

In practice, the Kemalist state–in terms of both political organization and class structure–had to remain nonmobilizational and antiparticipatory. Social mobility and membership in the urban and semiurban professional middle class (in particular, teachers, judges and state officials) depended on participation in the expansion of the Kemalist state. In turn, the achievement of higher social status necessarily involved the rejection of local hierarchies, organizations, and traditional ties. Social ascent, at least ideologically, was thus based on universalist institutions of the *Gesellschaft* society promoted by the radical republic.

This structural foundation meant that Kemalist ideology found its supporters among the classes that would benefit *not* from mass mobilization but from the expansion of state authority. The CHP's viability in the countryside rested on its ability to tap the political influence of rural elites and to project an urban image. As state officials, the promoters of the Republican ideology adopted a utopian vision of positivist social harmony.

In short, the republic was a clear rejection of the traditional *Gemeinschaft* society. There had been no social revolution; however, the CHP, basing its power on limited social participation and its ability to recruit a substantial part of the local elite, controlled the state by distancing the center from– rather than attempting to transform or incorporate–the cultural periphery in the countryside.

---

[5] Cf. Faruk Birtek,"The Turkish Adventures of the Durkheimian Paradigm: Does History Vindicate M. Labriola ?" *Il Politico* 61 (1991): 107-146.

The Challenge to Centrism: 1950-1980

By 1950, the monolithic, nonrepresentative state structure created by the CHP could no longer contain the considerable elite and middle class it had created. The postwar rise of liberal democracy on the international stage fueled the discontent of the diverse urban population. The CHP's timid, belated efforts to penetrate the countryside and establish ties with the peasantry could not be put into full effect because of the schisms within the party itself. The monolithic political structure which had emerged from the center's revolutionary mission and later from its "armed neutrality" in response to the atmosphere of international war in the early 1940s, had served its purpose. An increasingly diversified social order now posed a challenge to the raison d'être of the initial étatist policies.

In 1946, despite the CHP government's strong opposition, an economic congress was convened under the auspices of the mercantile and industrial chambers and associations of Istanbul. For the urban economic interests of the late 1940s, the question had become how to transform the center to their benefit. In defiance of the CHP government, the intelligentsia and urban professional middle classes supported the congress. This was an important show of force by the new urban groups that had emerged in the center and that now expressed their intention to transform that center.[6]

It is true that the opposition had not wanted to abolish the role of the state in economic policymaking. The congress saw the government's role as the coordinator of economic activity rather than as a direct player. This was the view expressed by the chair of the Istanbul Industrialists' Association. Direct state intervention in the economy, it was argued, was a primary cause of inefficiency. The congress recommended that the state play an active role in agriculture and rural development, transposing étatism to the countryside.

The opposition within the center as expressed by this congress had a significant impact on the younger cadres of the CHP. They shared the urban-based norms of respectability and positivist legitimacy and sympathized with the congress's arguments. The democratic elections of 1950 came about as a direct result of this opposition, which could not be easily dismissed or repressed by the CHP. Moreover, in the new postwar international political order, freely held elections would give Turkey added leverage with the West to offset mounting Soviet pressures.

The years between roughly 1950 and 1954 offered a crucial opportunity for Turkey to progress toward democracy, but this chance was ultimately missed. The urban opposition, which had so radically undermined the CHP's self-confidence and dominated public opinion, could not sustain its own momentum. By 1954, the new regime was largely in the hands of

---

[6]For an elaboration of this view and of how the Turkish economy might have traveled a road similar to Italy's, see Faruk Birtek, "The Rise and Fall of Etatism, 1930-1950," *Review* 7 (1985): 407-438.

the nonurban elite, which was composed of families that had come into their own after World War I in the western, more developed agricultural regions. Eastern areas developed only gradually from the 1970s on.

Had the urban bourgeoisie been able to present a united front, the republic would have been transformed. The chasm between the center and the periphery would have been gradually displaced as the defining paradigm of the Turkish political system, and 1950 would have been seen once and for all as the democratic watershed. The subsequent development of the Turkish economy and its position in the postwar international economic order might also have been different from what actually ensued.

Instead, the new government of the Democratic Party (DP) took shape as a party of provincial notables. The economic boom following the Korean War reversed the trend toward urban economic development, thus reinforcing the existing rubric of rural relations. The countryside was therefore not transformed according to the structural dynamics emanating from the urban centers, as both the CHP and the urban bourgeoisie had envisioned, and Western economic priorities were first realized in a rural context.

Turkish industrialization in its postétatism stage thus originated in the context of agricultural exigencies, expressed within the structure of the prerepublic communalist (*gemeinschaftlich*) society. Industrialization in an urban context only began two decades later, and it was heavily influenced by protectionism and import substitution. The delay in transforming the traditional rural economic structure, and the demographic imbalance due to high rates of childbirth in the urban areas, perhaps accounted for this uneven economic transformation. The increase in rural wealth in the 1950s therefore had two fundamental consequences for Turkey. First, it reinforced preexisting class relations. Second, having limited the economic emphasis to rural development and shaped industrial development according to agricultural needs, it left Turkey in a foreign exchange trap when world agricultural prices fell.

The emerging pattern of world economic integration created a category of half-developed economies stuck in a perennial state of "takeoff," in Walt W. Rostow's[7] terminology. For Turkey, the new pattern gave the rural town an advantage over both village and metropolis. It reinforced the position of the gateway to the countryside, extending its power into villages, as well as foreclosing urban political influence. The town became the true nest of the new *asabiyahs*, reinforcing the Turkish town's traditional role as the anchor of cultural conservatism.

Political change has not been entirely absent since the 1950s, but changes have only taken place in each of the disjointed contexts of village, town, and metropolis. I suggest that a new political ecology has emerged in the past twenty years due to economic factors, notwithstanding the absence of transformation of the overall structure. This political ecology, cast in the

[7] See Walt W. Rostow, *The Stages of Economic Growth: A Non-Communist Manifesto* (Cambridge: Cambridge University Press, 1966.)

mid-1950s, constructed the framework for the democratization of Turkish political life in the past four decades, as demonstrated clearly in the recent divisions of the political spectrum.

The Old and the New in the Post-1980 Polity

Economic transformation, limited by an unchanging, rural-centered framework, caused the disjointed development of the periphery. If the center-periphery dichotomy had been broken after the 1950 elections, a political ecology might have emerged that was based on class, for example.

In this segmented world, the only issue that could elicit a common political élan took the form of extreme nationalism.[8] This was basically due to the fact that with the rapid development of the economy in the 1970s, each segment had developed distinct economic policies and related political goals.

The ability to overcome the dichotomy between the center and the periphery required a political program that would appeal to all segments of society. In the 1980s, the town became the cultural linchpin of the segmented political scene, providing the only environment in which political transformation might be achieved. By transforming the nature of the town, the political agenda of the 1990s might be able to overcome the political segmentation. The manner in which that transformation is achieved will serve largely to address the critical questions of the current investigation: Whether the center-periphery dichotomy will be transcended, whether the 1950 elections were indeed the beginning of a democratic revolution, and whether the Republican institutions and democratic processes will achieve a stable synthesis. The central question to be pursued is whether the 1990s will be the decade of constructing a new institutional center or simply that of maintaining the dominance of the peripheral *asabiyah*.

A democratic republic, in our context, will have emerged when social location is no longer a result of political choice. The republic, in its progressive optimism, has become the universal terrain in which democracy is an integrative and not a divisive force. Thus, the agenda of the 1990s will either, in its success, prove itself as the retrospective savior of 1950 or, in its failure, condemn the 1950 elections as another episode of the peripheral *asabiyah*'s intrusion on its antimonious center.

---

[8] Cf. Emile Durkheim, *The Division of Labor in Society* (New York: Free Press, 1964), for the discussion of "segmented" structures and of how various social movements would more likely arise in the conditions of "mechanical solidarity."

PART EIGHT

Conclusion

19

Trials and Tribulations of Democracy in the Third Turkish Republic

Metin Heper

Since the installation of a multiparty regime in 1945, Turkish democracy has tended to display institutional monism. The bureaucratic, military, and academic–that is, the state–elites have considered themselves responsible for safeguarding the long-term interests of the community. According to them, politics had to be carried out in conformity with the norms they set. In their view, Atatürkism as an ideology–that is, as a political manifesto– constitutes the parameters for politics.

Thus, the 1961 and, to a lesser extent, the 1982 Constitutions, aimed to legalize this institutional monism. The former attributed the guardianship role to the state elites, who were based in the Constitutional Court, the Council of State (the Turkish version of France's *Conseil d'Etat)*, the National Security Council, and the higher institutions of learning. The latter gave this function to the president and the National Security Council.[1] The arrangements so effected could not be considered to be institutional pluralism, because the state elites felt they had to have the last word on all matters they considered vital to the long-term interests of the community. The three military interventions in 1960-1961, 1971-1973, and 1980-1983, but particularly the first two, were conducted because–in the eyes of the bulk of these elites–the political elites had acted, among other things, against the Atatürkian principles.[2]

The political elites reacted to such a categorical stance on the part of the state elites by placing sole emphasis on the horizontal dimension of democracy, or participation. They did this without realizing that a viable democracy has a vertical as well as a horizontal dimension– that is, prudent leadership should accompany political participation. Not only did they

---

[1] For an elaboration, see Metin Heper, *The State Tradition in Turkey* (Walkington, England: Eothen Press, 1985), Chapters 4 and 6.

[2] Ibid., Chapter 6.

oppose the idea of the state elites' acting as the guardians of the long-term interests of the community, but they also seemed to overlook the fact that "democracy is not just a form of politics or even of government but is a type of state" (Dodd).[3] After the 1960-1961 military intervention, for instance, despite prodding from the military, the political elites were unwilling to enter into pacts; they considered such arrangements undemocratic rather than viewing them as a means of facilitating the transition to democracy. During the 1970s, the political party leaders– at each end of the political spectrum–did not hesitate to collaborate with the "disloyal opposition" on the fringes.[4]

Viewed from this angle, the 1980s opened a new chapter in Turkey's transition to democracy. In fact, the post-1983 developments were seen as "releasing unprecedented social and political forces, including the rise of a new business class and a concerted attack on the entrenched étatist bureaucracy" (Rustow). Another observation was that "Turkish political institutions [were] at a potential threshold of a possible radical restructuration that could lead to a new consensus, a new political grammar, and a new political discourse" (Birtek).

One critical dimension of this restructuration was the weakening of what remained of institutional monism. First, the military interventionists themselves concluded that trying to regulate democracy from above was fraught with immense difficulties. One of the members of the junta that carried out the 1980-1983 military intervention, as well as the prime minister of the interregnum (a former admiral), told me in separate interviews in 1985 that the military comes to power; it tries to rebalance the political system by introducing a new constitution; but, once the military returns to its barracks, the politicians quickly revert back to their old ways. It must be noted that the military has always been reluctant to intervene, because this would have adverse effects on its professionalism and combat effectiveness.[5] The military has also felt that intervention creates havoc in the upper ranks and, in general, interferes with promotions based on merit. Intervention also increases the possibility of politicization and ideological polarization within the ranks–an anathema to the High Command which has consistently tried to keep the military a "total institution" with its own Weltanschauung and corporate culture.[6]

Second, the military faced increasing opposition from the bulk of the intelligentsia and the press. Most of the serious dailies and opinion weeklies

---

[3]Here and below, references in parantheses refer to the chapters in this volume. "Heper" refers to Chapter 15.

[4]Kemal H. Karpat, "Turkish Democracy at Impasse: Ideology, Party Politics and the Third Military Intervention," *International Journal of Turkish Studies* 2 (1981): 1-43.

[5]İlter Turan, "Cyclical Democracy: The Turkish Case," Paper delivered at the Annual Meeting of the Midwest Political Science Association, Chicago, 11-14 April 1984.

[6]Following the 1980 military intervention, General Kenan Evren, then head of the junta, told the officers at the lower ranks that the intervention was carried on out of necessity and that the military officers should preoccupy themselves with their own tasks as officers.

argued that the cleavage between the military and the "democrats" that developed in the mid-1980s had become the most significant conflict in Turkish politics. It was also argued that the "electorate, by solidly rallying behind Turgut Özal's Motherland Party [ANAP] in the 1983 general and the 1984 local elections [at the time, the ANAP was the most anti-military political party among the parties competing], had restrained the military's overly ambitious attempt to prescribe the personnel as well as the institutions of the new regime" (Rustow; also Evin). The voters' verdict could indeed have had an important impact; the military had always considered itself as the spokesperson of the people at large and not of specific groups, including the intelligentsia and the press. This was particularly the case during the 1980s, because–in the military's view–during the 1960s and 1970s, the intelligentsia, the press and the politicians had all contributed to the fragmentation and polarization of Turkish politics (Evin).

Third, the military was increasingly confronted with pressures from abroad, in particular from the European Community (EC). During the 1980s, more and more Turkish leaders realized that the country would have to live up to European standards of democracy if it wanted its full membership to be seriously considered by the Europeans (Steinbach). More specifically, the military's commitment to maintain Turkey's ties with the West prevented it from overlooking Western views on the regime problems in Turkey (Karaosmanoğlu).

Finally, the renewed emphasis on a multidimensional foreign policy and on market forces in the 1980s necessitated the adoption of more pragmatic policies in both areas. As Turkey's foreign relations became more diversified, different worldviews and ideologies began to compete with the Atatürkian principles (Steinbach).

In the process, the Atatürkian principles were reinterpreted by the military, and étatism was almost completely discarded. Turgut Özal, a proponent of liberal economic policies, was initially made vice-premier responsible for the economy in the 1980-1983 interregnum governments. The stance on secularism was considerably softened. President Kenan Evren even cited verses from the Koran in order to strengthen certain points he made in his public statements and speeches. Islam was increasingly recognized as an essential element in holding the social fabric together. The military concluded that "Islam, when viewed as a progressive faith and moral teaching, could play a critical role in combatting the ideological extremism of the left and the right and in promoting social unity" (Szyliowicz). Consequently, "it became permissable to search for a new, historically rooted sociocultural Turkish identity" (Steinbach).

The reinterpretation of the Atatürkian principles along the lines delineated here meant that there was now more scope for politics as compared to the sphere of the state. More specifically, President Evren and the National Security Council (the state elites) opted for a combination of institutional monism and institutional pluralism and gave the impression that their preference in the long run was for social pluralism. They wanted to maintain institutional monism concerning such matters as territorial integrity and the national unity of Turkey. Thus, they aspired to play a dominant role regarding what they considered to be external and internal threats to the country. They wanted to have the last word in such matters as law and order, foreign policy, and education of the young, because–in their opinion–these were vital for the long-term interests of the community. Their sensitivity on these issues was derived from Turkey's unfavorable geopolitical situation as well as from threats of separatist activities and Islamic fundamentalism–the latter two having strong transnational aspects, as delineated in this volume by Karaosmanoğlu. Thus, despite their increasingly conciliatory attitude toward the free play of politics, they could not refrain at times from adopting an undemocratic stand: "In May 1988, at a time of incidents of leftist violence, Evren warned that if the political authorities did not do their duty, the armed forces could not stay silent" (Dodd).

With regard to those matters they did not consider to be critical for the territorial integrity and the national unity of the country, the state elites did not insist upon institutional monism. On the contrary, they opted for institutional pluralism in those areas not related to security issues. President Evren, for instance, occasionally drew the government's attention to such problems as unemployment, inflation, foreign debt, frequent price hikes, and the like. In general, however, he refrained from suggesting specific remedies. His press secretary once reported (November 1986) that the president stayed on top of economic problems, but he felt that he should not directly interfere "because the economy was essentially government's responsibility." [7]

Despite their pessimism about the possibility of rational politics taking root in the short run (as revealed by the remarks made to me by the two leading members of the 1980-1983 interregnum already noted), the state elites considered even the kind of institutional pluralism they tried to develop to be a stopgap measure; that is, they would come into the picture only when absolutely necessary. In their view, government should be carried out essentially by the political executive. Thus, in the Third Turkish Republic (1982 to the present), the hand of that executive was strengthened; for instance, the government could more easily issue decree laws, and the prime minister could dismiss a minister without the entire Council of Ministers having to resign.

In sum, the state elites' primary concern was the establishment of an effective, as well as a prudent, government: "What the president stressed in his speeches was not the state but rather a variety of attitudes that were consonant with the role he clearly accepted of defender of the Constitution and of Atatürkism which, rightly or wrongly, was seen to underlie it–the

---

[7]Metin Heper, "The Executive in the Third Turkish Republic, 1982-1989," *Governance* 3 (1990), p. 312.

need for security and especieally for a firm stand to be taken against terrorism" (Dodd). Dodd has also argued (in this volume) that "the president was performing a service in the interest of realism and, in the longer term, in the interest of democracy." As already noted, the state elites wanted to gradually withdraw even from the limited sphere they had designated for themselves. They tried to inject into Turkish politics greater doses of rationality, less politicization, and a consensual political culture. Among other things, for a time they banned the former politicians from participating in active politics; they changed the electoral law to make it more difficult for the fringe parties to become members of the Parliament;[8] and, in his speeches, President Evren "tried to inculcate the moral and social behavior he considered appropriate for Turkish political life–that is, reasonable and sensible participation in public life" (Dodd). He wanted to alert the public to the "need for a 'civic' rather than just 'civil' society"; he also endeavored to ensure that such an approach to politics "permeated the spirit of the administration over which he had broad surveillance" (Dodd).

Although the elites in Turkey wanted the institutionalization of social pluralism and viewed institutional pluralism essentially as a stepping stone to achieving it, the bulk of the intelligentsia, the press, and politicians were concerned solely with democratization–that is, bolstering the horizontal dimension of democracy (Heper). Following the military's rise to power in September 1980, for a time, journalists considered themselves to be the "sole surviving standard-bearers of democracy," and referred to the post-1982 democracy in Turkey as "superficial" democracy (Groc). They tried "to push back . . . the limits imposed by censorship; consciously infringed on certain well-established taboos"; and were generally engaged in "hard-hitting reporting" (Groc). The bulk of the intelligentsia also pressed for the further democratization of the regime. In time, these endeavors paved the way for some constitutional and legal changes in a liberalizing direction, including the lifting of the ban on former politicians. The latter, too, quickly focused their attention on bringing about a genuine democracy (*tam demokrasi*), which to its proponents meant political participation virtually without limits.

The ANAP governments (and later the True Path Party [DYP]-Social Democratic Populist Party [SHP] coalition as well) aimed at further democratizing the regime by decreasing the role the civil bureaucracy, the president, and the military played in politics. These governments tried to curb the powers of the bureaucracy by liberalizing the economy, privatizing the state economic enterprises (SEEs), and decentralizing the government. The measures taken toward economic liberalization included the adoption of a monetarist approach (partially lifting controls on interest rates, foreign exchange, and the prices of the nonbasic commodities produced

---

[8]For an elaboration, see İlter Turan, "Political Parties and the Party System in Post-1983 Turkey," in *State, Democracy and the Military: Turkey in the 1980s*, Metin Heper and Ahmet Evin, eds. (Berlin: Walter de Gruyter, 1988).

by the SEEs, as well as those of the agricultural products) and the development of capital markets (Saracoğlu). The original intent behind the policy of privatizing the SEEs was that of basing the economic growth on the entrepreneurial spirit of individuals and on spreading capital to the masses (İlkin). The decentralization policy of governmmnet was aimed at decreasing the administrative, legal, and financial tutelage of the central government over the municipalities (Kalaycıoğlu).

During the early years of the ANAP governments,[9] Prime Minister Özal acted in a rather circumspect manner toward the president and the military. He rarely made public statements on subjects other than the economy. But he soon found himself on the spot when the press began questioning him concerning matters for which the state elites felt they were responsible–law and order, foreign policy, and the like. Also, with the passage of time, President Evren's detractors became increasingly assertive, and criticized him openly. Thus, Özal gradually began to use the prerogatives of the government vis-à-vis both the president and the National Security Council.[10] For instance, in January 1987, some higher civil servants–who were reputed to have the personal blessing of the president–were either appointed to positions of lesser significance or were dismissed. In the same year, the government appointed a new chief of the general staff, although the military had another candidate (Evin). Again in 1987, the National Security Council warned the government of the danger of Islamic revivalism in Turkey; Özal stated publicly that this was a potential and not an immediate threat and that it should not be exaggerated. As Özbudun points out in this volume, thus began a "marked shift of power from the president to the prime minister."

In sum, the state elites were not only forced, but also turned out to be willing, to end institutional monism in the Turkish polity. As already noted, they had wanted to substitute a mild form of institutional pluralism for institutional monism; however, even this institutional pluralism was perceived as undemocratic by the bulk of the intelligentsia, the press, and politicians. The latter groups wanted to place almost sole emphasis on the horizontal dimension of democracy, not unlike their colleagues of the pre-1980 period (Heper). Could Turkish democracy indeed be consolidated within the framework of social pluralism? That is, could civil societal elements and their representatives wield more influence in the polity and could a successful marriage between the horizontal and vertical dimensions of democracy be effected by the political elites?

The first condition of the consolidation of democracy as social pluralism is, of course, the autonomization of political elites and social actors from the dominance of the state elites. As already noted, during the 1980s, the political elites have gone a long way in freeing themselves from the control of the state elites. In addition, at least within the ranks of the ANAP, the

---

[9]The first ANAP government was formed in 1983.
[10]Heper, "The Executive in the Third Turkish Republic, 1982-1989."

technocratic elites began to replace the modernizing ones.

The modernizing elites had subscribed to radical secularism, legalism, and authoritarianism. They sought an enlightened public mind, which would result from a universal culture. Their Durkheimian vocabulary had no place for the vestiges of communal culture. They aimed at replacing the latter with a new mode of social solidarity based on "progress" and nationalism (Birtek, Mardin). In contrast, the technocratic elites endeavored to reconcile the former cultural orientations with requisites of economic growth, rather than trying to impose a new identity upon society by means of adopting certain Western values. Their aim was to synthesize communal culture and pragmatic rationality (Göle), a project that was facilitated by the increased interpenetration in Turkey of the secular and Islamic modes of thinking (Mardin).

Thus, for the first time in Turkey, a large number of politicians (within the government party) began to share the sentiments of the people at large. These were "entrepreneurial politicians" and not "politicians of conviction" (Göle). They had to be entrepreneurial because, during the same decade, support for political parties tended to be given in terms of the services delivered and not in terms of ideological conviction.[11] In Turkish politics one now came across the "fluidity of the votes based on calculations of economic interest and other similar pragmatic considerations" (Göle). If the gradual weakening of the influence of the state elites in the polity was the first step toward the freeing of civil society from the clutches of the state, the emergence of the technocratic elites was a second and, in fact, an even more significant step. The technocratic elites *did* introduce in Turkish politics a new discourse, which Birtek (in this volume) thought the post-1980 period might have brought about. They attempted to replace the modernizers' utopias "deriving from imagination undetermined by time and space" with their "ideologies" that were anchored in the present empirical reality (Göle). They emphasized more immediate problems–such as public health, tourism, and pollution–at the expense of such grand issues as democracy, the state, and the like (Göle).

Their efforts to establish a link between the everyday life of people and politics were paralleled by those of some segments of the press, which, during the 1980s, increasingly took up the conditions of life in different spheres of society. There was now a more detailed scrutiny of different social problems. A portion of the press began to turn the citizens' attention, which had habitually and for a long time turned on the issues of democracy and state, to the latter's day-to-day performance: "The press offered the citizen a true opening to information, knowledge, taste, and culture, thus beginning to prepare the ground for the emergence of a civil society not dominated by a monolithic state" (Groc).

---

[11] Üstün Ergüder, "Decentralisation of Local Governmnet and Turkish Political Culture," in *Democracy and Local Government: Istanbul in the 1980s,* Metin Heper, ed. (Walkington, England: Eothen Press, 1987), pp. 17ff.

Indeed, during the 1980s, responsibility for social engineering shifted perceptibly from the state elites, not only to the political elites but also to social actors. New issues were taken up and defended by such disparate civil societal groups as women, ecologists, Islamicists, veiled Muslim students, and homosexuals and transsexuals (Göle). One also observed the emergence of a greater number of better-organized groups, which included the "liberals," the Muslim intellectuals, and the new left. The "liberals" attempted to carve for themselves an economic sphere independent from the state. The Muslim intellectuals tried to do the same for religion. The new left came up with less "utopian" and more "ideological" formulations and sought a niche for itself in the emerging polity (Göle). These were all developments toward the autonomization of civil society along with that of politics.

Furthermore, disparate as well as more organized civil societal groups joined the ranks of the bulk of the intelligentsia, as well as the press and the Turkish democracy's critics in the EC, in demanding greater rights and freedoms. As already noted, the state elites themselves were not eager to maintain institutional monism and the authoritarian arrangements it would have entailed. The result was the series of constitutional and legal changes already noted. Among other things, political parties with links to their pre-1980 predecessors replaced the ones that had been created artificially following the reinstallation of the multiparty system in 1982 (Özbudun, Turan).

In the process, has the political system become more representative? It is difficult to respond in the affirmative. A large number of politicians within the government party did begin to share the sentiments of the people and, in fact, saw to it that these aspirations were reflected in public policies and legislation. Yet, the ANAP governments turned out to be responsive only to the sentiments of the people at large and not to the interests and views of specific social groups, including the organized economic interests. They were no less populist than the pre-1980 politicians.

The growth strategy of the ANAP governments *was* based on the entrepreneurial spirit of the private sector. The policies of these governments, which enabled the banks to finance investments, along with the development of capital markets for the same purpose, did bolster the financial autonomy of the private sector. However, the ANAP governments' policy of liberalization had an *economic* rather than a *political* rationale behind it. They wanted to inject dynamism into the economy; they were not interested in furthering political pluralism and bringing about a society-centered polity. Not unlike the pre-1980 political elites, they also tried to transform the earlier state-centered polity into a political party-centered one,[12] but insofar as certain issues–including the economy–were concerned, this polity bordered on an inner executive-centered govern-

---

[12]See Metin Heper, "The State, Political Party and Society in post-1983 Turkey," *Government and Opposition* 25 (1990): 321-333.

mental system.[13]

They could do this with impunity for reasons pointed out in this volume by İlkin and Birtek. The rising urban classes had forced the Republican People's Party government to convene the Turkish Economic Congress in 1948. At the congress, they had pointed out that one could not talk about freedom and democracy when the means of livelihood were in the hands of a political authority (İlkin). As Birtek in this volume cogently shows, these groups–the urban bourgeoisie, including the professional middle classes–continued their ascendance within the polity during the 1950-1954 period: yet, after 1954, they could not sustain this momentum. Consequently, the center-periphery cleavage could not have been replaced as the defining paradigm of the Turkish political system. Turkish industrialization with an urban content would begin two decades later and with a heavy dose of protection and import substitution. Turkey found itself in perpetual foreign exchange difficulties in view of the internationally declining agriculture prices and an industry that was appended to its agricultural output and accumulation–that is, an industry always in need of subsidy and support. In the process, the town became the locus of the new *asabiyah*–the town that had always emerged, in the Turkish case, as the ecological context of cultural conservatism. In this segmented world, emphasis was placed on an exaggerated form of nationalism.

Emphasis was placed on other hard or soft ideologies, one may add. This meant that in post-1980 Turkey there were still cultural, as well as economic, cleavages. Integration still had to be largely mechanical rather than organic. It was difficult for dynamic consensus to emerge in place of the static consensus.

Organic integration and dynamic consensus had difficulty taking root, because the emerging pluralism was based on "pragmatism" and not on "liberty in a more general sense, [that is] autonomy of the self, and on individualism in its Western connotation" (Göle). Dodd in this volume alludes to what instead might take place (and was, in fact, taking place): "Too much credence may unfortunately be placed in the notion that civil society, composed of free and interacting individuals and groups, will of itself create a viable democracy." Dodd's optimistic forecast is that "this development, coupled with a free market, may curb party domination (an intraelite conflict), by taking the pressure off government as the source of all bounty." Dodd's pessimistic prediction is that "it can lead to an irresponsible *enrichissez-vous* type of society, which will not please either the military or the now-stronger puritanical Islamic right."

One can argue that in post-1980 Turkey, the civil societal elements still could not act as agencies of "social coordination" through horizontal relations of adjustment and exchange or as factors of moderation for the polit-

---

[13] Ayşe Öncü and Deniz Gökçe, "Macro-Politics of De-Regulation and Micro-Politics Politics of Banks," in *Strong State and Economic Interest Groups: The Post-1980 Turkish Experience*, Metin Heper, ed. (Berlin: Walter de Gruyter, 1991).

ical elites–each a sine qua non for social pluralism. The technocratic elites within the ranks of the ANAP did attempt to introduce a new discourse–toleration rather than confrontion and emphasis on specific policy issues and not on the grand issues (Göle). They, too, however, were gradually drawn to the spheres of grand issues and confrontational politics by the bulk of the intelligentsia, the press, and the opposition politicians–all of which continued to focus exclusively on cultural issues and the questions of political legitimacy (Heper); and, in the process, contributed to the re-polarization of Turkish politics.[14]

It was, therefore, not surprising that "there was no interparty agreement on the electoral system, the proper role of the legislature in the political system, the powers of the president of the republic, limitations on fundamental rights and liberties, and political activities of the trade unions" (Özbudun). Electoral and political party laws were used by the governing party for partisan purposes (Turan). At least until the October 1991 general elections, one observed increasing intransigence, even on the part of political leaders such as then President Turgut Özal and Erdal İnönü (the then chair of the Social Democratic Populist Party, as of 1984, and then vice-premier, between 1991 and 1993); earlier in the decade, both had displayed conciliatory attitudes (Heper).

In the Turkey of the early 1990s, institutional monism had been largely eroded, institutional pluralism was considered undemocratic, and social pluralism was not to be found. The consolidation of democracy was still seen basically only in terms of its horizontal dimension; even the mention of its vertical dimension was perceived as a longing for authoritarian solutions. Moreover, the political economy of distribution had been neglected to an unprecedented degree (Kuruç); the educational system was perpetuating the existing inequalities (Szyliowicz); and class consciousness was sharpening.[15]

The only redeeming feature was that almost nobody seemed to opt for authoritarian solutions. The military was not interested in again becoming embroiled in politics. Politicians wanted to further democratize the regime, either for its own sake or as a means for dealing with other problems the country faced, such as the Kurdish issue. The fringe parties and groups, who could have other aspirations, were too weak to have influence. And increasing numbers of people began indicating the need for consensual politics. Following the October 1991 general elections, the leading politicians, also began opting for a politics of harmony.

There was, as a result, a gradual softening of attitudes nationwide, even on issues that had raised strong emotions in the recent past. As noted, all of Turkey's allies pressed for greater democratization throughout the

---

[14]Metin Heper and Jacob Landau, eds., *Political Parties and Democracy in Turkey* (London: I. B. Tauris, 1991).

[15]Çağlar Keyder, *State and Class in Turkey: A Study in Capitalist Development* (London: Verso, 1987).

decade. Such demands were no longer considered to be unacceptable foreign interference in Turkey's domestic affairs, and they ceased eliciting highly negative reactions from either official circles or the press.

Increased public observance of religion and of rising sectarian activity have been causes of concern among the secularist urban groups, who called into question the extent to which the state and political elites should have shown a relaxed attitude toward the use of religion in public life. The danger of unbridled growth of retrogressive religious movements in a democratic polity presented a dilemma for those who perceived the threat of a religious revival, but some observers, committed to secular democracy, claimed that Turkish Islam showed signs of developing into a civil religion (for instance, Mardin in this volume).

It could be said that in the early 1990s, areas of conflict in the Turkish polity have been substantially reduced, whereas societal prerequisites for consensus have not been commensurately strengthened. The future of Turkish democracy seems to depend on political elites' realization of the need not only for a politics of harmony but also for striking a balance between the vertical and horizontal dimensions of democracy.

Bibliography

Ahmad, Feroz. *The Turkish Experiment in Democracy: 1950-1975*. London: C. Hurst, 1977.

Akarlı, Engin D., with Gabriel Ben-Dor, eds. *Political Participation in Turkey: Historical Background and Present Problems*. Istanbul: Boğaziçi University, 1975.

Aktan, Coşkun Can. *Kamu İktisadi Teşebbülleri ve Özelleştirme*. İzmir: n.p., 1987.

Aktan, Tahir. "Mahalli İdarelerde Vesayet Denetimi," *Amme İdaresi Dergisi* 9 (1976): 3-24.

Aldan, Mehmet. "İdari Vesayet Denetimi," *İller ve Belediyeler*, nos. 475-467 (1985): 228-237.

Alkan, Türker. *12 Eylül ve Demokrasi*. Istanbul: Kaynak, 1986.

Allum, Peter. *Politics and Society in Post-War Naples*. Cambridge: Cambridge University Press, 1973.

Almond, Gabriel, and Sidney Verba. *The Civic Culture*. Princeton: Princeton University Press, 1973.

Altıntaş, Berra. *Kamu İktisadi Teşebbüslerinin Özelleştirilmesi ve Özelleştirmenin Sermaye Piyasasına Etkisi*. Ankara: Sermaye Piyasası Kurulu, 1981.

Arıcanlı, Tosun, and Dani Rodrik. *The Political Economy of Turkey: Debt, Adjustment and Sustainability*. London: Macmillan, 1990.

Badie, Bertrand, and Pierre Birnbaum, *The Sociology of the State*, trans. Arthur Goldhammer. Chicago: University of Chicago Press, 1979.

Barkey, Henri J. "Why Military Regimes Fail: The Perils of Transition," *Armed Forces and Society* 16 (1990): 169-192.

Ben-Dor, Gabriel. "Institutionalization and Political Development: A Conceptual and Theoretical Analysis," *Comparative Studies in Society and History* 7 (1975): 309-25.

Bendix, Reinhard. *Kings or People: Power and the Mandate to Rule*. Berkeley: University of California Press, 1980.

Bianchi, Robert. *Interest Groups and Political Development in Turkey*. Princeton: Princeton University Press, 1984.

Birand, Mehmet Ali. *The Generals' Coup in Turkey*. Trans. M.A. Dikerdem. London: Brassey's, 1987.

Birch, A. H. *Representation*. London: Macmillan, 1971.

Birtek, Faruk. "The Turkish Adventures of the Durkheimian Paradigm: Does History Vindicate M. Labriola?" *Il Politico* 61 (1991): 107-146.

———. "The Rise and Fall of Etatism, 1930-1950," *Review* 7 (1985): 407-438.

———. "Transition to Capitalism in England and Turkey. A Structural Model," Unpublished Ph.D. dissertation, University of California, Berkeley, 1978.

Birtek, Faruk, and Binnaz Toprak. "The Conflictual Agendas of Neo-Liberal Reconstruction and the Rise of Islamic Politics in Turkey: The Hazards of Rewriting

Modernity," *Praxis International* 13 (1993): 192-212.

Bölügiray, Nevzat. *Sokaktaki Asker*. Istanbul: Milliyet, 1989.

Boratav, Korkut. "Türkiye'de Popülizm: 1962-76 Dönemi Üzerine Bazı Notlar," *Yapıt* 46 (1983): 7-18.

Bourdieu, Pierre. *Outline of a Theory of Practice*. Cambridge: Cambridge University Press, 1977.

Burrows, Sir Bernard. "Turkey and the European Community," Working paper 3/87, Federal Trust for Education and Research, London, 1987.

Carnoy, Martin. *The State and Political Theory*. Princeton: Princeton University Press, 1984.

Castoriadis, Cornelius. *L'Institution imaginaire de la société*. Paris: Seuil, 1975.

Celasun, Merih. "A General Equilibrium Model of the Turkish Economy, SIMLOG-1," *METU Studies in Development* (Ankara) 13 (1986): 29-94.

Celasun, Merih, and Dani Rodrik. *Debt, Adjustment and Growth: Turkey*. Chicago: University of Chicago Press, 1989.

de Certeau, Michel. *The Practice of Everyday Life*. Berkeley: University of California Press, 1984.

Cizre, Ümit Sakallıoğlu, "Labour: The Battered Community," in *Strong State and Economic Interest Groups: The Post-1980 Turkish Experience*, Metin Heper, ed. Berlin: Walter de Gruyter, 1991.

Couloumbis, Theodore A. *The United States, Greece and Turkey: The Troubled Triangle*. New York: Praeger, 1983.

Dahl, Robert A. *Dilemmas of Pluralist Democracy: Autonomy vs. Control*. New Haven: Yale University Press, 1982.

Danielson, Michael N., and Ruşen Keleş. *The Politics of Rapid Urbanization: Government and Growth in Modern Turkey*. New York: Holmes and Meier, 1985.

Dodd, C. H. *The Crisis of Turkish Democracy*. Walkington, England: Eothen Press, 1983.

———. *Democracy and Development in Turkey*. Walkington, England: Eothen Press, 1979.

———. *Politics and Government in Turkey*. Manchester: Manchester University Press, 1969.

Doğan, Yalçın. *Dar Sokakta Siyaset: 1980-1983*. Istanbul: Tekin Yayınevi, 1985.

Doğramacı, İhsan. "The Turkish Universities," *Higher Education in Europe* 9 (1984): 74-82.

Donat, Yavuz. *Buyruklu Demokrasi, 1980-1983*. Ankara: Bilgi Yayınevi, 1987.

Dunleavy, Patrick, and Brendon O'Leary. *Theories of the State: The Politics of Liberal Democracy*. London: Macmillan, 1987.

Duran, Lütfi. "Cumhuriyetin 'Yürütmesi': Kuvvetli İcra mı? Kişisel İktidar mı?" in *Bahri Savcı'ya Armağan*, n.e. Ankara: Ankara Üniversitesi Siyasal Bilgiler Fakültesi, 1988.

Durkheim, Emile. *The Division of Labor in Society*. New York: Free Press, 1964.

Dyson, Kenneth H.F. *The State Tradition in Western Europe: A Study of an Idea and Institution*. Oxford: Martin Robertson, 1980.

Eisenstadt, S. N. *Traditional Patrimonialism and Modern Neo-Patrimonialism*. Beverly Hills: Sage, 1978.

Eke, Ali Erkan. "Anakent Yönetimi ve Yönetimlerarası İlişkiler," *Amme İdaresi Dergisi* 18 (1985): 41-62.

Ergüder, Üstün. 'Decentralisation of Local Government and Turkish Political Culture," in *Democracy and Local Government in Turkey: Istanbul in the 1980s*. Metin Heper, ed. Walkington, England: Eothen Press, 1987.

Ergüder, Üstün, and Richard I. Hofferbert. "The 1983 General Elections in Turkey: Continuity or Change in Voting Patterns?" in *State, Democracy and the Military: Turkey in the 1980s*, Metin Heper and Ahmet Evin, eds. Berlin: Walter de Gruyter, 1988.

Ete, Muhlis. *State Exploitation in Turkey*. Ankara: n.p., 1951.

Evans, Peter B., Dietrich Rueschemeyer, and Theda Skocpol, eds. *Bringing the State Back In*. Cambridge: Cambridge University Press, 1985.

Evin, Ahmet, ed. *Modern Turkey: Continuity and Change*. Opladen: Leske Verlag und Budrich, 1984.

Evin, Ahmet, and Geoffrey Denton, eds. *Turkey and the European Community* Opladen: Leske Verlag und Budrich, 1990.

Evren, Kenan. *Kenan Evren'in Anıları*, vol. I. Istanbul: Milliyet, 1990.

Findley, Carter V. "The Advent of Ideology in the Islamic Middle East," Part I, *Studia Islamica*, from fascicle LV: 143-169.

Frey, Frederick W. "Patterns of Elite Politics in Turkey," in *Political Elites in the Middle East*, George Lenczowski, ed. Washington, D.C.: American Enterprise Institute, 1975.

General Secretariat of the National Security Council. *12 September in Turkey: Before and After*. Ankara: Ongun Kardeşler, 1982.

Giner, Salvador, "Political Economy, Legitimation and the State in Southern Europe," in *Transitions from Authoritarian Rule: Southern Europe*, Guillermo O'Donnell, Philippe C. Schmitter, and Laurence Whitehead, eds. Baltimore: Johns Hopkins University Press, 1986.

Gökalp, Altan, ed. *La Turquie en transition: Disparités, identités, pouvoirs*. Paris: Maisonneuve, 1986.

Göle, Nilüfer. "Seçmen Davranışları Araştırması," June 1988, typescript.

——. "Anavatan Partisi Seçmen Davranışı Araştırmaları," July 1987, typescript.

——."Les Ingénieurs islamistes: une nouvelle forme de modernité turque?" Paper presented at the conference Horizons de Pensèe et Pratiques Sociales chez les Intellectuels du Monde Musulman, Fondation Nationale des Sciences Politiques, Paris, 1-2 June 1987.

——. *Mühendisler ve İdeoloji: Öncü Devrimcilerden Yenilikçi Seçkinlere*. Istanbul: İletişim, 1986.

Gönlübol, Mehmet. "A Short Appraisal of the Foreign Policy of the Turkish Republic, 1923-1973," *Turkish Yearbook of International Relations* 7 (1974): 1-19.

Groc, Gérard. "Aspects de la presse turque," Paper presented at the symposium Aspects de la Turquie Actuelle, Paris, October 1986.

Grothusen, Klaus-Detlev, ed. *Türkei: Südosteuropa-Handbuch. Volume IV.* Göttingen: Vandenhoeck und Ruprecht, 1985.

Gürkan, Celil. *12 Mart'a Beş Kala*. Istanbul: Tekin Yayınevi, 1986.

Hale, William. *Political and Economic Development of Modern Turkey*. London: Croom Helm, 1981.

Harris, George. *Turkey: Coping With Crisis*. Boulder, Colo.: Westview Press, 1985.

Hawking, Stephen, *A Brief History of Time*. New York: Bantam, 1988.

Henze, Paul B. *Goal: Destabilization, Soviet Agitational Propaganda, Instability and Terrorism in NATO South*. Marina del Rey, Calif.: European American Institute for Security Research, 1981.

Heper, Metin. "Extremely 'Strong State' and Democracy: The Turkish Case in Comparative and Historical Perspective," in *Democracy and Modernity*, S. N. Eisenstadt, ed. Leiden: Brill, 1992.

——, ed. *Strong State and Economic Interest Groups: The Post-1980 Turkish Experience*. Berlin: Walter de Gruyter, 1991.

——. "Transitions to Democracy Reconsidered: A Historical Perspective," in *Comparative Political Dynamics: Global Research Perspectives*. Dankwart A. Rustow and Kenneth P. Erickson, eds. New York: HarperCollins, 1991.

——. "The Executive in the Third Turkish Republic, 1982-1989," *Governance* 3 (1990): 299-319.

——. "The State and Debureaucratization: The Turkish Case," *International Social Science Journal* 42 (1990): 605-615.

——. "The State, Political Party and Society in post-1983 Turkey," *Government and Opposition* 25 (1990): 321-333.

——. "Turkish Democracy Reconsidered: Illusion Breeding Disillusion?" in *Institutional Aspects of the Economic Integration of Turkey into the European Community*, foreword by E. Kantzenbach. H. Körner and R. Shams, eds. Hamburg: HWWA, 1990.

——. "The Motherland Party Governments and Bureaucracy in Turkey, 1983-1988," *Governance* 2 (1989): 457-468.

——. "The State, the Military, and Democracy in Turkey," *Jerusalem Journal of International Relations* 9 (1987): 52-64.

——. "Introduction," in *The State and Public Bureaucracies: A Comparative Perspective*, Metin Heper, ed. New York: Greenwood Press, 1987.

——. ed. *Democracy and Local Government: Istanbul in the 1980s*. Walkington, England: Eothen Press, 1987.

——, ed. *Dilemmas of Decentralization: Municipal Government in Turkey*. Bonn: Friedrich-Ebert-Stiftung, 1986.

——. *The State Tradition in Turkey*. Walkington, England: Eothen Press, 1985.

——. "Islam, Polity and Society in Turkey: A Middle Eastern Perspective," *Middle East Journal* 33 (1981): 345-363.

——. "Center and Periphery in the Ottoman Empire with Special Reference to the Nineteenth Century," *International Political Science Review* 1 (1980): 81-105.

——. "The Recalcitrance of the Turkish Public Bureaucracy to 'Bourgeois Politics' : A Multi-Factor Political Stratification Analysis," *Middle East Journal* 30 (1976): 485-500.

Heper, Metin, and Jacob Landau, eds. *Political Parties and Democracy in Turkey*. London: I. B. Tauris, 1991.

Heper, Metin, and Ahmet Evin, eds. *State, Democracy and the Military: Turkey in the 1980s*. Berlin: Walter de Gruyter, 1988.

Hibbs, Douglas A., Jr. *The Political Economy of Industrial Democracies*. Cambridge: Harvard University Press, 1987.

Huntington, Samuel P. *Political Order in Changing Societies*. New Haven: Yale University Press, 1968.

İlkin, Selim. "Exporters: Favoured Dependency," in *Strong State and Economic Interest Groups: The Post-1980 Turkish Experience*. Metin Heper, ed. Berlin: Walter de Gruyter, 1991.

——. "Turkey's Attempts to Approach the Islamic Countries after 1974," in *Die Türkei auf dem Weg in die EG*, Werner Gumpel, ed. München: Oldenburg, 1979.

İnalcık, Halil. *The Ottoman Empire in Classical Age: 1330-1666*, trans. Norman Itzkowitz and Colin Imber. London: Weidenfeld and Nicholson, 1973.

———. "The Nature of Traditional Society: [Turkey]," in *Political Modernization in Japan and Turkey*, Robert E. Ward and Dankwart A. Rustow, eds. Princeton: Princeton University Press, 1964.

Jaros, Dean. *Socialization to Politics*. New York: Praeger, 1973.

Kalaycıoğlu, Ersin. "The 1983 Parliament in Turkey: Changes and Continuities," in *State, Democracy and the Military: Turkey in the 1980s*, Metin Heper and Ahmet Evin, eds. Berlin: Walter de Gruyter, 1988.

———. "Türk Yasama Sistemi ve Siyasal Temsil," in *Türk Siyasal Hayatının Gelişimi*, Ersin Kalaycıoğlu and Ali Yaşar Sarıbay, eds. Istanbul: Beta 1986.

Kaptan, Saim. *Türkiye'de Yüksek Öğretim ve İnsangücü Hedefleri*. Ankara: Devlet Planlama Teşkilatı, 1982.

Karaosmanoğlu, Ali L. "Turkey and the Southern Flank: Domestic and External Contexts," in *NATO's Southern Allies: Internal and External Challenges*, John Chipman, ed. London: Routledge, 1988.

Karataş, Cevat. *Privatization in Britain and Turkey*. Istanbul: Istanbul Chamber of Commerce, 1990.

Karpat, Kemal H. "Turkish Democracy at Impasse: Ideology, Party Politics and the Third Military Intervention," *International Journal of Turkish Studies* 2 (1981): 1-43.

———. "The Stages of Ottoman History," in *The Ottoman State and its Place in World History*, Kemal H. Karpat, ed. Leiden: Brill, 1974.

Kaya, Yahya K. *İnsan Yetiştirme Düzenimiz*. Ankara: Erk Basımevi, 1981.

Kazancı, Metin. "Yerel Yönetimler Üzerine Birkaç Not," *Amme İdaresi Dergisi* 16 (1983): 36-51.

Kazancıgil, Ali, and Ergun Özbudun, eds. *Atatürk: Founder of a Modern State*. London: C. Hurst, 1981.

Kesselman, Mark. "Over Institutionalization and Political Constraint: The Case of France," *Comparative Politics* 2 (1970): 21-44.

Keyder, Çağlar. *State and Class in Turkey: A Study in Capitalist Development*. London: Verso, 1987.

Kili, Suna. *Turkish Constitutional Developments and Assembly Debates on the Constitutions of 1924 and 1961*. Istanbul: Robert College Research Center, 1971.

Kirchheimer, Otto. "Confining Conditions and Revolutionary Breakthroughs," *American Political Science Review* 59 (1964): 964-974.

Kjellströrm, Sven B. "Privatization in Turkey," World Bank Working Paper, November 1990.

Koloğlu, Orhan. "La Presse turque, evolutions et orientations depuis 1945," in *La Turquie en transition*, Altan Gökalp, ed. Paris: Maisonneuve, 1986.

Kongar, Emre. *12 Eylül ve Sonrası*. Istanbul: Say, 1987.

Korpi, Walter. "Social Policy and Distributional Conflict in the Capitalist Democracies," *West European Politics* 3 (1980): 296-316.

Kramer, Heinz. *Die Europäische Gemeinschaft und die Türkei: Entwicklung, Probleme und Perspecktiven einer schwierigen Partnerschaft*. Baden-Baden: Nomos Verlagsgesellschaft, 1988.

Kushner, David. "Turkish Secularists and Islam," *Jerusalem Quartterly*, no.38 (1986): 86-106.

Landau, Jacob M., ed. *Atatürk and the Modernization of Turkey*. Boulder, Colo.:

Westview Press, 1984.

———. *Pan-Turkism in Turkey: A Study of Irredentism.* London: C. Hurst, 1981.

———. *Radical Politics in Modern Turkey.* Leiden: Brill, 1974.

Lewis, Bernard. *The Emergence of Modern Turkey.* London: Oxford University Press, 1961.

Lewis, Raphaela. *Everyday Life in Ottoman Turkey.* New York: Dorset Press, 1971.

Lijphart, Arend. *Democracies: Patterns of Majoritarian and Consensus Government in Twenty-One Countries.* New Haven: Yale University Press, 1984.

Lipset, Seymour M. *Political Man: The Social Bases of Politics.* Baltimore: Johns Hopkins University Press, 1981.

———. "Some Social Requisites of Democracy," *American Political Science Review* 53 (1959): 69-105.

Mackenzie, Kenneth. *Turkey in Transition: The West's Neglected Ally.* London: Institute for European Defence and Strategic Studies, 1984.

———. *Turkey Under the Generals.* London: Conflict Studies, no. 126, 1981.

Maddick, H. *Democracy, Decentralisation and Development.* Bombay: Asia Publishing House, 1963.

Manisalı, Erol, ed. *Turkey's Place in the Middle East: Economic, Political and Cultural Dimensions.* Istanbul: Üç-er, 1989.

Mardin, Şerif. "Freedom in an Ottoman Perspective," in *State, Democracy and the Military: Turkey in the 1980s,* Metin Heper and Ahmet Evin, eds. Berlin: Walter de Gruyter, 1988.

———. "The Transformation of an Economic Code," in *The Political Economy of Income Distribution in Turkey,* Aydın Ulusan and Ergun Özbudun eds. New York: Holmes and Meier, 1980.

———. "Ideology and Religion in the Turkish Revolution," *International Journal of Middle East Studies* 2 (1971): 197-211.

———. "Power, Civil Society and Culture in the Ottoman Empire," *Comparative Studies in Society and History* 11 (1969): 258-281.

———. "Opposition and Control in Turkey," *Government and Opposition* 1 (1966): 375-387.

———. *The Genesis of Young Ottoman Thought: A Study in the Modernization of Turkish Political Ideas.* Princeton: Princeton University Press, 1962.

Mawhood, Philip. *Local Government in the Third World: The Experience of Tropical Africa.* New York: John Wiley, 1953.

Muller, E. N., Seligson, M.A. and İ. Turan, "Education, Participation and Support for Democratic Norms," *Comparative Politics* 20 (1987) : 19-33.

Nadaroğlu, Halil, and Ruşen Keleş. *Fiscal Relations Between Central and Local Governments.* Istanbul: Marmara University Publication, 1991.

Naff, Thomas. "The Ottoman Empire and the European State System," in *The Expansion of International Society,* Hedley Bull and Adam Watson, eds. London: Oxford University Press, 1984.

Nas, Tevfik, and Mehmet Odekon, eds. *Liberalization and the Turkish Economy.* Westport, Conn.: Greenwood Press, 1988.

Newton, Ronald C. "On 'Functional Groups,' 'Fragmentation,' and 'Pluralism' in Spanish American Political Society," *Hispanic American Historical Review* 5 (1978): 1-29.

O'Donnell, Guillermo, and Philippe C. Schmitter. *Transitions from Authoritarian Rule: Tentative Conclusions About Uncertain Democracies.* Baltimore: Johns Hopkins University Press, 1986.

O'Donnell, Guillermo, Philippe C. Schmitter, and Laurence Whitehead, eds. *Transitions from Authoritarian Rule: Comparative Perspectives*. Baltimore: Johns Hopkins University Press, 1986.

————, eds. *Transitions from Authoritarian Rule: Latin America*. Baltimore: Johns Hopkins University Press, 1986.

————, eds. *Transitions from Authoritarian Rule: Southern Europe*. Baltimore: Johns Hopkins University Press, 1986.

Öncü, Ayşe. "The Potentials and Limitations of Local Government Reform in Solving Urban Problems: The Case of Istanbul," in *Dilemmas of Decentralization: Municipal Government in Turkey*, Metin Heper, ed. Bonn: Friedrich-Ebert Stiftung, 1986.

Öncü, Ayşe, and Deniz Gökce, "Macro-Politics of De-regulation and Micro-Politics of Banks," in *Strong State and Economic Interest Groups: The Post-1983 Turkish Experience*, Metin Heper, ed. Berlin: Walter de Gruyter, 1991.

Öniş, Ziya. "Privatization and the Logic of Coalition Building: A Comparative Study of State Divestiture in the United Kingdom and Turkey," *Comparative Political Studies* 24 (1991): 231-253.

Onulduran, Ersin. *Political Development and Political Parties in Turkey*. Ankara: University of Ankara, Faculty of Political Science, 1974.

[Özbudun, Ergun]. *Development and Consolidation of Democracy in Turkey*. Ankara: Turkish Democracy Foundation, 1989.

————, ed. *Perspectives on Democracy in Turkey*. Ankara: Turkish Political Science Association, 1988.

————. "The Status of the President of the Republic Under the Turkish Constitution of 1982: Presidentialism or Parliamentarism?" in *State, Democracy and the Military: Turkey in the 1980s*, Metin Heper and Ahmet Evin, eds. Berlin: Walter de Gruyter, 1988.

————. "Turkey," in *Competitive Elections in Developing Countries*, Myron Weiner and Ergun Özbudun, eds. Durham, N.C.: Duke University Press, 1987.

————. "Political Parties and Elections," in *Südosteuropa-Handbuch*, Grothusen Klaus-Detlev, ed. Göttingen: Vandenhoeck und Ruprecth, 1985.

————. "Turkish Party System: Institutionalization, Polarization, and Fragmentation," *Middle Eastern Studies* 17 (1981): 228-240.

————. *Social Change and Political Participation in Turkey*. Princeton: Princeton University Press, 1979.

Özbudun, Ergun, and Aydın Ulusan, eds. *The Political Economy of Income Distribution in Turkey*. New York: Holmes and Meier, 1980.

Özgediz, Selçuk. "Education and Income in Turkey," in *The Political Economy of Income Distribution in Turkey*, Ergun Özbudun and Aydın Ulusan, eds. New York: Holmes and Meier, 1980.

Özmen, Selahattin. *Türkiye'de ve Dünya'da KİT'lerin Özelleştirilmesi*. Istanbul: n.p., 1987.

Pevsner, Lucille. *Turkey's Political Crisis: Background, Perspectives and Prospects*. New York: Praeger, 1984.

Piscatori, James P. *Islam in a World of Nation-States*. Cambridge: Cambridge University Press, 1986.

Richards, Peter G. *Local Government Systems*. London: George Allen & Unwin, 1983.

Ricoeur, Paul. "L'Histoire comme récit et comme pratique," *Esprit* 6 (1981): 155-165.

Rustow, Dankwart A. *Turkey: America's Forgotten Ally*. New York: Council on Foreign Relations, 1987.

———. "Elections and Legitimacy in the Middle East," *Annals of the American Academy of Political and Social Science*, no. 482 (1985): 122-146.

———. "Turkey's Liberal Revolution," *Middle East Review* 17 (1985): 5-11.

———. "Turkey's Travails," *Foreign Affairs* 58 (1979): 82-102.

———. "Transitions to Democracy: Toward a Dynamic Model," *Comparative Politics* 2 (1970): 337-363.

———. "Atatürk as Founder of a State," in *Philosophers and Kings: Studies in Leadership*, Dankwart A. Rustow, ed. New York: G. Braziller, 1970.

———. "The Army and the Founding of the Turkish Republic," *World Politics* 11 (1959): 513-552.

Sartori, Giovanni. *The Theory of Democracy Revisited: Part Two: The Classical Issues*. Chatham, N.J.: Chatham House, 1987.

Sayarı, Sabri. "Generational Changes in Terrorist Movements: The Turkish Case." Santa Monica, Calif.: Rand Corporation, July 1985.

———. "Patterns of Political Terrorism in Turkey," *Terrorism, Violence and Insurgency* 6 (1985): 39-44.

———. "The Turkish Party System in Transition," *Government and Opposition* 13 (1978): 39-57.

Smith, B. C. *Decentralisation: The Territorial Dimension of the State*. London: George Allen & Unwin, 1985.

Smith, Gordon. "The Functional Properties of the Referendum," *European Journal of Political Research* 4 (1976): 1-23.

Stanyer, Jeffrey. *Understanding Local Government*. Oxford: Martin Robertson, 1976.

Steinbach, Udo. "Turkey-EEC Relations: Cultural Dimension," in *Turkey's Place in Europe: Economic, Political and Cultural Dimensions*, Erol Manisalı, ed. Istanbul: Üç-er, 1989.

———. "Turkey's Third Republic," *Aussenpolitik* 39 (1988): 234-51.

———. "Die sowjetisch-türkischen Beziehungen seit 1973," *Osteuropa* 34 (1984): 723-733.

———. "Perspectiven der türkischen Aussen- und Sicherheitspolitik," *Europa-Archiv*, 25 July 1978: 431-440.

Stewart, John. *Local Government: The Conditions of Local Choice*. London: George Allen and Unwin, 1983.

Sunar, İlkay. "Anthropologie politique et economique: L'Empire Ottoman et sa transformation," *Annales: Economies, Sociétés, Civilizations*, nos. 3-4 (1980): 551-579.

———. *State and Society in the Politics of Turkey's Development*. Ankara: Ankara Üniversitesi Siyasal Bilgiler Fakültesi, 1974.

Sunar, İlkay, and Binnaz Toprak. "Islam in Politics: The Case of Turkey," *Government and Opposition* 18 (1983): 421-441.

Szyliowicz, Joseph S. "Continuity and Change in Turkey's Educational Policies," *Journal of Turkish Studies* 8 (1984): 241-250.

———. *A Political Analysis of Student Activism: The Turkish Case*. Beverly Hills, Calif.: Sage, 1972.

Tachau, Frank. "The Political Culture of Kemalist Turkey," in *Atatürk and the*

Modernization of Turkey, Jacob Landau, ed. Boulder, Colo.: Westview Press, 1984.

———. *Turkey: The Politics of Authority, Democracy and Development*. New York: Praeger, 1984.

Tachau, Frank, and Metin Heper. "The State, Politics and the Military in Turkey," *Comparative Politics* 16 (1983): 17-33.

Toprak, Binnaz. *Islam and Political Development in Turkey*. Leiden: Brill, 1981.

Toynbee, Arnold J. *Change and Habit: The Challenge of Our Time*. London: Oxford University Press, 1966.

Tunaya, Tarık Zafer. *Türkiye'nin Siyasi Hayatında Batılılaşma Hareketleri*. Istanbul: Yedigün, 1960.

———. *Türkiye'de Siyasi Partiler, 1859-1952*. Istanbul: Doğan Kardeş, 1952.

Tuncay, Mete. *Türkiye Cumhuriyetinde Tek Parti Dönemi*. Ankara: Yurt, 1981.

Turan, İlter. "Political Parties and the Party System in Post-1983 Turkey," in *State, Democracy and the Military: Turkey in the 1980s*, Metin Heper and Ahmet Evin, eds. Berlin: Walter de Gruyter, 1988.

———. "Cyclical Democracy: The Turkish Case," Paper delivered at the Annual Meeting of the Midwest Political Science Association, Chicago, 11-14 April 1984.

———. "The Evolution of Political Culture in Turkey," in *Modern Turkey: Continuity and Change*, Ahmet Evin, ed. Opladen: Leske Verlag und Budrich, 1984.

Türkiye Sanayiciler ve İşadamları Derneği. *Türkiye'de Özelleştirme Uygulamaları*. Istanbul: TÜSİAD, 1992.

Uricoechea, Fernando. *The Patrimonial Foundation of the Brazilian Bureaucratic State*. Berkeley: University of California Press, 1980.

Vali, Ferenc A. *Bridge Across the Bosporus: The Foreign Policy of Turkey*. Baltimore: Johns Hopkins University Press, 1971.

Vaner, Semih. "Etat, société et parties politiques en Turquie depuis 1982," *Revue d'Etudes sur le Monde Méditerranéen et Musulman* 50 (1988): 87-107.

Walstedt, Bertil. *State Manufacturing Enterprises in Mixed economy: The Turkish Case*. Washington, D.C.: World Bank, 1989.

Weiker, Walter F. *The Modernization of Turkey: From Atatürk to the Present Day*. New York: Holmes and Meier, 1981.

———. *The Turkish Revolution, 1960-1961: Aspects of Military Politics*. Washington, D.C.: Brookings Institution, 1963.

Whitehead, Laurence. "International Aspects of Democratization," in *Transitions from Authoritarian Rule: Comparative Perspectives*, Guillermo O'Donnell, Philippe C. Schmitter, and Laurence Whitehead, eds. Baltimore: Johns Hopkins University Press, 1986.

Wincent, Andrew. *Theories of the State*. Oxford: Basil Blackwell, 1987.

Wolff, Peter. *Stabilisation Policy and Structural Adjustment in Turkey, 1980-1985*. Berlin: German Development Institute, 1987.

Yaşa, Memduh. *İktisadi Meselelerimiz*. Istanbul: n.p. 1966.

Yaşar, Muammer. *Paşalar Politikası*. Istanbul: Tekin Yayınevi, 1990.

About the Book

The consolidation of democracy depends upon striking a balance between political participation and prudent political leadership. During the Ottoman-Turkish period, state elites in Turkey emphasized political leadership; following the transition to democracy in the mid-1940s, the situation was reversed and the stress was on political participation. As a result, for decades Turkish politics has suffered from an imbalance between the two extremes.

This volume examines the process of democratization in Turkey after 1980 in light of these disproportions. Early chapters offer an overview of Turkish democracy from a comparative and historical perspective and outline the theoretical underpinnings of the book. Subsequent chapters focus on the withdrawal of the military from politics, the role of political and civil elites in the consolidation of democracy, liberalization and privatization of the economy, the emergence of Islam as a secular religion, and international influences on the democratization process. A final chapter analyzes the interplay of political leadership and participation in Turkish politics today.

About the Contributors

Faruk Birtek is Professor in the Department of Sociology, Boğaziçi University, Istanbul.

C.H. Dodd is Professor and the former director of the Turkish Studies Programme, School of Oriental and African Studies, University of London.

Dr. Ahmet Evin (coeditor) is affiliated as Professor with Deutches Orient Institut, Hamburg.

Nilüfer Göle is Associate Professor in the Department of Sociology, Boğaziçi University, Istanbul.

Dr. Gérard Groc teaches at Télliers les Plessis, Courtomer, France.

Metin Heper (coeditor) is Professor and is head of the Department of Political Science and Public Administration, Bilkent University, Ankara.

Selim İlkin is senior economist at the Statistical, Economic and Social Research and Training Center for Islamic Countries, Ankara.

Ersin Kalaycıoğlu is Professor in the Department of Political Science and International Relations, Boğaziçi University, Istanbul.

Ali L. Karaosmanoğlu is Professor and head of the Department of International Relations, Bilkent University, Ankara.

Bilsay Kuruç is Professor at the School of Political Science, Ankara University.

Şerif Mardin is Professor and holds a chair in Islamic Studies in the American University, Washington, D.C.

Ergun Özbudun is Professor in the Deparment of Political Science and Public Administration, Bilkent University, Ankara, vice-director of Turkish Democracy Foundation, and head of the Turkish Political Science Association.

Dankwart A. Rustow is Distinguished Professor at the City University Graduate School, New York.

Dr. Rüşdü Saracoğlu is former governor of the Central Bank of Turkey.

Udo Steinbach is Professor at the University of Hamburg and director of Deutches Orient Institut, Hamburg.

Joseph S. Szyliowicz is Professor at the Graduate School of International Studies, University of Denver.

İlter Turan is Professor in the Department of International Relations, Koç University, Istanbul.

Index